THE OFFICIAL
PRICE GUIDE TO
BEER
CANS
& COLLECTIBLES

**FROM THE EDITORS OF
THE HOUSE OF COLLECTIBLES**

FOURTH EDITION

**THE HOUSE OF COLLECTIBLES
NEW YORK, NEW YORK 10022**

© 1986 Random House, Inc.

All rights reserved under International and
Pan-American Copyright Conventions.

Published by: The House of Collectibles
201 East 50th Street
New York, New York 10022

Distributed by Ballantine Books, a division of Random House, Inc., New York and simultaneously in Canada by Random House of Canada Limited, Toronto.

Manufactured in the United States of America

Library of Congress Catalog Card Number: 85-647587

ISBN: 0-87637-539-5

10 9 8 7 6 5 4

TABLE OF CONTENTS

ACKNOWLEDGMENTS

The House of Collectibles extends sincere thanks to the following people and organizations for their support in putting out this book:

G. Heilman Brewing Co., Inc., La Crosse, WI; Geyer Bros. Brewing Co., Frankenmuth; MI; Jacob Leinenkugel Brewing Co., Chippewa Falls, WI; Moosehead Breweries, Dartmouth, NJ: Schoenling Brewing Co., Cincinnati, OH; Spoetzl Brewery, Inc., Shiner, TX; Thousand Oaks Brewing Co., Berkeley, CA; Walter Brewing Co., Eau Clive, WI; and Guernsey's Auctions, Tuxedo Park, NY.

We would also like to thank Mr. Dale Rogalsky of the Rogalsky Bros., Gainsville, FL; Mr. Tony Steffen, Elgin, OH; Mr. Paul K. Michel, Buffalo, NY; and Guernsey's, New York, NY, for supplying the photographs in this book.

Cover art was supplied by Richard Stoike, Knickerbocker Chapter, Beer Can Collectors.

NOTE TO READERS

MARKET REVIEW

Even a casual observer couldn't help but notice it; beer can collecting is expanding at a tremendous rate. The hobby is still forming and growing. It's especially exciting since no one really knows what direction the market will take. It's a relatively new hobby, having only become popular in the early to mid 1970's, and it's taken a few years for it to settle down into a steady enough market for collectors to really figure out. Many new collecting trends are developing even now. After extensive research, the editors of the House of Collectibles have tried to sort out the trends as they happen.

As was already mentioned, the most striking trend in beer cans is the large number of new people drawn to the hobby every day. One of the great things about this hobby is its accessibility. There are literally a couple of thousand cans out there that can be had for $25 or less, the vast majority of those usually selling for $10 or less. There's also the option of trading, in which case, after an initial investment, little or no money need be spent. One problem in most collectibles that beer cans really doesn't share is the difficulty of getting started. You don't have to look far for beer cans, the trade papers are full of mail order opportunities for trading and selling. One complaint raised by a few voices, however, is that beer cans is increasingly becoming a mail order hobby instead of a show- or sale-oriented hobby. There has been a gradual movement away from shows, no doubt due to the vast number of collectors and the distance between them. If one is willing to travel, however, there are definitely still lots of shows and conventions where one may go. The collector still has the choice.

What's selling and what isn't? No doubt about it, pull tabs are still the most collected beer can. Blame the large supply, the low prices and the interesting color and design variations. Those from the late '50's and '60's are doing especially well, showing strong price increases. At least one major dealer attributes this to people rounding out their collections and spending what they must to do it. The lower priced pull tabs ($10 and below) are staying steady in value and continue to be the major attraction for new collectors.

Flat tops are also doing well. Values are strong and the supply remains very good. Especially strong are the cans with opening instructions. Before World War II, when cans were first introduced, the can manufacturers printed directions for opening directly on the can. This practice didn't last long, but there are enough different types to be collectible. Standard flats are doing well, but the opening instruction cans are really going strong. Dealers report that collectors are lining up for them. Look for continued growth there.

Crowntainers and cone tops have really taken off in the past few years. Once thought of as relatively unattractive, collectors have discovered these cans and have really taken a liking to them. It is not at all uncommon for these cans to be in the $1,000 and up price range. Their values, especially for crowntainers, should continue to increase.

American 16 oz. cans are doing well, especially the older flat tops. They make interesting additions to any collection. The foreign 16 oz. cans are not doing nearly as well as the American cans. Dealers report a glut on the market that they don't expect to go away.

Foreign cans in general have slacked off. Until recently, their values were growing at a faster rate than American cans, but that has changed for now. The big news for the current European can collector was the recent changeover of European manufacturers from three-piece steel cans to aluminum. The color quality is not as good with aluminum so there has been a drop-off in collectibility. Dealers report, however, that the English 9 ⅔ oz. cans are holding their own in terms of value. It is, however, advisable to exercise caution with foreign cans now.

The large cans, quarts, half-gallons and gallons continue to be a specialty market. There aren't too many of these cans around. People can complete a full collection in a relatively short time. To some people, the fun is in the search, so this is a turn-off to them. There will always be a market for these cans, but it will never approach the 12 oz. cans. The little 8 oz. cans, on the other end of the size spectrum, share the same fate; there are just too few of them to be highly collectible.

Another interesting trend in beer cans is who's collecting and why. More collectors are getting interested in the investment qualities of beer cans. Of course, they enjoy their cans, but they're more aware of the financial aspects. This kind of collector knows they've got a real investment. The veteran collectors will say that they always knew about the investment possibilities, but it has become even more so now.

Beer can collecting is about as strong a collecting field as exists today. New collectors every day, a strong organization like the Beer Can Collectors of America (BCCA), and strong can values combine to make a viable hobby. If you haven't done it already, join the BCCA and one of its local chapters. The cost is very low, and they'll supply you with up to date collecting information. They'll also supply you with the greatest thing a collector can acquire; new friends with a common interest in beer cans. Good luck and good hunting!

EVOLUTION OF BEER

We don't have much in common with the ancient Egyptians these days. We've given up worshipping idols (at least the gold variety), and construction companies of the 1980's get very few calls to put up pyramids. But one very prominent holdover of the ancient Egyptian way of life remains: beer. It's survived about 60 centuries, through countless wars, plagues and famines, and it's as popular as ever.

Though historical records are a bit sketchy on the matter, it's believed that the Egyptians were brewing beer as early as 4,000 B.C. Thus the origin of beer predates the origin of such things as books, coins and indoor plumbing. Beer was being made and consumed before the Old Testament was compiled; before Rome was founded; a whopping 4,000 years before Julius Caesar lived.

It would be great to have a few beer cans from that era (can you picture the brand names—Pharaoh Light, maybe?). But, of course, it was a whole different ballgame in those days. There were no beer cans, no beer bottles, not even any taverns where the poor Egyptian could go and knock down a few, after a hard day of hauling 40-ton boulders. Beer was apparently a highly exclusive product in its pioneer stages. There was no way to get it unless you made it. The super-wealthy had it made for them, by their slaves; and they consumed it themselves, occasionally portioning out a few precious cupfuls to chosen guests. Average folk were lucky to get water to drink. The selling of beer did not begin, so far as we know, until thereafter. So even though beer existed, probably less than one-tenth of 1% of the world's population got a taste of it.

One of the strong clues about beer being highly regarded in ancient Egypt comes from tomb paintings. Servants are shown in procession, carrying vessels which presumably contain the beverage, and only the well-to-do got a burial complete with tomb paintings. Likewise, archaelogical digs into pharaohs' graves have uncovered many storage containers and cups that almost certainly were intended for beer. The Egyptians believed that the spirit might re-enter the body at any time, so they left plenty of food and drink within handy reach of the deceased.

From Egypt, the brewing, consuming and enjoyment of beer spread elsewhere. In fact it spread just about everywhere, eventually. Ancient Greeks maintained a preference for wine, so beer (though it was known in Greece) made no huge inroads there. In Rome, it was quite another story. Though the Romans were almost as fond of wine as were the Greeks, they liked variety. On the whole, beer was more expensive in Caesar's Rome than wine. There were some very costly wines—the modern equivalent of hundreds of dollars a bottle—but also some brands made from recycled fruit pulp that could be picked up for next to nothing. Beer had a more constant price, and it was high enough to confine it to the upper crusts of society. Commercial sale of beer was a major industry in Rome, though the total revenue probably did not equal that of wine sales. So far as can be determined, all the beer sold in Rome was domestic. That was not the case with wine, as about half the available brands (there were well over 100) were imports.

After the fall of Rome in 476 A.D., the commercial beer industry had its own fall. Times got tough and few citizens could indulge in any kind of luxury. Some enterprising souls did their own brewing, and chiefly the manufacture of beer during the long Dark Ages (up to about 1450 A.D.) was left to the monasteries. Every monastery had its winery and brewery, and for centuries not the slightest outcry was raised about monks consuming so much alcohol. Only in the 15th century, at the time of the Reformation, did the drinking (not to mention eating) habits of monks become a target for criticism. The Reformers sought—among many other things—to restrict alcoholic-beverage production in the church to wine only, and only so much as was needed for sacramental services. In this they were successful. Had the blow been struck earlier, say around 600 or 700 A.D., it might have meant temporary doom for beer brewing. By the 15th century, monastic brewers no longer had a monopoly on the trade. They had been joined by commercial brewers, who were supplying beer to innkeepers and "cook houses" (the early versions of restaurants), and in many cases by the proprietors of these establishments themselves. Once again, the public was tasting beer, after a lull of roughly a thousand years. There was a major difference this time, though. Late medieval beer (the 15th-century variety) was not the super-exclusive type it has been in Egypt or classical Rome. It was available at more moderate prices, and was reaching a much larger audience. The late medieval era was the first in which "the man in the street" got much of an acquaintance with beer. Of course it was still not within the grasp of everybody, cost-wise, but that time was rapidly approaching.

Living in the 15th century was ultimate paradise for any confirmed beer fan, by all recorded accounts. Since so much of the beer sold at public houses was brewed on the premises, it varied considerably from one establishment to the next. If there were 50 inns or hostelries within mule-riding distance (which there were, if you lived in London or Paris or any big town), you had your pick of many different beers. Quite a few of these places rose from rags to riches on the popularity of their beer. Guests gladly endured fleas and leaking roofs if the place served a good brew. The favorite inns became landmarks, and each hung out its distinctive shingle: Bull and Bear, Red Lion, Cross and Staff. They became the meeting places for the wits and rogues and storytellers of the day, and before long they inspired a kind of folklore all their own. To give just one example, the term "cock and bull story" originated with a London inn that was actually called the Cock and Bull. It was marked by a sign picturing a cock (rooster) and bull, and was, evidently, a wellspring for tall tales.

In time, taverns gradually divorced themselves from inns. They began springing up and multiplying all over Europe, and the independent tavern (with no rooms to let upstairs) quickly pulled business away from the innkeepers. Many of the tavernkeepers also brewed their own beer, as some continued doing until recent times. But frequently they were operating on low budgets or with limited space and facilities, so they brought in commercially brewed beer. This obviously proved a great boost for the beer industry, and with the proliferation of neighborhood taverns came a corresponding proliferation of commercial breweries.

Mountains of literature exist on the making and consumption of beer in Merrie Old England, as well as anecdotes and legends connected with it. Next to Germany, England had the heaviest consumption of beer in Europe, despite its small population. In the 17th century, when local taverns really got rolling, beer was not even too popular in some European countries. France and Italy consumed very little of it, preferring wine instead. But Holland—now there was a beer-laced land, if ever one existed! The Netherlanders made beer-drinking a national pastime in the days of Vermeer and Rembrandt. Tavern life was the life in old Holland. If you didn't make regular appearances at the tavern, you were automatically off the social register. Everybody who was anybody went there, from sea captains to majors to philosophers, and quite a few businessmen actually stayed all day and conducted their business right in the tavern. When they ran a newspaper ad, they gave the tavern's address. Obviously, this elevated the tavernkeepers to positions of social and political importance. Not only did they become wealthy, they often became influential residents in town. Tobacco smoking got its start in the early Dutch taverns, too—a newfangled idea brought to Europe via Christopher Columbus from the American "savages."

In London taverns of the 17th and 18th centuries, the most widely available types of beer or beer-related beverages were ale, porter, and "small beer" (light beer). By all odds, porter was the favorite. It was sometimes mixed with ale, as has been done occasionally by breweries in the 20th century. The standard "pint of porter" accompanied almost all meals, and was usually split between two diners. References to it in the literature of the period are endless, as for example in James Boswell's "Life of Samuel Johnson." The favorite meeting spot for these titans of culture was a Fleet Street tavern called the Mitre, and the pint of porter was automatically called for—followed often by another and another. Johnson was well known for taking a few too many, but overimbibing was a very common practice and it seemed to hurt nobody's reputation.

Since beer was being put up in glass bottles for the London tavernkeepers (so it could be brought to one's table in the same manner as wine), it was possible to get take-out packages. However, the tavern proprietors did not encourage take-out business, since customers who drank on the premises also ate food and did more spending. To balance the scales, they charged higher prices for take-out bottles, and this did the trick; while take-out sales provided a good source of revenue, they never seriously cut into tavern attendance. The liquor store, selling packages only, did not exist at that time. And, of course, beer was not available at the grocery, or anywhere except your local tavern. Out of consideration for the tavern owners (who were, of course, their best customers), the breweries would not sell individual bottles to private parties.

Beer became popular not only throughout the British Isles, but wherever the British went. Each land they colonized was automatically imbued with a taste for malt and hops. In the case of America, this came early. It has long been maintained that kegs of beer were among the possessions taken aboard the Mayflower and brought to Plymouth Rock in 1620, though there is no certain evidence of this. In any event, home brewing was thriving in colonial America from the earliest days. The history of beer drinking in America is quite different from that of European countries. It was almost as popular in early America as in England, Holland or Germany (since most of the settlers came from those countries); it was far more popular than in France or Italy. But the supply network that existed in the Old World was not to be found on this side of the Atlantic. There were no huge breweries turning out tons of barrels per year, and no clusters of neighborhood taverns until well into the 18th century. Being highly resourceful folk, the pioneer Americans brewed their own; and their unselfishness measured up to their industriousness, as they shared most of what they brewed. George Washington and Thomas Jefferson both had their own home breweries. The list of other illustrious citizens who did likewise would be long. Even if someone didn't really care for beer, it was mandatory to have it on hand for guests. So the practice of brewing was carried on by just about everyone who could afford it. Home brewing could provide the stepping stones to a career. Almost every colonist who brewed decent beer received requests to purchase it, from persons who did no brewing or were unsatisfied with the quality of their beer. This became a profitable sideline occupation which, with just a bit of push, could be turned into a full-time enterprise. When the age of taverns finally dawned in America, most of them were supplied by brewers who got their start in just such a fashion.

There was one enormous difference between the beer industry in 18th-century America and that of 18th-century England. While take-out beer was available in England, and on much of the continent, it could not be had in America. In the American tavern, beer was kept in kegs. If you took a table at the tavern and ordered beer, it did not arrive in a bottle but in a mug or stein. Naturally the tavern owners knew about bottled beer, and it would have been easy for them to put up beer in bottles, or for the breweries to do it. They did not choose to follow the reasoning used by their London counterparts, that take-out packages were good for business so long as you kept the prices high. It was their conviction that take-out sales would be damaging, since widespread home brewing was already keeping down tavern patronage. In fact, beer did not become widely available in bottles in this country until around the time of the Civil War, only about 120 years ago. When this happened, prophets of gloom and doom immediately predicted the collapse of the tavern business. Unlike in England, where the taverns were selling bottled beer, the trade in America was mostly in the hands of a very unwelcome rival—the liquor store. Previously, the liquor stores had been selling spirits and that was bad enough. If taverns had to depend on drawing customers strictly on the strength of their food, it was going to be tough sledding. The 1860's and more particularly the 1870's witnessed an all-out war between the taverns and liquor retailers, which carried on (though with decreasing ferocity) until after the turn of the century. The taverns were the underdogs and used every weapon in their arsenal to stay afloat. They offered free lunches with each purchase of a nickel glass of beer. They brought in entertainment. They installed nickelodeons, pool tables, dart boards, and anything they could think of in an effort to pull in customers. Much to the surprise of nearly everyone—including the tavernkeepers—it worked. But the gimmicks and promotions probably had little to do with the survival of taverns. The telling factor was the difference in quality—real or imagined—between draft and bottled beer.

As is usually the case when something new comes along, there were many skeptics who raised their eyebrows at bottled beer and concluded that it couldn't possibly be as good—even before giving it a try. The wood supposedly gave the beer a special mellowness; how could anything get mellow from setting in a glass bottle? The detractors went even further. Not only would bottled beer fail to measure up to the keg brew, but after a short time on the shelf it would deteriorate into an undrinkable mess. This was not a totally unfounded speculation. The liquor shops had no refrigeration equipment, and much of their stock was displayed on window shelving which received direct sunlight day after day. If a bottle did not sell fast, it was going to deteriorate in quality. Breweries tried to prevent this by using colored bottles, in hopes of filtering out the sun rays, but nothing really helped if a bottle remained on the dealer's shelf too long. Since the bottles were stopped with corks, it can be further inferred that some were not absolutely air-tight; and if air was leaking into a hot bottle, the contents were not going to be overly palatable. Even if bad bottles accounted for just one out of every ten sold, they created widespread bad publicity—for the liquor stores and the breweries. Many consumers swore off bottled beer upon hitting a sour bottle, and went back to the taverns.

Improvements were gradually made in bottling, and in the merchandising of bottled beer. But enough ill-feeling had been generated, at the outset, to insure that the tavern business would not be dealt a death blow by this new arrival on the American scene. By the time everyone concluded that bottled beer was here to stay, they had also concluded that taverns were here to stay.

As you might expect, the breweries also had some tricks up their sleeves. Of course they wanted to lure the tavern patron away from the tavern and into the liquor store. But this was not really of major importance to them, since they were selling to the taverns, too, and could catch the customer in either direction. If consumption of beer remained the same, but beer was merely bought in liquor shops rather than taverns, the breweries did not stand to benefit very much. What would benefit them would be increased consumption, wherever and however it occurred. How could that be accomplished?

Well, it could be pretty safely surmised that some people weren't drinking beer because they didn't like it. On draft or in bottle, light or dark, strong or light, they just didn't like it. Or they had moralistic objections to it. Or something. This was the hopeless portion of the potential audience. Oh, a few might become beer drinkers, but no worthwhile revenues were going to arise from that group.

But, just as certainly, there were others—it was hard to say how many, but maybe millions—who were not drinking beer because they hadn't tried it. Basically, these were individuals who would not frequent taverns, for one reason or another. Now that beer was available without going into a tavern, they suddenly became prospective customers. The question remained: how do you get them to try beer?

Breweries knocked that one around for a while, then concluded that a hard sell would do the trick—but one aimed at the head, not the stomach. It was decided to launch advertising campaigns extolling the medicinal properties of beer. The breweries ran ad after ad advising the public of the magnificent health benefits to be derived from their products. (The same thing, incidentally, was done by pioneer soft-drink manufacturers.) Whatever ailed you, it could be banished by a few swigs of the suds. David Nicholson of St. Louis called his beer "liquid bread," yet the only thing it had in common with bread was yeast. Another approach was to call beer "malt extract," as was done by Hoff's. The Hoff advertising claimed its product to be "a remedy recommended by European physicians for complaints of the chest, dyspepsia, obstinate cough, hoarseness, and especially consumption." Dyspepsia was the old-time word for indigestion; consumption was tuberculosis.

C. Conrad and Company, a wholesaler for Adolphus Busch in St. Louis, sold the original Budweiser from 1877 to 1890. The Budweiser name was a trademark of C. Conrad but in 1891 the company sold it to the Anheuser-Busch Brewing Association. By that time Adolphus Busch, founder of the company, had already established two companies to make beer bottles. In addition to furnishing bottles for Budweiser, they supplied other breweries from about 1880 to 1910.

Corks were replaced as stoppers on beer bottles with the invention by William Painter in 1891 of the "crown cork closure," containing a thin slice of cork within a tight-fitting metal cap.

Bottled beer sales soared in the early years of the 1900's. By this time nobody had any major complaints against bottled beer, but there were some minor ones, including the nuisance of bringing bottles back to the store to redeem the deposit. Also, bottles could break. Though nobody realized it at the time, these seemingly trivial strikes against the bottle were to lead (in part, anyway) to the eventual experimentation with, and adoption of, beer cans.

There is no space here to go into detail on the many companies active in the earlier days of bottled beer. They were scattered widely around the country, at first concentrated in the East and Upper Midwest, but later virtually everywhere. There were, of course, distribution problems because of the slowness of travel, and many companies came into being in an effort to win local business away from the big distant breweries. Such was the case with Aberdeen Brewing Co. of Aberdeen, Washington, which had distribution facilities in the Pacific Northwest and could supply the retailers in that area much more quickly than a brewer in St. Louis or Milwaukee or New York. American Brewing of Baker City, Oregon, could get its beer to the Rockies' clientele in short order. There were numerous such firms in the late 19th century, operating in small towns and taking advantage of their edge on the local distribution routes. By the same token, many breweries opened up in the South, which could of course be served very well by St. Louis but even better by a local manufacturer. There was the Alabama Brewing Company in Birmingham and the Augusta Brewing Company in the Georgia town of that name, two examples out of dozens that could be cited. Not all of them were successful by any means, as their product was not always on a par with that of the major established breweries; but they showed what could be accomplished in the distribution war, and encouraged others to get into the race. The local breweries were active even in small and medium-sized towns in New England, such as Bridgeport, Connecticut, even though there was competition rather close by in Boston. St. Louis was the first brewing capital of the country, but Milwaukee had taken the lead before the turn of the century and never relinquished it. However, a number of major breweries have been active elsewhere, notably the Jacob Ruppert in New York. "Colonel" Jacob Ruppert was the model for endless "beer baron" jokes during the 1920's, some of which are still being told today. His giant brewery, made of red granite and styled after a European fortress, stood on Lexington Avenue in upper Manhattan. It was a landmark for many years, before being taken down in 1971. In addition to his brewery interests, Ruppert also owned the New York Yankees baseball team, during the era of Babe Ruth and Lou Gehrig. Ruppert was the producer of Knickerbocker Beer, which for many years was one of the best-selling brands in the East.

Since they were the direct ancestors of beer cans, the collector cannot fail to take some interest in the old beer bottles. They were made in a vast variety of sizes, shapes and colors—not because of any necessity to do so, but simply because the makers wanted to have distinctive bottles that everybody would remember and recognize. Green was the predominant basic color, but was used in multitudes of shades ranging from a dark olive green to pale green mixed with blue. There were also a number of companies using cobalt blue bottles, such as the aforementioned David Nicholson of St. Louis (the maker of "liquid bread"). Amber bottles were likewise in use, but in general the popularity of amber was slow to take hold until after Prohibition. Following Prohibition, green was replaced as the most common color for beer bottles by brown. Colors other than these are scarcer. It was not considered prudent to do too much experimenting with colors, just for the sake of attracting attention, since the color and its intensity were related in some measure to the product's shelf life. It was believed in the early days that green did the best job of filtering out light, and manufacturers who used other colors were going against the grain. Actually, there was probably no difference in the preservative powers of colors; it was the deepness of color, rather than the color itself, which mattered.

Supplying bottles to breweries was one of the major (and most profitable) activities for the glass companies. Since the bottles were washed and reused until they broke (or until somebody failed to redeem the deposit), the manufacture of bottles was not nearly as great as the overall sale of beer. But, nevertheless, it was a major industry in itself; the number of people engaged in making, packing and shipping beer bottles was a fair share of the American work force, and in some small towns this was the chief source of employment. By 1930, the beer bottle had been on the scene for 70 years or more, and it was not seriously believed that a challenger to its dominance would appear.

What happened to unseat the beer bottle?

Basically, the Depression, which got everybody thinking of ways to make things cheaper and faster. But it's vital to realize—for any beer can historian —that the beer can was far from an instant hit. It received considerable negative reaction at first, and not only from quarters where such opinion would be anticipated (the bottle makers). For fully a decade after beer cans were introduced, they remained a "maybe" product—gaining wider acceptance but still leagues behind the bottle in overall use, and without any kind of firm future. The beer can was called a novelty and a fad, and it was really not until after World War II that a majority of beer drinkers were taking it seriously. It had a very tough uphill climb, tougher in fact than the beer bottle in its early days.

DEVELOPMENT OF THE HOBBY

By the 1930's, when beer cans came on the scene, the concept of canning perishables in metallic containers was nothing new. This had been done with foodstuffs since the mid 1800's. Canning beer called for a much thicker type of can, however, since the pressure in pasteurization was much greater. With bottles apparently doing the job of selling beer very satisfactorily, nobody rushed to put beer into cans.

There were two factors basically responsible for the beer can's birth. One was the Great Financial Depression, which brought forth many new merchandising innovations in an effort to trim costs. Another was the matter of "deposits." Just like soda bottles in those days, beer bottles were sold on the deposit system. When buying beer, you paid a couple of extra pennies as a deposit on the bottle. This was refunded when you returned the empties. Since there was a certain amount of bother attached to lugging back your empty bottles, a packaging method that eliminated "deposits" was sure to be popular.

The American Can Company was the first maker of beer cans. Its first can model was called Keglined, used by the Krueger Brewing Co. early in 1935. The name Keglined referred to the fact that the can's interior was specially coated, to prevent the beer from acquiring a metallic taste. These first beer cans were not the "cone top" types, which many people erroneously believe were the earliest. They were ordinary "flat tops," very similar to the flat tops that continued to be sold until the era of pull tabs. The cone top can, which looked like an inverted funnel, made its debut later in that same year (1935). It was a product of the Continental Can Co. As soon as American started making beer cans, Continental (the leading rival maker) naturally wanted to compete, and tried to devise a type that would be different from American's and hopefully more appealing. Supposedly the cone top had two big advantages. It was easier to drink from the cone spout, and you could pry off the cap with a common soda bottle opener, whereas the top of a flat top can had to be punctured. These features won many followers for the cone top. Though cone top cans continued to be made for about 20 years, and were very successful, the flat top eventually won out. At the same time, beer continued to be marketed in bottles, too, for the benefit of those who believed that canned beer just didn't taste the same. During most of World War II (1941–1945), bottled beer enjoyed a renaissance, as the materials needed to make cans were in short supply. But this was only temporary and the war's conclusion saw beer cans in greater production than ever before.

The early cans were made of tin. The industry's interest in reducing the weight of cans turned its attention to aluminum. There was no big general rush to make aluminum cans, but gradually the change came about. By the late 1950's, Coors was placing aluminum tops on its steel cans. Other makers followed along, and in time the all-aluminum, seamless can was the order of the day. Since they could be recycled, there was a hope—that aluminum cans would result in less littering. By the early 1970's aluminum "redemption centers" had opened all across the country, buying aluminum beer and soft-drink cans by the pound.

The next innovation, and really the biggest of all, was the self-opening can. This made its debut in 1962 with Iron City Beer, and in the following year one of the major brewers, Schlitz, started using pull tabs. There were many problems at first with pull tabs, mainly in the form of cut fingers and lips from sharp edges. By 1965 these had been ironed out, and it was apparent that the pull tab can was here to stay.

GETTING INTO THE HOBBY

Beer can collecting is one of the most social of hobbies. For more transactions are made by trading and swapping than by cash buying. The swap meets are great get-togethers for collectors, who invariably meet other collectors that they never would have met through correspondence or advertising. The early organizers of beer can collecting firmly advocated "keeping the dollar out" of the hobby—they envisioned this as a unique hobby in which collectors' items would change hands but not cash. While that lofty concept has not proven 100% workable, since some collectors have nothing to trade and want to spend money on beer cans, it definitely established the tone for beer can collecting. Even today, many individuals who don't have a spare nickel to spend on hobbies get into beer can collecting, a statement which can be made about precious few collecting pastimes. There is real solid encouragement to do so, because you can accumulate plenty of beer cans without buying them on the collector market. Every time you buy a six-pack, you've got six cans; and if you buy a different brand each time, you have one specimen for yourself and a trading stock of five duplicates. Don't worry about the duplicates. You need them, if you're going to engage in trading and swapping to build the the majority of your collection. There is no such thing as a wasted can, unless it's in poor condition. Somebody else is going to want it, and you're going to want that person's duplicates.

Get the picture?

In a sense it's like chain letters, with the big exception that in beer can collecting there are no schemes and no losers. You profit from what other hobbyists are doing, and they profit from what you're doing. Everybody ends up with a collection that's worth money, without having to spend much or any money.

There must be a gimmick behind it, you say. Well, it's not exactly a gimmick. It's really just a matter of circumstances—circumstances which prevail as the result of American marketing techniques, and which just happen to be very favorable for amassing an outstanding beer can collection. Hundreds of brands of beer, ale and related beverages are produced in this country. Some of them have nationwide distribution but these are vastly in the minority. By and large the selection of brands you find in Portland, Oregon, is quite different from that in Augusta, Georgia. Most of them will be local brands, brewed right in that area (perhaps right in the city itself). Then there are regional brands, which enjoy whopping annual sales but still are not sold nationwide. Until fairly recently, Coors was not available on the East Coast, despite the fact that it was one of the country's best-selling brands. Brands—and, consequently, cans—that are common for you in your locality are not easy to get for a collector 1,000 or 2,000 miles away. He can't find them in his local store, so for him they're new and different and appeal, despite the fact that you see them every day.

Thus, even if a can type is still being produced, it has collector desirability and trading value. Obviously, nobody is going to pay $50—or even $10—for a current can. Maybe all they'd pay in a cash transaction would be 50¢ or 75¢. But the current cans are perfect as "traders." When currently manufactured cans are swapped amongst collectors, it's almost always on a one-for-one basis, which eliminates the necessity for bargaining or hashing it out. If another hobbyist has six cans that you don't have, and you have six that he doesn't, you have a smooth even-up trade. Assuming of course that all specimens involved have been properly drained by opening them from the bottom, which is the standard etiquette of the hobby, and that none are defective in any way.

Without any doubt, that is the best and simplest way (not to mention least expensive) of getting into the hobby. Start small, but start smart. When you buy beer, avoid the huge national brands and buy those with local or regional distribution. Don't buy the same brand each time. When you've exhausted the selection in one store, try elsewhere. The selections will be different from one to the next, though you may not have noticed this when you were buying beer as a consumer rather than as a collector. Some stores simply stock more brands than others. Others—a growing number these days—are collector-oriented, possibly because the manager collects beer cans, and purposely offer a few unusual brands. Just by buying in this way, you will build up a pretty sizable arsenal of cans in no time at all. When you have a few dozen different types available for trading, the real fun begins.

Beginning collectors sometimes shudder at the prospect of encountering a space problem. Where are they going to put 100, 200 or 500 cans, each of which takes up several dozen cubic inches of space? Don't fret. This has a knack of working itself out. If you do a lot of trading, which nearly every beer can hobbyist does, you will be disposing of cans at approximately the same pace you acquire them. During your first six months or so, you will be accumulating cans at a rapid rate. If that ratio of acquisition, without trading, were kept up for five or six years, you would, indeed, be inundated with beer cans. In most cases, the typical collection will not get too much larger after it's reached 100 cans (unless your goal is quantity), and the rate of growth will be much, much slower than in the beginning. As the result of trading you will build a better collection and a more varied collection, but in terms of size it will stay well within reasonable bounds. Your first 100 cans are likely to include as many as 80 duplicates. You may still acquire some duplicates thereafter, but mostly you will be getting different cans by trading them off. You will reach the point (a point you might have thought was unattainable!) where half the cans in your collection are different and only half are duplicates. And gradually the stockpile of duplicates will dwindle down even more, though it's always good to have some on hand; zero duplication is not a wise ambition, since your trades then have to be made with cans from your primary collections. The difference is that as an advanced hobbyists you will be having better duplicates. Your duplicates will no longer be ones from the grocery store, with a "common in-production can" trading value, but more desirable obsolete specimens. Theoretically you could go on forever, stockpiling duplicates from the grocery store and using them for trading. But this is not very satisfactory for an advanced collector, as he wants to get the scarcer cans when he trades. If he has nothing but current cans to give in return, he may have difficulty finding hobbyists who will trade with him; and even if trades can be made on that basis, you will need to give five, six or more current cans to get a decent obsolete one. This means more expense for postage if the trades are being conducted by mail, and more of a hassle all the way around. The best trades in this hobby are those which can be made one-for-one or as close as possible to one-for-one. For example, if you have two obsolete cans worth three dollars each, they can be traded for one obsolete can with a six-dollar market value. You are giving equal value for what you receive, and there is no problem with the packing and shipping. To sum it up: to be successful in trading, you have to think just as much of what you're giving as what you're getting. You must put yourself in the other person's shoes. When you become an advanced collector, you will not think highly of someone who wants to swap 20 of his 50¢ current cans for one of your $10 duplicates. The cash value may balance out in a swap of this nature, $10 in value for $10 in value, but the $10 obsolete can is much more desirable than all 20 of the current cans put together. Thus, to make a fair and equitable trade for a $10 obsolete can, it's necessary to give (say) two five-dollar cans, in lieu of another $10 specimen. This holds true all the way down the line, for cans worth $20, $50, $100 and up.

So as you can see, the space problem is generally not a problem at all. Quality and gradually quantity are desirable in the average collection; it grows in value, importance, and collector enjoyment, but not too greatly in actual size after reaching a given level. If you do have boundless space available and want to shoot for a huge general collection, encompassing all current brands and as many of the obsoletes as possible, this is another way of approaching the hobby. It's a matter of circumstances and personal motivation. When thinking of space and the opportunities (or lack of them) that it offers you, don't forget that the space consumed by beer cans will depend largely on the manner of storage. You can't make a can any smaller than it is, but you can store and/or display it so that it takes up the least possible room. Consider the size of your room or rooms, then get a paper and pencil and do a little arithmetic. You should be able to determine very accurately just how many beer cans could be comfortably housed in your quarters. Chances are you will want to use wall shelving. This is by far the most economical from a space-saving point of view, and also economical financially compared to most other storage equipment. Even if you have just a single wall to use for shelving, this will provide accommodations for more cans than you might imagine. Three inches of shelf space is all you will need for most cans, and six inches between the shelves. Actually you could get away with slightly less than six inches between shelves, and perhaps fit in an extra shelf, but over-crowding doesn't make for a very attractive display. Assuming the wall is 12 feet by 9 feet, this gives you the potential for over 200 feet of shelving. At three inches per can, you could house more than 800 cans on a wall 9 $\times$ 12. Certainly that's a sizable collection by anybody's standards, though some collections numbering 5,000 cans and more have been assembled.

If you're going to build your collection mainly by swapping, two-for-one swapping (with you giving two cans and receiving one in return) is the best way to improve the quality of your holdings. Whenever you can give two one-dollar cans for a two-dollar specimen, or two fives for a ten, you have accomplished something to be satisfied about. You've brought scarcer, more desirable cans into your collection without spending any money in the process. Of course this cannot be done indefinitely or exclusively. If you start with a trading stock of 100 cans, and make nothing but two-for-one transactions, you will hit bottom after 50 trades. Some can buffs engineer that many swaps in a month's time or less! There are various ways of getting around this. Mostly it's a question of being loose in your approach and not restrictive in the way you collect or acquire cans. If an attractive opportunity comes along to buy, buy! If you must make a one-for-one trade to obtain a desirable can, by all means make it, if the can you're trading away is a duplicate. There is no logic in getting too sentimental about one's duplicates. The only good reason for having duplicates in the first place is for use in trading.

You will meet many traders in this hobby, in person and through the mails. You will meet experienced collectors who want to trade—people who've been in the hobby for a number of years and who virtually "having everything." You cannot impress them with recent obsoletes, and even a five-dollar or ten-dollar can is likely to already be in their collection (not to mention another twelve duplicates in their trading stock). By the same token you will encounter intermediate collectors, and many, many raw beginners who have nothing of any particular merit to offer in trade. Most—or all—the cans they have are "currents." As you can easily surmise, traders usually pair off at their own level. It is not a matter of age or personal wealth or anything except the quality of one's trading stock. Thus you will see 11-year-old beginners trading with 60-year-old beginners. If cash was real force in this hobby, the youngsters would be left far behind; but their trading cans are as good as anyone else's on their collecting level.

In trading you have to be logical. You should not expect to receive less value than you give, and you should not expect to receive more. The objective is to get different cans—different from those already in your possession, and which would add to your collection. If you have current brands for trading, most of your trades will be conducted with others who have current duplicates. Occasionally you will find someone who is willing to give an obsolete can for some of your "currents." Maybe he has a number of duplicates of that can. Maybe his brother-in-law worked for the brewery. Who knows? In any case, this is regarded by most collectors as a golden opportunity which should not be bypassed under any circumstances. In this kind of situation, you would of course be justified in giving away more value than you receive, which you will undoubtedly have to do.

Be a smart trader and a respected trader. Don't think of other collectors as your competition; it isn't a Macy's vs. Gimbel's kind of game. We're all in this together, and we have the power to help the hobby, help ourselves, and help each other if we use some common sense. The overall health of the hobby is (or should be) of paramount importance to every serious collector, and obviously it can't be too healthy if there are numerous traders trying to "beat the other guy." There is an etiquette in can trading as in most other aspects of life! The basic tenets are: 1. Do not make a fool out of yourself; 2. Do not try to make a fool out of anybody else; 3. Be at least slightly humble; 4. Be gracious, and accept "no" for an answer when no is inevitable; 5. Do not be pushy; 6. Think of yourself as a shopkeeper and of the person with whom you're trading as a customer; make sure he wants to keep coming back for more; 7. Be reputation-conscious and strive to maintain a good reputation within the hobby. Rule #7 bears some elaboration. Word gets around about traders and the way they conduct themselves, thanks to the massive communication within this hobby. If you advertise, your name is being read by thousands of collectors and it's going to come up in conversation. You don't want people saying negative things about you and word-of-mouth advertising is even more influential than what appears on the printed page. If somebody can say, "Gosh, I got a really good trade from him," this is going to encourage others to come forward and trade with you.

Etiquette is all-important in this hobby. If you don't conduct yourself along the established, accepted lines, you will become noticeable for not doing so. You will either be marked as a greenhorn or someone who is purposely trying to play by his own rules. The considerations about etiquette in beer can collecting extend all the way down to the "SASE." In the event you are unaware, SASE stands for "self-addressed stamped envelope." You might not think this is something worth debating about, but the SASE has been the subject of quite a bit of coverage in club bulletins and other beer can literature. Actually it's no trivial matter. Someone running a national ad might receive a hundred replies (or he might receive just two, depending on luck and conditions). If he has to spend 22¢ postage replying to them, this means a 22¢ bite out of his hobby budget. For most collectors, spending 22¢ and not getting any beer cans for it is not a noble prospect. So it has become the accepted practice, though not really an ironclad rule, for everyone who answers an ad or makes any kind of inquiry, to enclose a SASE. You may ask, "Why should I have to pay double postage, to send my letter and get a response?" Well, that might not be wholly fair, but it's even less fair for the advertiser to foot the bill. It boils down to the fact—sad but true—that many people who send in inquiries are not wholly serious in the first place. Many of them are just soliciting information, to determine the trading potential of their cans, and have no real intention of completing a trade. The advertiser must spend time to answer these letters, which of course is wasted if no deal results; so for him to waste postage in addition to time seems like asking a bit much. Of course when you establish any kind of on-going trading (or corresponding) relationship with another hobbyist, the SASE formality can be dropped. It applies only to the initial correspondence with any advertiser. To look on the bright side: the use of the SASE will benefit you, if you advertise, so don't feel too badly about it!

In placing a trading ad, you can do it in either of two ways. You can run a short ad simply announcing that you have a trading list available, and possibly giving some indication of the type of cans it contains (cone tops, obsoletes, quarts, etc.). This kind of ad will save you some money because of its brevity, but then of course you will need to produce the list. If you have a list professionally printed or even run out on a xerox machine by a printing service, you can expect to pay at least 5¢ per page. In other words, 100 copies of a three-page list (300 pages) would run a minimum of $15, and many printing services charge more than this. If you instead spent the $15 on the ad, you could buy quite a bit of space—not enough to run a three-page list, of course. This is something you have to decide for yourself. If you don't really have a great many cans to list, it could be smarter to run a large ad. This is especially true if you have numerous duplicates of each one. Running a large ad is also worthwhile if you have cans of moderate to high value to trade, since they will attract considerable attention when listed in an ad. Many people will probably trade with you, on the basis of seeing the cans listed in the ad, who would not have bothered to write for a list. So the saving of a few dollars in operating expenses should really not be your major consideration in deciding which way to go. The goal is to make the most possible trades and the best possible trades.

There are right and wrong ways to prepare an ad. You will learn a lot by studying the ads now appearing in beer can club bulletins and in the hobbyist press in general. See how the others do it. Take note of which ads grasp your attention, and what is appealing about them. You will see good ads and bad ads. There are plenty of bad ones because some are being run by first-timers who have no previous advertising experience. Some of these individuals will receive little response from their ads, and will conclude that advertising is a waste of money and time—not realizing that many of the advertisers in that very same publication are enjoying excellent results. With a little experience you will become adept at this. Don't try to be flashy. Don't model your ads after those for commercial products in big magazines. Imagination doesn't count for as much in beer can advertisements as getting the information across. Make an easy-to-read listing of what you have, pointing out the condition grade if any of the cans are not A-1. If you have scarce cans, attention should be called to them. Many readers are interested only in the scarcer types such as cone tops, and scan the listings merely to see if anyone is offering them. If this is not pointed out prominently it may slip by unnoticed. Plan your ad as if every reader was in a hurry and was just skimming through the publication. Get as many facts as you can into the ad, and trim down the unnecessary words. Leave out all the traditional advertising lingo such as "super," "exciting," "limited time," etc.

In making up a list, you can list all the cans alphabetically by brand name (not brewery), but it's generally better to take a little time and separate them into groups. The cone tops should be listed by themselves, and the flat tops should not be mixed in with the pull tops. Even if you identify the type of can next to its brand name, this is not as convenient for readers as grouping them by type. If someone wants just flat tops, for example, he will need to sift through the entire list to locate them, and he may miss some (or not bother in the first place). You should state a value next to each can, at least in terms of what you want to receive in trade for it. The common practice today is to indicate a cash value, and you can do this simply by using the values as given in this book. Just let your readers know where the values came from, so they won't imagine you arrived at them yourself. You can state the type of cans you would be interested in trading for, or specific cans if you have an actual "want list." Naturally you will get somewhat more response if your requirements are fairly general. Some of your correspondents will have swap lists of their own, and will send them to you. You can save a little time by telling the correspondent which cans interest you, among those on his list, when you send him your list. This helps. This helps in another way, too, as the collector might put these cans aside for you, pending a possible swap, rather than swapping them with someone else.

You can refer to the condition of your cans by the standard grading system. This is perfectly acceptable, but in the case of a really scarce can you might want to go into more detail and mention the specific type of damage or defect. This pays off because some collectors (don't ask why!) are turned off by one kind of damage but not by another, even though both types may be of equal severity. You certainly want to keep returns at a minimum as this is very wasteful in terms of labor and postage, not to mention possible missed trades that you could have engineered with other collectors.

The rule in swapping through the mail is that everybody pays the postage on his own cans. In other words, if you send it out, you pay the postage on it, regardless of what sort of arrangements are involved in the transaction. The only exception is when you buy a can through the mail, in which case the seller may charge you for the postage. Usually the size of the order and the value of the cans will determine whether the seller will pay the postage. It would be unfair to expect any seller to pay postage on a shipment of 20 or 30 cans having a value of under one dollar apiece. In fact this is really an unprofitable shipment no matter how you look at it—even from the buyer's viewpoint. With sturdy packaging and postal insurance, the cost of sending out a carton of 30 cans will run five dollars or more. This is adding about 20% to the price, so if you could swap for those cans locally and avoid paying postage (not to mention avoiding a cash payment for them), you would probably do much better. With scarcer cans it is quite a different story, as the postage is about the same whether the cans are valuable or not—it is only slightly higher for rare specimens because of the higher insurance.

Wait a while for your list to circulate thoroughly before entering into trades, certainly before making major ones. The first few offers you receive may not be as attractive as those arriving later. The mails are slow and some of your correspondents are apt to be pretty slow themselves. If you've never done any prior trading, there will be a natural inclination to jump at the first "nibble," but this is unwise.

Trading in person is something else again. In-person trading is far preferable in many ways, the chief being that both parties see the cans and can decide just how appealing they are. There are no disappointments and no returns when you trade face-to-face. If all trades could be conducted this way, there's no question but that everyone in the hobby would welcome it. The problem is, they can't be. There is no way for all the country's beer can collectors to meet each other. Without mail trading, less than half of the trades now taking place would occur, and collections would not get built up as rapidly or impressively.

The two major opportunities for in-person trading occur at club shows and in personal meetings between collectors. Sometimes there's chance for trading at flea markets, as beer can collectors are often on hand selling and swapping duplicates from their trading stock. You will need to determine in advance whether the particular flea market will have a beer can person at it. Even if it does, this is not a guarantee that the individual will be in a mood to trade. On some occasions, it's a "cash only" ballgame with no trades entertained. You have to understand that the flea market exhibitors are paying a fee to show their merchandise, and if they trade rather than sell they could end up losing money. At a club show or any commercially sponsored hobby show it is, of course, quite a different situation. Trading is always in vogue at these gatherings, and at club shows there may even be a restriction against cash sales (or against trading a beer can for anything other than another beer can).

You probably won't be able to lug along every can in your trading stockpile, so select the best ones. Two or three dozen is about right, and even that number will require a bit of juggling dexterity as you move through crowded aisles and tables. Do not take more than one specimen of any can. Do not take cans in poor condition. Do not take any cans that are even mildly defective, unless the value is high. If the can would bring $120 or $25 in very fine condition, you can assume that it will still have some trading appeal even if slightly defective. Naturally it's high-caliber action at a show. You will see rare cans that you had read about, but never saw in the flesh. You will see hundreds and hundreds of cone tops and many brands that you never heard of—possibly some brands that nobody but the owner has ever heard of! The exhibitor and swappers at these gatherings represent the cream of the hobby, in terms of their holdings and expertise. Many of them have been collecting for a long while and know the hobby inside out. What you see on display may be a tiny fraction of the total number of cans they actually possess. You can't very well expect these people to be excited about current cans or recent obsoletes (brands on which the label design has changed within the past year). They either already have plenty of them, or don't want them. If this is the only type of can you have to trade, it might be difficult or impossible to work out a swap with the exhibitors, unless some of them have brought along batches of common cans specifically for swapping with beginners and making new friends. However this does not mean you cannot swap at a show, as there should be ample opportunity to swap with others attending the show, and who have brought along cans similar in value to yours. They, too, will find that they cannot negotiate swaps with the exhibitors, and will be anxious to swap with somebody. So keep an open mind, look around, and always be prepared to talk business with anybody interested in swapping.

Chances are you will want to supplement your trading with some buying—and possibly selling, too. The same basic rules apply. In buying for cash or selling for cash, you must have a reliable knowledge of the values; not just the value of a can, but the value of your particular can in terms of its condition. This could be very different from the overall market value. Beginners have a tendency to pay too little attention to condition and, at the same time, to pay too much cash for specimens that are not in the best state of preservation. If they can get a $20 can for $15 they feel they've saved five dollars and are content with the deal. They do not stop to realize that inferior-grade specimens detract from the appeal of one's collection, and that the real value of such a specimen might be much less than they've paid. If a can is badly corroded or faded, the $20 established market value might translate into one dollar and fifty cents or two dollars. Certainly you would be overpaying by giving even one half the market value for a can with serious rusting and loss of paint. When a can is advertised as "restored," this can usually be taken to mean "repainted" or touched up. The word "restored" sounds reassuring, as if all the negative factors about the can's condition had been wiped away. There is nothing illegal or devious about restoring collectible cans, and such specimens are to be found in many of the leading collections. The point to keep in mind is that you can restore the can but not its value. You can (if you have the skill and proper equipment) make the can look almost as it did before deterioration, but this does not bring it in line, price-wise, with a specimen that has never been damaged. Such a can is worth more, of course, than a damaged specimen on which no restoration work has been done, since it displays more attractively and is closer to the original appearance. It might be worth one half the market value of a well-preserved specimen. This varies and has to be judged on an individual basis. In some repair jobs, the rust is not totally eliminated.

CANS IN THE FIELD

Not everyone you see picking up beer cans by the roadside is a recession victim looking to make a few cents on the aluminum. While these do indeed account for the bulk of can-hunters, there are also some collectors out in the field, who would think no more of recycling a beer can than of selling the Gutenberg Bible as scrap paper.

The possibility definitely exists for making prospector-type "finds" in this hobby. You can certainly get plenty of different brands of modern commons in this way, and even sometimes an obsolete or a real oldie—depending on where you look and how diligently you look. For this, the litterbugs of America have to be thanked. They make it all possible.

Naturally, you're going to run into some disappointments in prospecting, chiefly in terms of the condition of the cans located. You will occasionally come upon a can that isn't in your collection, but which has obviously been reposing by the roadside for many, many months and is far the worse for wear. Mother Nature is not too kind to beer cans. Nor were many of the people who flung them from their car windows—they crunched them up before giving them the heave-ho. What with dents, crumpling, and rust, most of the outdoor cans leave a lot to be desired. Nevertheless, you will come upon some in almost pristine store-condition, and when such a specimen is a brand needed for your collection it makes all the disappointments worthwhile. Since you aren't spending anything—except on gas—you won't be taking a loss regardless of how your fling at amateur prospecting turns out.

Prospecting for modern commons and recent obsoletes can be done just about anywhere. Chances are you will do better as you get further and further away from your own locale, as the number of out-of-state brands ought to increase. Roads leading to and from beaches and picnic sites are usually fruitful; so are those in the vicinity of camping grounds and wherever people are apt to have done some drinking. You'll encounter plenty of stray cans here and there, but it's rarely worthwhile to stop and inspect them. What you'll be looking for essentially are piles of them, and these do turn up. Anyone who's done more than a few weeks of can prospecting has stumbled upon piles of 50–100 or more specimens. If you can get to a popular picnic area on a Monday morning in mid-summer, you might find 1,000 cans. Yes, most of them will be duplicates, and most will already be in your collection, but—who knows?

Going after obsolete cans (defunct brands, or those which have changed the color or configuration of their can) will require more ingenuity and maybe more traveling. The place to find them is in a location that was once occupied, but has been unoccupied—and untouched—for several years at minimum. Old vacant houses are a possibility—don't neglect to peer under the porch. Also worth checking out are abandoned railroad stations and rail yards, if they've been out of use for a few years. They saw a great deal of activity in their day, so there should be some beer cans around.

Finding cone tops is the dream of most beer can prospectors. These won't be at the picnic or camping grounds, and they're not too likely to surface in abandoned buildings, either—they're just too old for that. The only real hope for finding cone tops, except for a once-in-a-while lucky find, is by digging. There are millions of buried cone tops (not to mention flat tops). Don't forget that these cans were in production for 20 years, and nobody was recycling them. They got buried en masse when town dumps were filled in with landfill and paved over. They got buried during roadwork operations and all kinds of earth moving with heavy equipment. They got buried when landscaping was done on city parks, and they even got buried during the construction of private homes (there may be some right in your yard!). Most buried cans are badly rusted, but look at it this way: quite a few cone tops on the beer can market are badly rusted, too. So you might get just as collectible a specimen by digging, as you could by trading or buying.

For digging you will need a metal detector and some idea of where to take it. You needn't spend a great deal of money on the instrument; $250 will buy one that's perfectly suitable for beer can prospecting. You don't need an ultra-sensitive $900 model, since beer cans are large, usually buried in clusters, and generally found quite near the surface. It's different with old coins, which might have been underground since the 1800's and worked their way very deep down. You can easily test out a metal detector in the dealer's showroom by bringing a non-aluminum can with you. Place it on the ground and hold the instrument about two feet above it. If you get a reaction, the detector will be fine for locating most can deposits.

Hunting with a metal detector is becoming more and more popular among beer can hobbyists. There are many advantages, above and beyond making finds of valuable old cans. It's great way to spend a summer's day, and you're almost guaranteed to find something of interest or value, even if no beer cans turn up on a given outing. Metal detector prospectors often build a sideline collection of the miscellaneous objects they uncover in the quest for beer cans. You'll find jewelry, coins, kitchen utensils, sad irons, knives, and what-not. Most metal detectors pay for themselves eventually, in the value of relics unearthed with them. But, as we said, you must know where to use them. Aimless or random use of a metal detector is going to get you absolutely nothing but fresh air and sunshine. Concentrate on areas like beaches and parks where there's been plenty of activity over long periods of time. If there were not too many people using or occupying an area, there won't be many beer cans. Raccoons and squirrels are not noted for their beer consumption. Construction sites are excellent, if you're allowed in. Whenever the foundation of an old building is taken up, you can be sure there will be relics to find. This is especially true of public buildings in large cities. When these were built, the site was generally a vacant lot to begin with—littered with mounds of trash. The trash was just mixed in with earth as the foundation was bulldozed, and yesterday's trash is, as we all know, the treasure of today.

Use common sense with your metal detector, or when prospecting in general. Don't put life and limb in danger. Vacant mine shafts are inviting, and relics are often found in them, but for the amateur they're dangerous and best left alone. This also applies to caves.

CONDITION

Condition is an important consideration with beer cans, as with most hobby items. Collectors not only want their cans in the best obtainable condition, but are willing to pay higher prices for top-grade condition. This sharply influences the values. In most cases there will be little demand for a damaged can, and a dealer may be able to sell it for only five dollars, even if scarce. But the very same can in well-preserved condition is likely to be highly sought-after, enabling the dealer to place a high value on it.

Even a beginner who is not personally "turned off" by poor condition should learn to be very attentive to condition. He will probably overpay for some of his cans, if he takes condition lightly.

On the other hand, becoming *too* critical of condition is inadvisable. All the modern pull tabs and most flat tops can be had in excellent "as new" condition, and this is the way you should be aiming to get them; not dented, rusted, scratched or harmed in any other way. This is not the case with many cone tops and the early flat tops. Sometimes the only available specimens are deteriorated in one way or another. The scarcer and older the can, the less likely it is that any perfect specimens exist or could be found for purchase. If you hold out for a Grade One specimen of these cans, the result is apt to be a gap in your collection that never gets filled! The logical approach is "middle of the road." That is, taking the best one that comes along, provided the price is in line with its condition. Prices shown in this book are set for Grade One cans. A can in lesser condition (even if rare) would always qualify for a discount in price, though it is often difficult to agree on the proportion of discount. The personal opinions of the buyer and seller are sure to enter the picture. Some collectors do not want restored cans in their collection; in their opinion, a restored can is worth no more than if it had not been restored. But the majority of collectors are receptive to restored specimens of *scarce, older* cans, and the market values bear this out: a well-restored can does sell higher than if it had not been restored, even though there may be some hobbyists who are not interested in it.

Grading within the hobby is based upon guidelines drawn up by the B.C.C.A. (Beer Can Collectors of America), in which any can—old or new, excellently preserved or dilapidated—falls into one of six grading categories. Correct grading is important to mutual satisfaction in trades, as well as in buying and selling. Anyone who trades or sells cans through the mail should pay special attention to the correctness of his grading. By the same token he should expect correct grading in the cans he obtains through the mail from dealers and other hobbyists. The "over-graders" (those who boost their cans into a higher-condition grade than they deserve) soon get a reputation and are not well thought of. Fortunately it is much easier to grade cans than coins, in which there are over a dozen possible categories!

The six condition categories, and their standards, are:

MINT. A new-appearing can. Small dents and handling marks can sometimes be tolerated, but anything that mars the can's appearance should disqualify it to Grade One. Very few cans fall into this category and the term has become overused. A new collector should be wary of a can advertised as Mint condition. It is not always so. These cans, when they are sold or traded, obviously bring top dollar.

GRADE ONE. Very good condition. Small handling marks and dents are common in Grade One cans, but the can's appearance is still very "displayable." Cans in this condition are very close to Mint.

GRADE TWO. Should still be in good condition, although the imperfections are starting to become more apparent. Cans in Mint or Grade One condition should have flaws noticeable only upon close inspection. Grade Two cans will have flaws more easily noticed. Some fading in color is acceptable, as is some rim rust. The sides should be clean with a minimum of rust.

GRADE THREE. Large amounts of rust, spotting or scratches. The brand name should be legible though the colors would probably be faded. The difference between this and a Grade Four can is that Grade Three cans have a more or less even appearance.

GRADE FOUR. Heavy dents, peeling or rusting. The vast majority of the lettering should be legible. This can is ugly but can be used as a "filler" until a better specimen comes along.

GRADE FIVE. Not "displayable." Majority of can surface is pitted, rusted or peeled. Lettering is illegible. Large dents. The only way a Grade Five can could have any value at all would be if it were very rare to begin with.

RESTORATION

Restoration is an accepted part of the beer can hobby. In some hobby fields, any effort to restore a specimen is looked upon as tampering, no matter how skillful. This is not the case with beer cans. Many specimens of the scarce early cans have been restored, and many more will be! Restoration of a beer can may elevate it into the next higher-condition category, but this is possible only with raising a Grade Four can to Grade Three level. It is not possible to raise a Grade Three can to Grade Two, or a Grade Two to Grade One, since Grades One and Two automatically exclude restored specimens.

Just as the grade can be elevated from Four to Three, the monetary value of a restored can may likewise be increased. To understand the reason for this, you must realize that the attraction of beer cans as collectibles is largely physical. While beer cans do have a historical and scarcity interest, many of their owners are more interested in the display qualities than anything else. If a good restoration job succeeds in improving the display qualities of a can, making it more appealing to look at and less obvious for its faults, it has more sales attraction and thus can be sold at a higher price. Of course it will never command as high a price as if no damage had ever occurred, and no restoration had been necessary.

Restoration usually takes the form of rust removal, touching up areas of missing or faded color, and flattening out dents. It is delicate work and not to be attempted on a rare can by an inexperienced hobbyist! You might pay $50 for a Grade Four can, expecting to elevate it into Grade Three and raise the value to $75 or $80. But if your restoration project is unsuccessful, your Grade Four can will become a Grade Five, and worth only a fraction of the sum you paid for it.

Learn about restoration before attempting it. If you become a member of B.C.C.A., you will find that the club's literature contains much helpful information about restoration.

CARE AND STORAGE

Beer cans are no problem to care for, compared to most hobby items. They are not delicate and will remain in top condition for a lifetime, with just a bit of reasonable care.

Most collectors like to display their cans on wall shelves. You can build the shelving yourself without too much expense. Since empty cans are light, the shelves need not be heavy-duty. When shelving cans, do not let them touch each other, as they can scratch. Also, a bit of space beside each can improves the appearance of your display. Preferably the shelves should not be painted, as paint can become sticky in humid weather and your cans might pick up some traces of the paint. Plain unfinished wood is perfectly acceptable.

Of course you have the option of collecting full or empty cans, but there is much more to be said for "empties." Sooner or later, full cans become a nuisance. A shelf of them is very heavy; they "sweat" in warm weather; they are liable to develop rust spots or actual leaks; and the accumulation of alcohol gas within them may lead to bloating. Also, you are handicapped in trading or selling if you have full cans. They're much more costly to mail, and you need a license to sell full cans. If you sell a full can, you're an alcoholic beverages dealer in the eyes of the law—even if you're really just a beer can hobbyist. In light of all these considerations, it is unthinkable that anybody would really choose to collect full cans.

A pull tab can should be emptied by simply removing the tab. A flat top can should be emptied by making a neat V-shape puncture, with an opener, on the bottom. After emptying the can, rinse the inside several times to remove alcoholic residue. If you fail to do this, the can will have an odor and will attract insects.

RUST

One of the most commonly asked questions is, "If I acquire a can without any traces of rust, can I be certain that it will not develop rust in time? Also, if I have a can with light rust, will it get more serious?"

Generally speaking, rust will not start, or increase, among cans in a display —so long as some simple precautions have been taken. When you have rinsed out a can (as described above), it should be thoroughly dried with a towel rather than left to dry by itself. Wooden shelving for your collection is a better rust preventative than other forms of shelving, though plastic would be acceptable. Metal shelving, though used and endorsed by some hobbyists, is not to be recommended, because of the temperature changes which metal undergoes. Do not keep your collection in a damp room. Collections stored in a basement are at a disadvantage in this respect, as the humidity level is usually quite a bit higher there than in other areas of the house. If the humidity in your collection room is frequently above 70%, you may want to consider the use of a dehumidifier. Excessively high humidity can lead to formation of rust, or encourage spread of rust in cans where light rusting exists. Humidity can also be controlled by the use of chemical preparations which draw moisture out of the air in a very localized area of a room. Such products are used by coin collectors to prevent corrosion in coins, and would be equally useful for beer can hobbyists.

Do not stack cans one on top of the other. One layer to a shelf, please!

ORGANIZATIONS AND PUBLICATIONS

The major organizations for beer can collectors are:

Beer Can Collectors of America (B.C.C.A.)
747 Merus Court
Fenton, Missouri 63026

American Breweriana Association, club and bimonthly journal
P.O. Box 6082
Colorado Springs, Colorado 80934
(303) 633-3220

American Can Collector, monthly newspaper
Box 291 Station B
Anderson, Indiana 46011

National Association of Breweriana Advertising
For information, write:
Robert Jaeger
2343 Met-To-Wee Lane
Wauwatosa, Wisconsin 53226

Beer Drinkers International, club and journal
PO Box 6402
Ocean Hills, California 92056
Dept. ACC.

Readers are urged to expand their knowledge and enjoyment of the hobby by joining one of the clubs. Information on memberships can be had by contacting them directly. The clubs have local chapters in many parts of the country, and by attending the local meetings you have the opportunity to meet many fellow collectors in your area.

HOW TO USE THIS BOOK

The beer cans portion of *The Official Price Guide to Beer Cans* is divided into three sections: Cone Tops, Flat Tops, and Pull Tabs—the three standard types of beer cans. Within each section, the cans are listed by brand names, in alphabetical order.

Information provided in each listing is as follows:

BRAND NAME. This may or may not be the same as the manufacturer's name. For example, Knickerbocker is a brand name of a beer that was made by Jacob Ruppert. But Jacob Ruppert also made Ruppert beer (brand name).

In all cases, the word "beer" has been omitted from the brand names in the listings, though it usually will appear on the can itself. If the product is something other than ordinary beer—such as ale, draft, bock, etc.—this will be noted in the listings.

MANUFACTURER. Name of the manufacturer directly follows the brand name. It will be shown even if identical to the brand name.

SIZE. Capacity of the can is stated after the manufacturer: 8 oz., 12 oz., gallon, etc.

ADDITIONAL INFORMATION. In most cases, no additional information is given, if the above three items (brand name, manufacturer, size) are sufficient for a positive identification. But usually, two or more different cans exist, which are identical in brand name, manufacturer, and size. They differ in color, or wording, or the place of canning, or some other respect. In these instances, additional information is given, to arrive at a positive identification. If the listing states, "Word 'beer' in red lettering," this is the key to identifying that particular can. Read each description thoroughly, and compare the description to details of your specimen.

VALUE. A value range (such as, six dollars–nine dollars) is given for each specimen, except for certain very rare cans on which values have been omitted. The stated values represent the current retail prices at which these cans are being sold by professional dealers, and are for cans in Grade One condition. A collector selling to a dealer could expect to receive about half of these sums for the scarcer, more desirable cans. Cans with a retail value of less than $10 are not appealing for dealers to purchase, since these cans are not particularly scarce and can be obtained by trading. Generally, when a dealer does agree to buy a low-value can, he will pay only a fraction of the retail price. On the other hand, if you have a rare can worth $500 or more, you may succeed in receiving 60% or 70% of its retail value from a dealer. Currently manufactured cans are not purchased by dealers under any circumstances.

Any can that was found to have an average market value of $1000 or more is listed in this book as "rare." These cans appear so infrequently on the market that it is unrealistic to fix a set value on them. It is true of all beer cans, but especially this type, that value is up to the individual. A can is worth only what it is worth to you.

Obviously, with so many thousands of varieties of beer cans in existence, it is impossible for any book to include them all. But before you conclude that any particular can is not listed in *The Official Price Guide to Beer Cans,* be sure you have looked thoroughly for it. The brand name may consist of several words, and you could be looking for it under the wrong word.

CONE TOPS

In a sense, cone tops are the aristocrats of the beer can hobby. Can for can, the values of cone tops are much higher than for flat tops and pull tabs. They have not been made (except for an occasional novelty) since the mid 1950's, which means that every specimen is at least about 30 years old. Since cone tops were introduced in 1935, some have reached their 50th birthday. There are no common cone tops. It is very difficult to acquire cone tops by swapping modern cans for them, as most hobbyists who have cone tops for trading want other cone tops in exchange for them. If cone tops are your field of interest, you will probably want to think in terms of building a small, well-chosen collection, rather than attempting a really large wall-wide display. Even if you collect just a few dozen of them, you'll be the envy of many other beer can hobbyists!

The term "cone top" is applied to all cans with the pyramid or inverted-funnel top. Technically, however, some of these cans went by a special name—CROWNTAINER. The Crowntainer type has a shorter body and the cone is taller. Crowntainers are much less common than standard cone tops; however, the values vary quite a bit, specimen by specimen (it is not automatically valuable by being a Crowntainer). We have called attention to the Crowntainers in the following listings, to aid in identification.

	Price Range	
☐ **Aero Club Pale Select,** East Idaho Brewing, 12 oz., gold and blue, shield with wings at upper center	85.00	110.00
☐ **Altes Brisk Lager,** Altes Brewing, 12 oz., green, white and silver	70.00	90.00
☐ **Altes Lager,** Altes Brewing, 12 oz., silver and gray	120.00	160.00
☐ **Altes Golden Lager,** Altes, 12 oz., "Altes" in red, "Golden Lager" in gold	175.00	210.00
☐ **Altes Lager,** Tivoli, 12 oz., silver and black CROWNTAINER	40.00	50.00
☐ **Ambassador Export,** Ambassador, 12 oz., dark blue, "The Beer with the Diplomatic Flavor"		RARE
☐ **American,** American, 12 oz., red, white, blue and gold, brand name in blue script lettering	100.00	125.00
☐ **Apache,** Apache Brewing Co., 12 oz., gold and blue, portrait of Indian facing left		RARE
☐ **Apex,** Apex Brewing, 12 oz., red, white and black, pyramid symbol with slogan, "The Peak of Perfection"		RARE
☐ **Arbee Lager,** Rochester Brewing, 12 oz., blue, brown and yellow, brand name in yellow against brown background, "beer" in white		RARE
☐ **Arrowhead Pale Lager,** Louis Ziegler Brewing, 12 oz., white with pink lettering		RARE

Price Range

☐ **Associated Lager,** Associated Brewing, 12 oz., red, white and blue, brand name in blue on white banner, logo at upper left .... **RARE**

☐ **Associated Lager,** Aztec Brewing, 12 oz., red, white and blue .... **RARE**

☐ **Atlantic Ale,** Atlantic Brewing Co., 12 oz., red, black and gold, small illustration of black waiter (or butler) in uniform carrying tray with glasses 120.00 150.00

☐ **Atlantic Beer,** Atlantic Brewing, 12 oz., blue, white and gold, gold "A" in blue oval in upper center, "Full of Good Cheer" on label. 140.00 180.00

☐ **Augustiner,** A. Wagner, 12 oz., white, red and gold, medals hanging from ribbons, brand name in red 175.00 210.00

☐ **B and B Special Export,** Rainier Brewing, 12 oz., black and orange .... 250.00 300.00 (Unusual label art in which the beer looks like a glass of orange juice.)

☐ **Barbarossa,** Red Top Brewing, 12 oz., gold with multicolor scenic design 110.00 150.00

☐ **Bartels,** Greater New York Brewing, 12 oz., gold, white and red 250.00 310.00

☐ **Bavarian Premium,** Mt. Carbon Brewing, 12 oz., beige, red and black with gold top, vignette of smiling man drinking from glass 60.00 80.00

☐ **Bavarian's Old Style,** Bavarian, 12 oz., white, gold and red, brand name in gold lettering (very ornate) with red initials 70.00 85.00

☐ **Becker's Uinta Club Mellow,** Becker, 12 oz., silver, blue and red, bucking bronco symbol ...... 135.00 165.00 *Note: This is the correct spelling: Uinta. But it frequently appears as "unita" on trade lists.*

☐ **Ben Brew,** Franklin Brewing, 12 oz., gold, red and blue, "Kraeusen Beer" on label, "Ben Brew" in white script on red banner on label 160.00 200.00

☐ **Berghoff 1887,** Berghoff, 12 oz., black, red and white 65.00 85.00

☐ **Berghoff 1887 Pale Extra Dry,** Berghoff Brewing, 12 oz., white and gold with brand name in black, three stars above brand name, eagle and shield symbol at center with initial B 600.00 750.00

☐ **Beverwyck Ale,** Beverwyck, 12 oz., red, white and green 105.00 130.00

☐ **Beverwyck Cream Ale,** Beverwyck, 12 oz., gold with green shamrock and silver trim 450.00 550.00

Top, Left to Right: **Altes Golden Lager**, *12 oz., $170–$210;* **Arrowhead Pale Lager Beer**, *12 oz.* **RARE**. *Bottom, Left to Right:* **Atlantic Ale**, *12 oz., $120–$150;* **Berghoff 1887 Beer**, *12 oz., $65–$85.*

Price Range

☐ **Beverwyck Famous,** Beverwyck Brewing, 12 oz.,
cream and green–CROWNTAINER 130.00 160.00

☐ **Beverwyck Famous,** Beverwyck, 12 oz., silver,
red and bluish green, brand name in red 105.00 125.00

☐ **Beverwyck Irish Brand Cream Ale,** Beverwyck,
12 oz., light green and dark green, illustration of
shamrock–CROWNTAINER .... **RARE**

☐ **Billings Pale Beer,** Billings Brewing, 12 oz., red,
gold and white, brand name in white on label .. 300.00 400.00

☐ **Billings Rap Beer,** Billings Brewing, 12 oz., white,
gold and red, "Tap" appears largest on label ... 160.00 210.00

☐ **Black Forest Light,** Cleveland Home Brewing, 12
oz., white and red, no lettering beneath address 230.00 275.00

☐ **Black Forest Light,** Cleveland Home Brewing, 12
oz., white and red, statement of alcohol content
beneath address 300.00 375.00

☐ **Blackhawk,** Blackhawk Brewing, 12 oz., black,
yellow and red, colored profile portrait of Indian at
upper center 100.00 125.00

☐ **Blackhawk Pilsener,** Blackhawk Brewing, 12 oz.,
gold and white 95.00 115.00

☐ **Blatz Ale,** Blatz Brewing, 12 oz., brown and yellow, "English Type" in banner across label, shield
design on label 160.00 210.00

☐ **Blatz Beer,** Blatz brewing, 12 oz., first Blatz can,
blue and white, "Blatz" in blue on white background, "Pilsener" in white on blue banner,
"Beer" in large letters in bottom center .... **RARE**

☐ **Blatz Beer,** Blatz Brewing, 12 oz., dark blue and
white, "Select Lager" appears along top, brand
name in script on label in white 40.00 50.00

☐ **Blatz Beer,** Blatz Brewing, 12 oz., light blue and
white, brand name in white, "Special Pilsener" in
red along top, "Old Heidelberg" in red banner on
label 40.00 50.00

☐ **Blatz Beer,** Blatz Brewing, 12 oz., light blue and
white, brand name in white, "Pilsener Type" in red
on top, "Old Heidelberg" in red banner on label 40.00 50.00

☐ **Bluebonnet Extra Pale,** Dallas-Ft. Worth Brewing
Co., 12 oz., gold and blue with multicolored picture
of mallards in flight 425.00 500.00

☐ **Bohemian,** Enterprise, 32 oz., red, white and blue,
brand name in white, "Beer" in white against red
ribbon .... **RARE**

Price Range

☐ **Bohemian Club,** Bohemian Brewing, 12 oz., red and white, vignette of man in Tyrolean outfit, gold tracery at lower part of can (which is not found on any other version) 90.00   110.00

☐ **Bohemian Club Light Export Lager,** Bohemian Brewing, 12 oz., multicolored, brand name in red on white background 110.00   135.00

☐ **Bon Premium,** Spearman Brewing, 12 oz., orange, blue and white, accent marks over O in "Bon" 200.00   250.00

☐ **Boston Light Ale,** Boston, 12 oz., white and black, word "Light" in red, illustration of lighthouse, Colonial-style lettering–CROWNTAINER 750.00   900.00

☐ **Braumeister Pilsener,** Independent, 12 oz., blue, gold and yellow 53.00   67.00

☐ **Breidt's Half and Half,** Breidt, 12 oz., yellow, red and green, silver top .... **RARE**

☐ **Breidt's Pilsner,** Breidt, 12 oz., gold 400.00   500.00
☐ **Breidt's Pilsner,** Breidt, 12 oz., yellow and red 100.00   130.00
☐ **Breidt's Pilsner,** Breidt, 12 oz., yellow and brown 110.00   140.00

☐ **Breunig's Lager,** Rice Lake, 12 oz., gold and blue, brand name in white, slogan "3 Generations of Brewing Experience" 40.00   60.00

☐ **Brewer's Best Premium Pilsener,** Atlantic Brewing, 12 oz., white, red and gold, gold lions at either side, gold crown at upper center 140.00   170.00

☐ **Brockert Pale Ale,** Brockert Brewing, 12 oz., cream, blue and red, brand name in cream lettering on blue banner 250.00   300.00

☐ **Brucks,** Brucks Brewing, 12 oz., red, white and blue, does not read "Jubilee" (Brucks was not yet calling its beer Jubilee at the time of this can) .. 200.00   250.00

☐ **Bruck's Jubilee,** Bruckman, 12 oz., silver and blue–CROWNTAINER 70.00   90.00

☐ **Bruck's Jubilee Ale,** Bruckman, 12 oz., silver, black and red–CROWNTAINER 375.00   425.00

☐ **Bub's,** Peter Bub, 12 oz., white with brand name in red and white 25.00   35.00

☐ **Bub's Strong,** Peter Bub Brewing, 12 oz., white, blue and gold, brand name has large red initial letter but remainder of lettering is blue, no gold bands at top and bottom 75.00   100.00

☐ **Buckeye Sparkling Dry Ale,** Buckeye Brewing, 12 oz., green, white and gold, brand name in green on white background 100.00   130.00

Price Range

☐ **Buckeye,** Buckeye Brewing, 12 oz., gold and blue, high stepping waiter with tray, red banner reading, "A toast to you" .... **130.00**　**160.00**

☐ **Buckeye,** Buckeye Brewing, 12 oz., gold and blue, high stepping waiter with tray, does not have red banner, reads "Dependable" in white lettering at bottom .... **110.00**　**135.00**

☐ **Buckeye Export,** Buckeye, 12 oz., cream white and blue with illustration of waiter carrying tray in exaggerated pose with one foot raised in air ... **115.00**　**150.00**

☐ **Buckeye Kraeusen Brewed Pilsener,** Buckeye Brewing, 12 oz., gold, white and blue, pair of high stepping waiters with trays at either side facing each other .... **150.00**　**180.00**

☐ **Buffalo Extra Pale,** Buffalo Brewing, 12 oz., red and white, slogan, "Pride of Sacramento" (where the brewery was located) .... **190.00**　**230.00**

☐ **Burgemeister Pilsener,** Warsaw Brewing, 12 oz., red, white and gold, name in black script lettering on red banner .... **70.00**　**90.00**

☐ **Burger Beer,** Burger Brewing, 12 oz., white, red and black, brand name in black, "Pale" and "Dry" appear above center, shield design in upper center, "Cincinnati" under shield .... **80.00**　**110.00**

☐ **Burger,** Burger, 12 oz., white and red, "Distinctively Light, Deliciously Dry" .... **175.00**　**210.00**

☐ **Burger Beer,** Burger Brewing, 12 oz., red, yellow and black, reads, "Vas you efer in Zinzinnati?" (Cincinnati—or Zinzinnati, as it's spelled on this can—was headquarters of the brewery. This slogan was inspired by Jack Pearl, radio comedian of the 1930's who specialized in German dialect routines. His famous line was, "Vas you dere, Sharlie?") **210.00**　**260.00**

☐ **Burger Bohemian,** Burger Brewing, 12 oz., red and blue, brand name in white, silver top ...... **90.00**　**115.00**

☐ **Burger Bohemian,** Burger Brewing, 12 oz., black and red, silver top .... **75.00**　**95.00**

☐ **Burger Bohemian Style,** Burger Brewing, 12 oz., black and red, gold top .... **85.00**　**115.00**

☐ **Burger Brau,** Burger Brewing, 12 oz., multicolored with illustration of bearded man in green hat holding glass which reads "beer" .... **190.00**　**245.00**

☐ **Burger Premium Quality,** Burger Brewing, 12 oz., white, brand name in tall thin block letters ...... **65.00**　**85.00**

Top, Left to Right: **Beverwyck Cream Ale,** 12 oz., **$175–$210;** Braumeister Pilsener, 12 oz., **$53–$67.** Bottom, Left to Right: **Bubs Beer,** 12 oz., **$25–$35;** Buckeye Sparkling Dry Beer, 12 oz., **$65–$85.**

Price Range

☐ **Burger Sparkling Ale,** Burger, 12 oz., brand name
on green medallion 250.00   335.00

☐ **Burkhardt's Export,** Burkhardt Brewing, 12 oz.,
yellow and red with brand name in blue 55.00   75.00

☐ **Burkhardt's Master Blended,** Burkhardt Brewing, 12 oz., red, yellow and white, brand name in
small dark blue lettering 80.00   100.00

☐ **Burkhardt's Special,** Burkhardt Brewing, 12 oz.,
yellow and red with brand name in blue 85.00   110.00

☐ **Bushkill,** Bushkill Brewing Co., 12 oz., cream yellow and black with red highlighting, word "Lager"
in thin red script lettering . . . .   **RARE**

☐ **Butte Special,** Butte Brewing, 12 oz., gold with red
lettering on white background 75.00   100.00

☐ **Butte Special,** Butte Brewing, 12 oz., gold, red
and black, brand name in red "Old English" letter-
ing, logo with initial at center . . . .   **RARE**

☐ **Canadian Ace,** Canadian Ace Brewing, 12 oz.,
brown, green and white, woodgrained to resemble
keg, small shield logo at upper center "Made in
U.S.A." in red banner near bottom 25.00   35.00

☐ **Canadian Ace,** Canadian Ace Brewing, 32 oz.,
same design as the 12 oz. 130.00   160.00

☐ **Cardinal Premium,** Standard Brewing, 12 oz.,
white and gold with brand name in red script letter-
ing 60.00   80.00

☐ **Carling Red Cap Ale,** Brewing Corporation of
America, 12 oz., dark green and yellow, illustration
of horse and rider 85.00   105.00

☐ **Carling Red Cap Ale,** Brewing Corporation of
America, 12 oz., dark green and yellow, illustration
of man wearing cap, no horse 75.00   100.00

☐ **Carling Red Cap Ale,** Brewing Corporation of
America, 12 oz., black and yellow, illustration of
man wearing red cap, no horse 75.00   95.00

☐ **Carling Red Cap Ale,** Carling Brewing, 12 oz., red
and yellow, illustration of man wearing red cap, no
horse 130.00   160.00

☐ **Carling's Black Label,** Brewing Corporation of
America, 12 oz., black and white with red emblem
at upper center 75.00   95.00

☐ **Carnegie Beer,** Duquesne Brewing, 12 oz., red
and white, illustration of man carrying tray laden
with glasses followed by dog . . . .   **RARE**

☐ **Carnegie Beer,** Duquesne Brewing 32 oz., same
design as the 12 oz. . . . .   **RARE**

Price Range

☐ **Century Lager,** Schneider Brewing, 12 oz., orange and gold, brand name in white, logo of hops in gold on blue circular background 250.00   300.00

☐ **Champagne Pilsener,** Harold Johnson Brewing, 12 oz., red and white, silver top 215.00   260.00

☐ **Champagne Velvet,** Terre Haute, 12 oz., gold and yellow, "CV" in white on red circle at upper center   25.00   35.00

☐ **Champagne Velvet Premium Pilsener,** Terre Haute, 12 oz., gold and yellow, "The Beer with the Million Dollar Flavor" 25.00   35.00

☐ **Champagne Velvet Premium Pilsener,** Terre Haute, 32 oz. 385.00   445.00

☐ **Chester Pilsner,** Chester, 12 oz., pink and cream white, slogan "The Beer that Makes Friends" –CROWNTAINER . . . .   **RARE**

☐ **Chevalier Premium,** White Eagle Brewing, 12 oz., white, gold and red, gold top 160.00   200.00

☐ **Chevalier Premium,** White Eagle Brewing, 12 oz., white, gold and red, silver top 170.00   210.00

☐ **Chevy Ale,** Hudepohl, 12 oz., blue with brand name in red, "Ale" in white 300.00   400.00

☐ **Chief Oshkosh Supreme Pilsener,** Oshkosh, 12 oz., white and red, illustration of Indian with feather headdress, "Oshkosh" in white lettering on black background–CROWNTAINER 700.00   800.00

☐ **City Club,** Schmidt, 12 oz., white, yellow and red, horizontal bands 65.00   80.00

☐ **City Club,** Schmidt, 12 oz., gold and red 70.00   90.00

☐ **City Club Strong,** Schmidt, 12 oz., white, yellow and red, horizontal bands 70.00   90.00

☐ **City Club Strong,** Schmidt, 12oz., gold and red   80.00   100.00

☐ **Clipper Pilsner,** Renner, 12 oz., red, white and black, illustration of airplane . . . .   **RARE**

☐ **Clyde Cream Ale,** Enterprise, 12 oz., pink and white, top of can is gray 200.00   250.00
(This can also exists in a very similar style in which the top of the can is gold-colored. The value is about the same.)

☐ **Cold Spring Lager,** Cold Spring Brewing, 12 oz., bright gold and white, silver top 65.00   85.00

☐ **Cold Spring Lager,** Cold Spring Brewing, 12 oz., gray with silver top 75.00   95.00

☐ **Cold Spring Pep Lager,** Cold Spring Brewing, 12 oz., grayish white with gold tracery decoration . .   70.00   90.00

☐ **Cold Spring Strong,** Cold Spring Brewing, 12 oz., yellow and white, "strong" in red lettering 70.00   100.00

Price Range

☐ **Cold Spring Strong Lager,** Cold Spring Brewing, 12 oz., cream white with gold tracery decoration, gold top 75.00 100.00

☐ **Condon's Modern Style,** Condon, 12 oz., green and red, brand name in pale green–CROWN-TAINER 550.00 650.00

☐ **Cook's Goldblume,** Cook Brewing, 12 oz., white, blue and red, "beer" in white 125.00 160.00

☐ **Cook's Goldblume,** Cook Brewing, 12 oz., gold and multicolored, illustration of paddle wheel steamer, silver top, brand name in dark red 125.00 160.00

☐ **Cook's Goldblume,** Cook Brewing, 12 oz., gold and multicolored, illustration of paddle wheel steamer, dark gray top, brand name in orange-red 120.00 150.00

☐ **Cooper's Old Bohemian,** Liebert and Obert, 12 oz., white, brown and gold 300.00 400.00

☐ **Cooper's Old Bohemian,** Liebert and Obert, 12 oz., silver, red and blue–CROWNTAINER . . . . . . RARE

☐ **Cooper's Old Bohemian,** Liebert and Obert, 32 oz., red, white and blue against solid gold, insignia with three horses near top 595.00 695.00

☐ **Copper Club Pilsner,** Copper Club, 12 oz., gold and green 60.00 75.00

☐ **Cremo,** Cremo Brewing, 12 oz., gold, white and blue 130.00 160.00

☐ **Cremo Ale,** Cremo Brewing, 12 oz., gold, cream and red 230.00 270.00

☐ **Cremo Ale,** Cremo Brewing, 32 oz., red and brown, "Connecticut's Best" appears in red on bottom of "C" in "Cremo," CROWNTAINER . . . RARE

☐ **Cremo Lager,** Cremo Brewing, 12 oz., brown and silver, woodgrained to resemble keg–Crowntainer VERY RARE

☐ **Cremo Sparkling,** Cremo Brewing, 12 oz., red and brown–Crowntainer 200.00 250.00

☐ **Croft All Malt Cream Ale,** Croft, 32 oz. 390.00 435.00

☐ **Croft Cream Ale,** Croft, 12 oz., green with yellow lettering, three faces at bottom with words "Dry, Pure, Sparkling" 275.00 345.00

☐ **Dawson's,** Dawson, 12 oz., gold with black brand name, word "Beer" in red script lettering, slogan "A Royal Brew" 600.00 750.00

☐ **Dawson's Beer,** Dawson Brewing, 12 oz., silver, black and red, illustration of king in upper center, brand name in black, "Beer" in red 110.00 140.00

☐ **Dawson's Beer,** Dawson Brewing, same king of diamonds design, 12 oz. . . . . RARE

Top, Left to Right: **Butte Special Beer,** *12 oz.,* **$75–$100;** *Carling Red Cap Ale, 12 oz.,* **$75–$100.** *Bottom, Left to Right:* **Champagne Velvet,** *12 oz.,* **$25–$35,** *Chief Oshkosh, 12 oz.,* **$110–$140.**

Price Range

☐ **Dawson's Master Ale,** Dawson, 12 oz., king of diamonds playing card occupies entire front of can — 250.00 / 325.00

☐ **Dawson's Pale Ale,** Dawson, 12 oz., tan with name in black .... — 65.00 / 85.00

☐ **Dee Light,** Cleveland Home Brewing, 12 oz., maroon and gold, silver top .... — 170.00 / 210.00

☐ **Deer Brand,** Schell, 12 oz., blue and cream white — 95.00 / 120.00

☐ **Diamond State Light,** Diamond State Brewing, 12 oz., dark gold and white .... — 200.00 / 250.00

☐ **Diehl,** Christian Diehl, 12 oz., greenish white and gold, dark gray top .... — 60.00 / 70.00

☐ **Diehl,** Christian Diehl, 12 oz., cream, gold and blue, "Seventy years of quality" .... — 45.00 / 55.00

☐ **Diehl,** Diehl Brewing, 12 oz., cream, gold and blue, "Quality since 1870" appears in bottom center, brand name in gold with blue outline .... — 45.00 / 55.00

☐ **Diehl Five Star Select Premium,** Diehl, 12 oz., red, white and yellow .... — 40.00 / 60.00

☐ **Dixie 45 Beer,** Dixie Brewing, 12 oz., white, red, maroon and gold, brand name in black lettering, "45" in red lettering, gold and maroon stripes on top and bottom of can .... — 170.00 / 210.00

☐ **Dorquest Quality Beer,** Schaeffer Brewing, 12 oz., brown, gold and white, brand name in gold — 200.00 / 260.00

☐ **DuBois Budweiser,** DuBois, 12 oz., white, yellow and silver, "Budweiser" in blue, crown at upper center–CROWNTAINER .... — **VERY RARE**

☐ **DuBois Export Lager,** DuBois, 12 oz., white and red–CROWNTAINER .... — 140.00 / 170.00

☐ **DuBois Famous Light,** DuBois Brewing, 12 oz., yellow and blue, words "famous" and "light" in script lettering, logo at upper center .... — **RARE**

☐ **DuBois Light,** DuBois, 12 oz., gray and blue–CROWNTAINER .... — 120.00 / 150.00

☐ **Duquesne Can-O-Beer,** Duquesne, 12 oz., brown with white lettering, designed to resemble keg–CROWNTAINER .... — **RARE**

☐ **Duquesne Can-O-Beer,** Duquesne Brewing, 12 oz., can is all gold, lettering all in blue, "The Finest Beer In Town" appears along top .... — **RARE**

☐ **Duquesne Keg-O-Beer,** Duquesne Brewing, 12 oz., brown and gold, woodgrained to resemble keg — 140.00 / 170.00

☐ **Duquesne Pilsener,** Duquesne, 12 oz., white with gold stripes, red and gold diamond with name in blue .... — 40.00 / 50.00

Price Range

☐ **Dutch Club,** Pittsburgh Brewing, 12 oz., two shades of blue, brand name in white lettering, large illustration of Dutch boy (this was the second version). 170.00   210.00

☐ **Dutch Club,** Pittsburgh Brewing, 12 oz., blue and white, brand name in black gothic lettering, Dutch boy in wooden shoes carrying tray 260.00   335.00

☐ **E and B Light Lager,** E and B Brewing, 12 oz., blue, yellow and red 40.00   50.00

☐ **E and B Premium,** E and B Brewing, 12 oz., blue, white and red 45.00   60.00

☐ **E and B Special,** E and B Brewing, 12 oz., black, gold and red 80.00   105.00

☐ **Eagle,** Albion Brewing, 12 oz., red, white and blue, large spreadwing eagle 700.00   800.00

☐ **Eastside,** Los Angeles, 12 oz., blue, red and gold, illustration of eagle (colored) 35.00   45.00

☐ **Ebling's,** Ebling, 12 oz., gold and yellow, brand name in black, slogan "That Grand Old Beer" on red background 375.00   440.00

☐ **Ebling Bock,** Ebling, 12 oz., silver and cream, vignette of ram's head–CROWNTAINER 400.00   550.00

☐ **Ebling Premium,** Ebling, 12 oz., red and silver–CROWNTAINER 120.00   150.00

☐ **Ebling's White Head Ale,** Ebling, 12 oz., silver and red, illustration of horse's head–CROWNTAINER 250.00   300.00

☐ **Edelweiss Light,** Schoen Edelweiss Brewing, 12 oz., red and white, does not say "secret brew"   40.00   50.00

☐ **Edelweiss Secret Brew Light,** Schoen Edelweiss Brewing, 12 oz., red and white, silver top 45.00   55.00

☐ **Ehret's Extra,** Ehret Brewing, 12 oz., red, white and gold 90.00   115.00

☐ **El Rey,** El Rey Brewing, 12 oz., yellow and gold with brand name in large red-bordered script letters. Translated, "el rey" means "the king" 400.00   500.00

☐ **English Lad,** Westminster Brewing, 12 oz., green and yellow, horseshoe enclosing jockey and horse   175.00   210.00

☐ **English Lad Ale,** Prima Brewing, 12 oz., green and yellow, horseshoe enclosing jockey and horse . .   175.00   210.00

☐ **Erlanger's Deluxe Pilsner,** Erlanger Brewing, 12 oz., white, word "deluxe" printed in large letters diagonally over brand name, to give the appearance of being stamped on afterward 110.00   140.00

☐ **Erlanger's Pilsner,** Erlanger Brewing, 12 oz., green and gold illustration of bellhop carrying tray   140.00   170.00

Top, Left to Right: **Dawson's Ale,** *12 oz.,* **$65–$85;** *Dawson's Pale Ale,* 12 oz., **$65–$85;** *Bottom, Left to Right:* **Duquesne Can-O-Beer,** *12 oz.,* **$45–$60;** *Duquesne Pilsener* **Beer,** *12 oz.,* **$40–$50.**

Price Range

☐ **Esslinger's Premium,** Esslinger, 12 oz., all gold
with brand name in blue, illustration of bellhop car-
rying tray, winking–CROWNTAINER 600.00   725.00

☐ **Esslinger's Premium,** Esslinger, 12 oz., dark orange and gold, illustration of bellhop holding tray,
winking 500.00   625.00

☐ **Eureka Beer,** Eagel, 12 oz., same design as Eu-
reka Pale Ale . . . .   RARE

☐ **Eureka Extra Pale,** Eagle, 12 oz., cream white and
rust brown, illustration of eagle, "Brewed with Ar-
tesian Well Water" . . . .   RARE

☐ **F and S Pilsener,** Fuhrmann and Schmidt, 12 oz.,
silver and black, no scroll (first version of this
brand's cone top) 300.00   400.00

☐ **F and S Pilsener,** Fuhrmann and Schmidt, 12 oz.,
red and white with scroll (second version) 120.00   150.00

☐ **F and S Pilsener,** Fuhrmann and Schmidt, 12 oz.,
red, white and gold, "beer" in white, gold top (third
version) 80.00   100.00

☐ **Falstaff Beer,** Falstaff Brewing, 12 oz., brown,
gold, red and white, brand name in red block letter-
ing, label is a shield design 50.00   60.00

☐ **Falls Premium Pilsner,** Falls Brewing, 12 oz., gold
and white, no red slogan at upper right 60.00   75.00

☐ **Falls Premium Pilsner,** Falls Brewing, 12 oz., gold
and white, red slogan at upper right 75.00   100.00

☐ **Falls Velvet,** Falls Brewing Co., 12 oz., gold and
black with gray top 130.00   165.00

☐ **Falls Velvet,** Falls Brewing Co., 12 oz., gold and
black with white top 130.00   165.00

☐ **Fauerbach Centennial,** Fauerbach Brewing, 12
oz., red and white, large "CB" 55.00   70.00

☐ **Fehr's XL,** Fehr, 12 oz., red, white and blue, vi-
gnette at center with shield below 90.00   115.00

☐ **Fehr's XL,** Fehr, 12 oz., orange, white and blue,
horses racing 90.00   115.00
(The racehorses were inspired by the fact that
Fehr was located in Louisville, Kentucky.)

☐ **Fehr's XL,** Fehr, 12 oz., –CROWNTAINER 32.00   40.00

☐ **Fitger's Nordlager Natural Brewed Beer,** Fitger,
12 oz., beige and very pale brown 200.00   250.00

☐ **Fitger's Nordlager Natural Brewed Strong
Beer,** Fitger, 12 oz., beige and very pale brown   200.00   250.00

☐ **Fitger's Rex Imperial Dry,** Fitger, 12 oz., yellow
and red 45.00   55.00

Price Range

☐ **Fitzgerald Lager,** Fitzgerald, 12 oz., blue and white 65.00   80.00

☐ **Fitzgerald's Burgomaster,** FitzGerald, 12 oz., light brown and dark brown–CROWNTAINER . . .   **RARE**

☐ **Fitzgerald's Burgomaster,** FitzGerald, 12 oz., silver and blue–CROWNTAINER 180.00   220.00

☐ **Fitzgerald's Garryowen Ale,** FitzGerald, 12 oz., green and cream–CROWNTAINER 150.00   190.00

☐ **Fitzgerald's Garryowen Ale,** FitzGerald, 12 oz., silver and green–CROWNTAINER 290.00   320.00

☐ **Fitzgerald's Lager,** FitzGerald, 12 oz., cream and blue–CROWNTAINER 140.00   170.00

☐ **Fitzgerald's Pale Ale,** Fitzgerald, 12 oz., white and red 120.00   150.00

☐ **Fitzgerald's Pale Ale,** FitzGerald, 12 oz., cream and red–CROWNTAINER 100.00   130.00

☐ **Fitzgerald's Pale Ale,** FitzGerald, 12 oz., silver and red–CROWNTAINER 60.00   80.00

☐ **Five Hundred Ale,** Cook Brewing, 12 oz., green, white and red, racing car and flag (Indy 500) . . .   160.00   200.00

☐ **Fort Schuyler Light Ale,** Utica Brewing, 12 oz., gold and green, "Light" appears in block lettering, "Ale" in script 120.00   150.00

☐ **Fort Schuyler Lager,** Utica Brewing, 12 oz., gold and red, "Lager" appears in script 100.00   130.00

☐ **Fort Schuyler Light Ale,** Utica, 12 oz., gold and greenish gray, illustration of "minuteman" 45.00   65.00

☐ **Fort Schuyler Light Ale,** Utica Brewing, 12 oz., green and white–CROWNTAINER 160.00   190.00

☐ **Fountain Brew,** Fountain, 12 oz., yellow, white and green, snowscape scene 80.00   110.00

☐ **Fountain Brew,** Fountain, 12 oz., green, red and yellow, banner in light green, background in light yellow, white top 80.00   110.00

☐ **Fountain Brew Export,** Fountain Brewing, 12 oz., yellow, white and pastel green, snowscape scene.   80.00   110.00

☐ **Fountain Brew Strong,** Fountain Brewing, 12 oz., yellow, white and green, snowscape scene 80.00   110.00

☐ **Fox Deluxe,** Fox Brewing, 12 oz., gold and white, man in red fox hunting jacket blowing horn 80.00   100.00

☐ **Frankenmuth,** Frankenmuth Brewing, 12 oz., yellow and white, slogan, "Dog gone good," portrait of dog 65.00   80.00

☐ **Frankenmuth Air Free,** Frankenmuth Brewing, 12 oz., yellow and white, portrait of dog 70.00   90.00

Price Range

☐ **Frankenmuth Old English Brand Ale,** Frankenmuth Brewing, 12 oz., black and yellow, silhouette of man in top hat holding foaming glass .... | 110.00 | 140.00

☐ **Frederick's Extra Pale,** Frederick Brewing, 12 oz., red and white .... | 230.00 | 260.00

☐ **Free State,** Free State Brewing, 12 oz., blue and red .... | 130.00 | 160.00

☐ **Fritz Brew,** Fritz Brewing, 12 oz., brown and orange, brand name in white .... | 150.00 | 185.00

☐ **Ft. Pitt,** Ft. Pitt Brewing, 12 oz., green–CROWNTAINER .... | 500.00 | 600.00

☐ **Ft. Pitt,** Ft. Pitt, 12 oz., red, white and blue, states "Contains 12 Fl. Ozs., Same as Bottle"–CROWNTAINER .... | 245.00 | 310.00

☐ **Ft. Pitt Pale Ale,** Ft. Pitt, 12 oz., white and blue | 85.00 | 105.00

☐ **Ft. Pitt Special,** Ft. Pitt, 12 oz., red and white, gold decoration .... | 60.00 | 80.00

☐ **Fuhrmann and Schmidt Pilsener,** Fuhrmann and Schmidt, 12 oz., red, yellow and gold, medallion logo with company initials at upper center, eagle at bottom but not in medallion .... | 200.00 | 300.00

☐ **Fuhrmann and Schmidt Pilsener,** Fuhrmann and Schmidt, 12 oz., red, eagle medallion near bottom, no F & S medallion .... | 500.00 | 600.00

☐ **Fuhrmann and Schmidt Pilsener,** Fuhrmann and Schmidt, 32 oz., red and yellow, eagle at lower center but no medallion .... | 200.00 | 250.00

☐ **Gam,** Wagner Brewing Co., 12 oz., white, red and gold, picture of young man holding glass .... (There was another version of this can, showing an old man holding the beer can. Values are about equal. Gam was short for Gambrinus.) | 80.00 | 105.00

☐ **G.B. Premium Pale Lager,** Grace Brothers, 12 oz., red and white .... | 100.00 | 125.00

☐ **Gerst Brew 77 Extra Dry,** Gerst Brewing, 12 oz., gold, red and white....................... | 90.00 | 125.00

☐ **Gerst Fifty-Seven Premium,** Gerst Brewing, 12 oz., silver, brand name in red–CROWNTAINER | 225.00 | 300.00

☐ **Gettelman,** Gettelman, 12 oz., beige with beige name in brown oval .... | 32.00 | 42.00

☐ **Gibbons,** Lion, 12 oz., dark red and dark gold, words "premium quality" do not appear above "beer" .... | 55.00 | 70.00

☐ **Gibbons Ale,** Lion, 12 oz., gold and black ..... | 225.00 | 300.00

☐ **Gibbons Premium Quality,** Lion, 12 oz., red and gold .... | 55.00 | 70.00

Top, Left to Right: **Eastside,** *12 oz.,* **$40–$52; E and B Light Lager,** *12 oz.,* **$40–$50.** *Bottom, Left to Right:* **Ebling White Head Ale** *(Crowntainer),* *12 oz.,* **$275–$325; Falstaff,** *12 oz.,* **$50–$60.**

Price Range

☐ **Gipps Amberlin,** Gipps Brewing, 12 oz., yellow, red and green 85.00 100.00

☐ **Gipps Amberlin Light Lager,** Gipps Brewing, 12 oz., white, red and green, word "beer" in red ... 100.00 130.00

☐ **Gipps Premium Quality,** Gipps Brewing, 12 oz., yellow, white and silver, brand name in red 200.00 250.00

☐ **Glasgo Select,** Glasgo, 12 oz., dark green with yellow lettering .... RARE

☐ **Gluek's,** Gluek, 12 oz., silver with name in red on red square–CROWNTAINER 30.00 40.00

☐ **Gluek's Pilsener,** Gluek, 12 oz., white with brand name in dark blue, "Pilsener" near top 550.00 650.00

☐ **Gluek's Pilsener Pale,** Gluek Brewing, 12 oz., blue and silver–CROWNTAINER 110.00 140.00

☐ **Gluek's Pilsener Pale,** Gluek Brewing, 12 oz., purple and silver–Crowntainer 85.00 105.00

☐ **Gluek's Stite,** Gluek Brewing, 12 oz., silver and black–CROWNTAINER 160.00 190.00

☐ **Goetz Country Club,** Goetz Brewing, 12 oz., red, white and silver 35.00 45.00

☐ **Goetz Country Club Lager,** Goetz Brewing, 12 oz., black and white, slogan, "Famous for its flavor" 275.00 375.00

☐ **Goetz Country Club Lager,** Goetz Brewing, 12 oz., green and white 80.00 100.00

☐ **Goetz Pale Near Beer,** Goetz Brewing, 12 oz., yellow and red 85.00 105.00

☐ **Gold Medal,** Stegmaier Brewing, 12 oz., purple and white 90.00 115.00

☐ **Gold Seal,** Mutual Brewing, 12 oz., silver and blue 130.00 160.00

☐ **Gold Seal Extra Dry Premium Beer,** Southwestern Brewing, 12 oz., gold, red, blue and white, "Gold Seal" appears in white block lettering in upper center, "Extra Dry" appears in blue script in lower center, red star on yellow background in blue circle 600.00 700.00

☐ **Gold Star,** Hoffbrau, 12 oz., red and gold with brand name in blue 90.00 115.00

☐ **Gold Star,** Hoffbrau Brewing, 12 oz., gold, red and white 85.00 105.00

☐ **Gold Top,** Reisch Brewing, 12 oz., silver and gold, illustration of peacock at lower right–CROWNTAINER 370.00 420.00

Top, Left to Right: **Fehrs XL**, *12 oz.,* **$32–$40;** **Fehrs XL**, *12 oz.,* **$90–$115.** *Bottom, Left to Right:* **Fitgers Nordlager**, *12 oz.,* **$200–$265;** **Fitzgerald's Burgomaster**, *12 oz.,* **$180–$220.**

Price Range

(Gold Top's can had a silver top.)

☐ **Goldcrest Beer,** Tennessee Brewing, 12 oz., blue, white, gold and red, can is mostly blue with white stripes, brand name appears in white on a blue banner on gold label, "Over 51 Years" appears in white on a red circle on bottom right of can 200.00   250.00

☐ **Goldcrest Beer,** Tennessee Brewing, 12 oz., blue, white, gold and red, can is white, brand name appears in white on blue banner on white label, "Over 51 Years" appears in white on a red circle on bottom center of can 175.00   225.00

☐ **Golden Age,** Fernwood, 12 oz., white, red and black, white and black alternating vertical stripes, slogan "The only beer brewed from pure Springfield water" .... RARE

☐ **Golden Age,** Golden Age Brewing, 12 oz., gold and gray, shield supported by lions at upper center (first cone top of this brand) 300.00   400.00

☐ **Golden Age Premium,** Golden Age, 12 oz., red, white and gold, "beer" in black 120.00   150.00

☐ **Golden Age Premium,** Golden Age, 12 oz., white, blue and gold, "beer" in red (believed to be the second cone top of this brand) 190.00   230.00

☐ **Golden Age Select Export,** Golden Age Brewing, 12 oz., white and red, shield at upper center ... 100.00   130.00

☐ **Golden Amber,** Renner Brewing, 12 oz., red and white 75.00   100.00

☐ **Golden Bud Genuine Top-Fermented Ale,** E and B, 12 oz., gold and red 400.00   500.00

☐ **Golden Creme,** Vernon Brewing, 12 oz., pumpkin and black, shield logo with company's initials letters at upper center, slogan, "None better" .... RARE

☐ **Golden Creme English Style Ale,** Vernon Brewing, 12 oz., white and green 250.00   300.00

☐ **Golden Old Topper,** Rochester Brewing, 12 oz., white and red, small vignette of man wearing top hat at lower right 100.00   130.00

☐ **Golden Old Topper Ale,** Rochester Brewing, 12 oz., white and red, silhouette of man wearing top hat 70.00   90.00

☐ **Gotham,** Cincinnati Brewing Co., 12 oz., red, white and silver with view of city skyline showing tall buildings 170.00   210.00

*Top, Left to Right: **Fountain Brew**, 12 oz., **$80–$100**; Frankenmuth Old English Brand* ***Ale**, 12 oz., **$110–$140**. Bottom, Left to Right: **Gettelman**, 12 oz., **$32–$42**; Gluek's* ***Beer**, 12 oz., **$30–$40**.*

Price Range

☐ **Grain Belt Beer,** Minneapolis Brewing, 12 oz., black, gold and red, can is mostly black with red label and gold lettering, "The Minneapolis Beer" appears along bottom 40.00   50.00

☐ **Grain Belt Beer,** Minneapolis Brewing, 12 oz., black, gold and red, can is mostly black with red label and gold lettering, "The Friendly Beer" appears along bottom 40.00   50.00

☐ **Grain Belt Beer,** Minneapolis Brewing, 12 oz., black, gold and red, can is mostly black with red label and gold lettering, "Strong Beer" appears along bottom 40.00   50.00

☐ **Grain Belt Beer,** Minneapolis, 12 oz., "The Friendly Beer with the Friendly Flavor" appears on bottom of label 40.00   50.00

☐ **Grain Belt Strong Premium Ale,** Minneapolis, 12 oz., red and white, slogan "The Friendly Ale" .. 350.00   450.00

☐ **Graupner,** Robert Graupner, 12 oz., red and gold   600.00   750.00

☐ **Graupner's Old German,** Robert Graupner, Inc., 32 oz., white and orange .... **RARE**

☐ **Gretz,** Gretz Brewing, 12 oz., cream and red, brand name in red lettering, logo of man on bicycle appears directly above brand name 100.00   130.00

☐ **Gretz,** Gretz Brewing, 12 oz., silver and blue, large red illustration of man on bicycle at center, brand name in blue 150.00   200.00

☐ **Gretz,** Gretz Brewing, 12 oz., silver and yellow, brand name in blue–CROWNTAINER 200.00   250.00

☐ **Gretz,** Gretz, 32 oz., yellow and blue front, silver and blue back, illustration of man riding 1890s bicycle, slogan "Made the Old Fashioned Way" .. 775.00   900.00

☐ **Griesedieck Bros. Double Mellow Light Lager,** Griesedieck Bros. Brewing, 12 oz., silver and blue–CROWNTAINER 75.00   100.00

☐ **Grossvater,** Renner, 12 oz., silver, blue and red–CROWNTAINER 45.00   60.00
Note: Literally translated, the brand name means "grandfather."

☐ **Grossvater,** Renner, 12 oz., silver, blue and red   150.00   200.00

☐ **Grossvater Special,** Renner, 12 oz., brown, yellow and white 100.00   135.00

☐ **Gunther's Special Dry Lager,** Gunther, 12 oz., reddish salmon, brand name in brown 550.00   650.00

☐ **Gus' Premium Topper,** Kalispell Brewing, 12 oz., white and red 150.00   200.00

Price Range

(This is believed to be the only brand of beer ever known by the brewer's first name, Gus Kallspell.)

☐ **Haas Beer,** Haas Brewing, 12 oz., gold, white, red and black, brand-name in white in red oval, "Pilsener Style" appears in red script 85.00   105.00

☐ **Haberle's Congress,** Haberle, 32 oz., gold and aqua, vignette of Capitol Building . . . .   **RARE**

☐ **Haberle's Light Ale,** Haberle, 32 oz., dark gold and green 600.00   750.00

☐ **Haberle's Light Ale,** H.C., 12 oz., red and light gray (later version, not quite as valuable, has greenish gray) 120.00   150.00

☐ **Hanley's Extra Dry Lager,** Hanley, 12 oz., red and white, illustration of bulldog–CROWNTAINER   280.00   335.00

☐ **Hanley's Extra Pale Ale,** Hanley, 12 oz., white and blue, illustration of bulldog–Crowntainer 120.00   150.00

☐ **Hanley's Extra Pale Lager,** Hanley, 12 oz., red and white, illustration of bulldog–CROWNTAINER   300.00   350.00

☐ **Hanley's Extra Pale Peerless Ale,** Hanley, 12 oz., silver and violet–CROWNTAINER 65.00   80.00

☐ **Hauenstein's New Ulm,** Hauenstein, 12 oz., white and red, brand name in red 50.00   65.00

☐ **Hauenstein's New Ulm,** Hauenstein, 12 oz., all red with white lettering 80.00   100.00

☐ **Hauenstein's New Ulm Strong,** Hauenstein, 12 oz., all red with white lettering 70.00   85.00

(Ulm was a town of some importance in the early German brewing industry.)

☐ **Heidel-Brau,** Sioux City Brewing, 12 oz., orange and gold 65.00   80.00

☐ **Heidelburg Extra Dry,** Valley Brewing, 12 oz., red, white and green 450.00   550.00

☐ **Heileman's Old Style Lager,** G. Heileman Brewing, 12 oz., red, yellow and black, label is shield-shaped, "Heileman's" appears in yellow banner on top of label 120.00   150.00

☐ **Heileman's Old Style Lager,** Heileman, 12 oz., white, red and black, scenic illustration 75.00   100.00

☐ **Highlander,** Missoula Brewing, 12 oz., reddish gold and blue, eagle at upper center 145.00   175.00

☐ **Hoff-Brau,** Hoff-Brau, 12 oz., white with gold trim, red ribbon with name in white 375.00   475.00

☐ **Hoff-Brau,** Hoff-Brau Brewing, 12 oz., white and red–CROWNTAINER 140.00   170.00

☐ **Hoff-Brau Ale,** Hoff-Brau Brewing, 12 oz., white, green and gold 130.00   155.00

Price Range

☐ **Hoff-Brau Dry Pilsener,** Hoff-Brau Brewing, 12 oz., white, red and gold 115.00   145.00

☐ **Hohenadel,** John Hohenadel, 12 oz., cream white, orange and gold, slogan "Well earned supremacy" near top 200.00   265.00

☐ **Hohenadel,** Hohenadel Brewing, 12 oz., cream–CROWNTAINER 170.00   215.00

☐ **Hohenadel,** Hohenadel Brewing, 12 oz., silver–CROWNTAINER 160.00   200.00

☐ **Hohenadel Indian Queen Ale,** Hohenadel Brewing, 12 oz., white, black and red, portrait of Indian female at upper center 250.00   300.00

☐ **Hohenadel Light,** Hohenadel Brewing, 32 oz., cream, black and red, silver top 700.00   850.00

☐ **Honer's Special Pilsener Type Lager,** Honer Brewing, 12 oz., gold, red and white 700.00   850.00

☐ **Hornung Light,** Jacob Hornung, 12 oz., gold and cream, wording, "Diamond anniversary brew" at top 160.00   200.00

☐ **Hornung's Light,** Hornung Brewing, 32 oz., gold and yellow with blue lettering .... **RARE**

☐ **Horton,** Horton, 12 oz., pinkish orange, brand name in dark blue, vignette of two glasses being touched together in a toast 140.00   175.00

☐ **Horton Ale,** City Brewing, 12 oz., red with brand name in white, wording, "America's finest" 90.00   115.00

☐ **Horton Ale,** Horton Brewing, 12 oz., bright pink with brand name in white, logo at center with slogan, "America's finest" 375.00   450.00

☐ **Horton Old Stock Ale,** Horton, 12 oz., brown and silver, vignette of two glasses being touched together in a toast 140.00   170.00

☐ **Horton Pilsener,** Pilsener Brewing, 12 oz., dark orange 130.00   160.00

☐ **Horton Pilsener,** Horton, 12 oz. 180.00   220.00

☐ **Huber All Grain,** Joseph Huber, 12 oz., red, white and gold, slogan, "Wisconsin made" 70.00   90.00

☐ **Hudepohl Chevy Ale,** Hudepohl, 12 oz., silver and blue–CROWNTAINER 300.00   400.00

☐ **Hudepohl Old 85 Ale,** Hudepohl, 12 oz., white and brown with red and gold bands at top and bottom 170.00   210.00

☐ **Hudepohl Pure Lager,** Hudepohl, 12 oz., red and white, word "beer" in red, "pure lager" in script lettering 70.00   85.00

*Top, Left to Right: **Grossvater Beer**, 12 oz., **$45–$60**; Hanley's Extra Pale Ale, 12 oz., **$65–$80**. Bottom, Left to Right: **Heidel-Brau**, 12 oz., **$65–$80**; **Hoff-Brau Beer**, 12 oz., **$375–$475**.*

Price Range

☐ **Hudepohl Pure Lager,** Hudepohl, 12 oz., red and white, "beer" in white, "pure lager" in block lettering (second version of this cone top) 50.00   60.00

☐ **Hudepohl Pure Lager,** Hudepohl, 12 oz., brown and black–CROWNTAINER 200.00   250.00

☐ **Hudepohl Pure Lager,** Hudepohl, 12 oz., white and red–CROWNTAINER 75.00   100.00

☐ **Hull's,** Hull Brewing, 12 oz., silver and blue–CROWNTAINER 225.00   275.00

☐ **Hull's Ale,** Hull Brewing, 12 oz., silver and blue–CROWNTAINER 150.00   200.00

☐ **Indian Queen Ale,** Hohenadel, 12 oz., yellow, brand name in blue, "Ale" in red, small illustration of Indian female, slogan "Well earned supremacy" .... RARE

☐ **Iron City,** Pittsburgh, 12 oz., red with name in white on black banners 135.00   165.00

☐ **Iron City Beer,** Pittsburgh Brewing, 12 oz., white, gold and red, can is mostly white with brand name in white on red circular label, "Select Quality" appears in gold lettering on black banner near bottom 95.00   115.00

☐ **Iron City Beer,** Pittsburgh Brewing, 12 oz., white gold and red, can is mostly white with brand name in white on red circular label, "It's Real Beer" appears on top 110.00   140.00

☐ **Iroquois Half and Half,** Iroquois Brewing, 12 oz., orange and yellow .... RARE
(This was an ale and porter mixture, such as many brewers were offering in the late 1930s and early 1940s.)

☐ **Iroquois Indian Head,** Iroquois Brewing, 12 oz., gold and blue (first version) 300.00   400.00

☐ **Iroquois Indian Head,** Iroquois Brewing, 12 oz., yellow with blue lettering (second version of this cone top) 170.00   210.00

☐ **Iroquois Indian Head,** Iroquois Brewing, 12 oz., gold and red, crosshatch design (third version) 95.00   115.00

☐ **Iroquois Indian Head,** Iroquois Brewing, 12 oz., red and white with colored Indian portrait, brand name in red, "beer" in blue (fourth version) 80.00   100.00

☐ **Iroquois Indian Head,** Iroquois Brewing, 12 oz., silver, red and blue, large Indian profile within circle–CROWNTAINER 80.00   105.00

Price Range

☐ **Iroquois Indian Head,** Iroquois Brewing, 12 oz., silver, red and blue, small Indian profile with no circle around it–CROWNTAINER 80.00   105.00

☐ **Iroquois Indian Head Ale,** Iroquois Brewing, 12 oz., silver, green and red–CROWNTAINER 100.00   130.00

☐ **John Bull,** New Philadelphia Brewing, 12 oz., cream and red, small vignette of man in straw hat at upper center 350.00   450.00
(John Bull is the British equivalent of Uncle Sam. The name was popularized by eighteenth-century caricaturist Thomas Rowlandson.)

☐ **Jolly Scot Ale,** Robert Graupner, Inc., 12 oz., gold and red, portrait of kilted Scotsman with plaid cape, leaning on walking stick .... **RARE**

☐ **Jolly Scot Ale,** Robert Graupner, Inc., 12 oz., silver, yellow and red, kilted Scotsman–CROWNTAINER .... **RARE**

☐ **Jolly Scot Ale,** Robert Graupner, Inc., 32 oz., gold and red, kilted Scotsman .... **RARE**

☐ **Jung Pilsener,** Jung Brewing, 12 oz., silver and green–CROWNTAINER 115.00   145.00

☐ **Jung Pilsener,** Jung Brewing, 12 oz., silver and violet–CROWNTAINER 135.00   165.00

☐ **Kaier's Special,** Charles Kaier, 12 oz., cream, red and white, castle battlement in red 80.00   100.00

☐ **Kamm's Pilsener Light,** Kamm, 12 oz., red and silver checkerboard–CROWNTAINER 70.00   85.00

☐ **Kamm's Pilsener Light,** Kamm & Schellinger Brewing, 12 oz., red and white, checkerboard design, slogan, "The quality beer" 325.00   425.00
(An example, and not a unique one, of the cone top version of a can outselling the Crowntainer version.)

☐ **Karlsbrau Old Time,** Duluth, 12 oz., red and white 80.00   100.00

☐ **Kato Gold Label,** Mankato Brewing, 12 oz., pink and dark blue 475.00   575.00
(Although the color of this can is classified as pink, which it most definitely appears to be, it was intended as a classy reddish shade of gold. Too much red was used.)

☐ **Kato Gold Label,** Mankato Brewing, 12 oz., gold and blue, brand name in gold script on blue banner 475.00   575.00

☐ **Kato Lager,** Mankato Brewing, 12 oz., blue and silver, brand name in silver script on blue banner 475.00   575.00

☐ **Keeley,** Keeley Brewing, 12 oz., red and white, "Just right" 80.00   100.00

*Top, Left to Right: **Hudepohl** (Crowntainer), 12 oz., **$75–$100**; **Iron City Beer**, 12 oz., **$135–$165**. Bottom, Left to Right: **Jax Pilsner**, 12 oz., RARE; **Kamm's Pilsener Light**, 12 oz., **$70–$85**.*

Price Range

☐ **Kessler,** Kessler Brewing, 12 oz., light blue and
dark blue, brand name in white 75.00   90.00

☐ **Kiewel's,** Kiewel, 12 oz., red and dark blue, brand
name in white, "Beer" in blue on red background   **RARE**

☐ **King's Head Ale,** Franklin Brewing, 12 oz., red
and dark blue, ornate lettering, portrait of king from
deck of playing cards 700.00   850.00

☐ **King's Taste,** Rainier Brewing, 12 oz., red, yellow
and blue 400.00   550.00
(Will be found imprinted with the names of various
West Coast retail dealers.)

☐ **Kingsbury,** Kingsbury Brewing, 12 oz., silver and
cream, shield at upper center–CROWNTAINER 65.00   80.00

☐ **Kingsbury,** Kingsbury Brewing, 12 oz., white and
green–CROWNTAINER 120.00   150.00

☐ **Kingsbury Pale,** Kingsbury Brewing, 12 oz., silver
and pale beige–CROWNTAINER 75.00   90.00

☐ **Kingsbury Pale,** Kingsbury Brewing, 12 oz., silver
and yellow–CROWNTAINER 75.00   90.00

☐ **Koch's Old Vienna,** Koch Brewing, 12 oz., pinkish
violet, view of street in Vienna 130.00   160.00

☐ **Koehler Select,** Erie Brewing, 12 oz., white, blue
and gold 90.00   120.00

☐ **Koehler's,** Erie Brewing, 12 oz., blue and gold,
brand name in white lettering on red banner, slo-
gan, "There is no better beer" 100.00   130.00

☐ **Koehler's,** Koehler, 12 oz., white with name in
white on red band 175.00   225.00

☐ **Koenig Brau Premium,** Prima Bismarck, 12 oz.,
white and gold, "premium" in red 80.00   100.00

☐ **Koenig Brau Premium,** Prima Bismarck, 12 oz.,
gold and white, gray top 70.00   85.00

☐ **Koller's Topaz,** Koller Brewing, 12 oz., silver–CROWNTAINER 65.00   80.00

☐ **Kopper Kettle,** LaFayette Brewing, 12 oz., gold
and yellow 175.00   225.00

☐ **Kraeusen Ben Brew,** Franklin Brewing, 12 oz., orange, blue and red, small star at upper center .. 150.00   200.00

☐ **Krueger Cream Ale,** Krueger Brewing, 12 oz.,
green 80.00   100.00

☐ **Krueger Finest,** Krueger Brewing, 12 oz., violet 110.00   140.00

☐ **Krueger Finest,** Krueger, 12 oz., wine red and
gold–CROWNTAINER 95.00   115.00

☐ **Krueger Light Lager,** Krueger Brewing, 12 oz.,
pale yellow and red 55.00   70.00

Price Range

☐ **Krug Pilsener,** Rainier Brewing, 12 oz., blue, red and white, illustration of beer stein ornamented with female figure . . . .   **RARE**

☐ **Kuebler Bock,** Kuebler Brewing, 12 oz., red and gold, illustration of man in top hat and goat drinking from mug of beer . . . .   **RARE**

☐ **Kuebler Cream Ale,** Kuebler, 12 oz., green and gold, illustration of man in top hat **490.00**   **580.00**

☐ **Kuebler Cream Ale,** Kuebler, 12 oz., white and green, illustration of man in top hat–CROWNTAINER . . . .   **RARE**

☐ **Kuebler Pilsener,** Kuebler, 32 oz., same design as 12 oz., with silhouette of man sitting in chair drinking tankard of beer . . . .   **RARE**

☐ **Kuebler Cream Ale,** Kuebler, 32 oz., red and yellow, top-hatted man pouring from can into glass   **RARE**

☐ **Kuebler Pilsener,** Kuebler, 12 oz., white with brand name in red–CROWNTAINER **325.00**   **400.00**

☐ **Kuebler Pilsener,** Kuebler, 12 oz., blue and red, illustration of man in top hat–CROWNTAINER . .   **475.00**   **575.00**

☐ **Lebanon Valley Pilsner,** Lebanon Valley Brewing, 12 oz., cream white, gold and blue, brand name in blue lettering with thin gold borders, "pilsner" in red **250.00**   **300.00**

☐ **Lebanon Valley,** Lebanon Valley Brewing, 32 oz., same design as 12 oz. **650.00**   **800.00**

☐ **Leidig's Deluxe,** Rainier Brewing, 12 oz., gray, black and red, brand name in gothic lettering, "deluxe" in red block letters, company address in white on red banner . . . .   **RARE**

☐ **Leidig's Dutch Mill,** El Rey Brewing, 12 oz., red, blue and white, star at top center, illustration of two windmills on side . . . .   **RARE**

☐ **Leinenkugel's Chippewa Pride,** Leinenkugel Brewing, 12 oz., yellow and silver, Indian profile–CROWNTAINER **115.00**   **145.00**

☐ **Leisy's Dortmunder Style,** Leisy Brewing, 12 oz., red and gold **150.00**   **200.00**

☐ **Leisy's Light,** Leisy Brewing, 12 oz., blue and white **130.00**   **170.00**

☐ **Lifestaff Pale Lager,** Rainier, 12 oz., pink and blue **150.00**   **200.00**
(On trade lists this name is often spelled as two words (Life Staff), but on the can it appears as one.)

Price Range

☐ **Lion Ale,** Greater New York Brewing, 32 oz., red, blue and silver, can is mostly red with circular blue label with silver lion resting one paw on medallion bearing name of brewer .... **RARE**

☐ **Lion Pilsener,** Lion Brewing, 12 oz., white, red and blue, logo of lion at upper center, slogan "New York's famous"–CROWNTAINER 500.00 600.00

☐ **Lisco Lager,** Sil's Food Co., 12 oz., gold and black 350.00 450.00

☐ **Little Dutch,** Wacker Brewing, 12 oz., blue and gold, illustration of Dutch boy and windmill, red bands at top and bottom .... **RARE**

☐ **Little Dutch Lager,** Wacker Brewing, 12 oz., white, yellow and silver, Dutch boy and windmill–CROWNTAINER .... **RARE**

☐ **Little Dutch Lager,** Wacker Brewing, 32 oz., Dutch boy and windmill .... **RARE**

☐ **London Bobby,** Miami Valley, 12 oz., white and red–CROWNTAINER 75.00 100.00

☐ **London Bobby Ale,** Miami Valley, 12 oz., green and cream white, coat of arms near top–CROWNTAINER 75.00 100.00

☐ **London Tavern Ale,** El Dorado Brewing, 12 oz., multicolor with central scene of a Victorian carriage led by four horses approaching a tavern .. **RARE**

☐ **Maier Export,** Maier, 12 oz., cream and gray, brand name in red 150.00 185.00

☐ **Maier Gold Label,** Maier, 12 oz., gold and red .. 140.00 165.00

☐ **Maier Gold Label Ale,** Maier, 12 oz., green, gold and silver, brand name in silver 220.00 260.00

☐ **Maier Select,** Maier, 12 oz., red and white 75.00 95.00

☐ **Martin's,** Yalsime Valley Brewing, 12 oz., blue and white, slogan, "Make mine Martin's" 200.00 250.00

☐ **M.C. Deluxe Pilsener,** Mount Carbon, 12 oz., gold and blue, "Brewers since 1887" 550.00 650.00

☐ **Menominee Champion Light,** Menominee Brewing, 12 oz., red and white 75.00 90.00

☐ **Metz Jubilee,** Metz Brewing, 12 oz., orange with white lettering 80.00 100.00

☐ **Michel Bock,** Ebling Brewing, 12 oz., silver and red–CROWNTAINER 500.00 600.00

☐ **Michel Light Dry,** Ebling Brewing, 12 oz., silver and red–CROWNTAINER 400.00 500.00

☐ **Milwaukee Club,** Schlitz, 12 oz., red and cream 100.00 130.00

☐ **Milwaukee Club,** Schlitz, 12 oz., brown and cream 70.00 90.00

☐ **Mineral Springs,** Mineral Springs, 12 oz., light brown and white, horse head symbol in red 57.00 69.00

	Price Range	

☐ **Monarch,** Monarch, 12 oz. . . . . — 85.00 — 100.00

☐ **Montery Beer,** Monterey, 12 oz., black and white pictorial with rodeo rider on bucking bronc, yacht on lake, etc. . . . . — 700.00 — 800.00 ·

☐ **Morlein Premium,** Burton Brewing Co., 12 oz., gold and dark green . . . . — 475.00 — 600.00

☐ **Muehlebach,** Muehlebach Brewing, 12 oz., white, gold and red, ornate shield with pair of facing lions at center . . . . — 120.00 — 150.00

☐ **Mug Ale,** Burkhardt Brewing, 12 oz., cream and blue, illustration of beer mug and smoking pipe — 200.00 — 250.00

☐ **Murphy's Ale,** Star Brewing, 12 oz., red and green, heraldic shield at upper center . . . . — 250.00 — 300.00

☐ **Namar Premium,** Cooper, 12 oz., gold and blue, brand name in white on blue background, "Carefully Blended on the Finest Ingredients" . . . . — 225.00 — 300.00

☐ **Namar Premium,** Cooper Brewing, 12 oz., silver and blue–CROWNTAINER . . . . — 200.00 — 250.00

☐ **Narragansett Banquet Ale,** Narragansett Brewing, 32 oz., gold and yellow . . . . — 800.00 — 925.00

☐ **National Ale,** National, 12 oz., silver and blue, word "Genuine" beneath brand name, map of U.S. in blue . . . . — 325.00 — 425.00

☐ **National Ale,** National, 12 oz., red, white and blue, eagle against blue background, states "New York office: 67 West 44th Street, N.Y.C." . . . . — 500.00 — 600.00

☐ **National Beer,** National Brewing, 12 oz., red and gray, map of U.S. appears in red in upper center, "Light" appears in red underneath brand name — RARE

☐ **National Bohemian Bock,** National Brewing, 12 oz., red, brand name in white lettering on black banners, "Bock" in yellow script, ram's head at upper right, slogan, "First brewed in 1885" . . . . . — RARE

☐ **National Bohemian Pale,** National, 12 oz., red and black, illustration of one-eyed man with moustache (company symbol)–CROWNTAINER . . . . . — 450.00 — 550.00

☐ **National Pale Dry,** National, 12 oz., violet and white, shield with lions–CROWNTAINER . . . . — 280.00 — 330.00

☐ **Neuweiler's Pilsener,** Neuweiler Brewing, 12 oz., silver, red and orange, German eagle symbol–CROWNTAINER . . . . — 20.00 — 30.00

☐ **Neuweiler's Pilsener,** Neuweiler, 32 oz., yellow, black and blue, eagle symbol at center . . . . — 325.00 — 425.00

Price Range

☐ **Nick Thomas Pilsner Pale,** Miami Valley Brewing, white, red and blue, brand name in red, logo of an arrow in bullseye with "Finest Quality" in white—CROWNTAINER 600.00   700.00

☐ **Noch-Eins Pale,** Washington Brewing, 12 oz., white and orange, vignette of rotund smiling man   225.00   275.00

☐ **Northern,** Northern, 12 oz., yellow with name in white on brown rectangle 150.00   180.00

☐ **Northern,** Northern, 12 oz., white with gold trim, multicolor scene with name in red 90.00   125.00

☐ **Northern Strong,** Northern Brewing, 12 oz., cream and brown 60.00   75.00

☐ **Old Anchor,** Brackenridge Brewing, 12 oz., white, red and navy blue, logo of anchor with rope and star at upper center, slogan, "Brewed from pure mountain spring water" .... **RARE**

☐ **Old Bohemia Pilsner,** Philadelphia Brewing, 12 oz., gold and blue 200.00   250.00

☐ **Old Bohemia Pilsner,** New Philadelphia Brewing, 12 oz., cream, black and red, red lettering 160.00   200.00

☐ **Old Bohemia Pilsner,** New Philadelphia Brewing, 12 oz., cream and blue, brand name in blue 160.00   200.00

☐ **Old Dutch,** Aztec Brewing, 12 oz., brown and gold, vignette in full color of a portrait by Franz Hals   170.00   210.00

☐ **Old Dutch,** Eagle Brewing, 12 oz., white and brown with colored illustration of moustached man and foaming glass—CROWNTAINER .... **RARE**

☐ **Old Dutch,** Old Dutch Brewing, 12 oz., cream and red, logo of windmill 500.00   600.00
(This brewery was located in Brooklyn, N.Y., in the 1930s and the name Old Dutch was inspired by the fact that many local streets had Dutch names.)

☐ **Old Dutch,** Old Dutch, 32 oz., white and brown   675.00   800.00

☐ **Old Dutch Ale,** Old Dutch, 12 oz., white and green, brand name in black 800.00   925.00

☐ **Old Dutch Ale,** Old Dutch, 32 oz., white and green   775.00   900.00

☐ **Old Dutch Brand Ale,** Old Dutch, 32 oz., same design as green and white, 12 oz. .... **RARE**

☐ **Old Dutch Lager,** Metropolis Brewing, 12 oz., red and white, small vignette of windmill at upper center 80.00   100.00

☐ **Old England Cream Ale,** Old England Brewing, 12 oz., gold, red and black, silver top 260.00   310.00

☐ **Old England Cream Ale,** Old England Brewing, 12 oz., yellow and dark blue, elaborate central logo of castle wall with shield .... **RARE**

Top, Left to Right: **Kingsbury Pale**, 12 oz., **$75–$100**; **Koehler's**, 12 oz., **$75–$100**. Bottom, Left to Right: **Neuweiler's Cream Ale**, 12 oz., **$100–$130**; **Neuweiler's Pilsener**, 12 oz., **$22.50–$32.50**.

Price Range

☐ **Old Export,** Cumberland Brewing, white can with red label, brand name in white, "Mountain Water Makes The Difference" in red lettering along the bottom 80.00   100.00

☐ **Old Fashioned,** Northampton Brewing, 12 oz., cream and black–CROWNTAINER 120.00   150.00

☐ **Old German,** Lebanon Valley, 12 oz., cream and brown, yellow lettering 150.00   180.00

☐ **Old German,** Queen City Brewing, 12 oz., white, red and yellow, silver top 95.00   120.00

☐ **Old German Lager,** Renner Brewing, 12 oz., green with white lettering 140.00   170.00

☐ **Old German Style,** Renner Brewing, 12 oz., white and red, vignette of man in German costume hoisting glass 70.00   90.00

☐ **Old German,** Graupner, 12 oz., red and white, brand name in red, "Beer" in black, "Brewed and Packaged by" in red . . . .   RARE

☐ **Old India Vatted Pale Ale,** Cremo Brewing, 12 oz., green 450.00   550.00

☐ **Old Ox Head Ale,** Standard Brewing, 12 oz., orange and red–CROWNTAINER 400.00   500.00

☐ **Old Oxford Ale,** Renner Brewing, 12 oz., pale green and yellow 90.00   110.00

☐ **Old Oxford Ale,** Renner Brewing, 12 oz., dark green and yellow, symbol at upper center of two men in fancy dress walking side by side 75.00   100.00

☐ **Old Oxford Ale,** Renner Brewing, 12 oz., dark green and yellow, symbol at upper center of man in Tyrolean costume hoisting glass 80.00   100.00

☐ **Old Reading,** Old Reading Brewing, 12 oz., violet and red, laughing man with handlebar moustache hoisting foaming tankard . . . .   RARE

☐ **Old Reading,** Old Reading Brewing, 12 oz., silver and dark green, moustached man raising glass (the first Old Reading cone top)–CROWNTAINER   150.00   200.00

☐ **Old Reading Pilsener,** Old Reading Brewing, 12 oz., silver and brown–CROWNTAINER 75.00   100.00

☐ **Old Reading Pilsener,** Old Reading Brewing, 12 oz., cream and brown–CROWNTAINER 75.00   100.00

☐ **Old Shay,** Ft. Pitt Brewing, 12 oz., silver, black and red–CROWNTAINER 75.00   100.00

☐ **Old Style Lager,** G. Heileman Brewing, 12 oz., green, brown and white, illustration of old-style brewery 90.00   115.00

Price Range

☐ **Old Style Lager,** Heileman, 12 oz., black, red and
yellow, brand name in white gothic lettering 140.00   180.00

☐ **Old Tap Bohemian,** Enterprise Brewing, 12 oz.,
gold and black..................................   200.00   250.00

☐ **Old Tap Select Stock Ale,** Enterprise Brewing, 12
oz., gold and white 180.00   230.00

☐ **Old Tap Select Stock Ale,** Enterprise, 12 oz.,
multicolored pictorial can with illustration of grin-
ning, toothless man holding glass 600.00   750.00

☐ **Old Topper,** Rochester Brewing, 12 oz., silver and
red–CROWNTAINER 130.00   170.00

☐ **Old Topper Ale,** Rochester Brewing, 12 oz., silver
and violet–CROWNTAINER 100.00   140.00

☐ **Old Topper Ale,** Rochester Brewing, 12 oz., green
and brown–CROWNTAINER 325.00   425.00

☐ **Old Topper Bock,** Rochester, 12 oz., silver and
gold, silhouette of man in top hat–CROWN-
TAINER ....   **RARE**

☐ **Old Topper Lager,** Rochester Brewing, 12 oz., silver and red, silhouette portrait against silver background–CROWNTAINER 95.00   120.00

☐ **Old Topper Lager,** Rochester Brewing, 12 oz.,
red and yellow, silhouette portrait against yellow
background–CROWNTAINER 130.00   160.00

☐ **Old Topper Lager,** Rochester, 12 oz., brown, silhouette of man in top hat–CROWNTAINER 200.00   250.00

☐ **Old Topper Snappy Ale,** Rochester Brewing, 12
oz., cream and brown with silhouette portrait of
man in tall hat 70.00   95.00

☐ **Old Vienna Premium Quality,** Koch Brewing, 12
oz., cream and red 80.00   100.00

☐ **Old English 600 Malt Liquor,** People's Brewing,
12 oz., white and gold 120.00   150.00

☐ **Olde Virginia,** Virginia Brewing, 12 oz., white and
blue 70.00   90.00

☐ **Olde Virginia Special Export,** Virginia Brewing,
12 oz., red, white and blue, "special" in white
against red background, horizontal stripes along
center of can 75.00   100.00

☐ **Old Style Pale Export,** Silver Springs Brewing, 32
oz., white and red ....   **RARE**

☐ **Oldtimer Premium,** Henry Ortlieb, 12 oz., red,
white and gold 100.00   130.00

☐ **Ortlieb's Ale,** Ortlieb Brewing, 12 oz., silver and
pale yellow–CROWNTAINER ....   **RARE**

Top, Left to Right: **Northern Beer,** *12 oz.,* **$95–$130;** *Northern Beer,* *12 oz.,* **$150–$180.**
Bottom, Left to Right: **Oertels 92 Lager Beer,** *12 oz.,* **$35–$47;** *Old Style Lager,* Heileman's, *12 oz.,* **$140–$180.**

Price Range

- ☐ **Ortlieb's Export Lager,** Ortlieb Brewing, 12 oz., silver and red–CROWNTAINER .... 475.00 | 575.00
- ☐ **Ortlieb's Lager,** Henry Ortlieb, 12 oz., yellow and red, slogan, "Packaged at the brewery" .... 275.00 | 350.00
- ☐ **Ortlieb's Lager,** Henry Ortlieb, 12 oz., silver, black and red–CROWNTAINER .... 225.00 | 275.00
- ☐ **Ortlieb's Lager,** Henry Ortlieb, 12 oz., silver, gold and red–CROWNTAINER .... 140.00 | 170.00
- ☐ **Pabst Blue Ribbon,** Pabst Brewing, 32 oz., gold, blue and white, "Snap-cap Full Quart" in blue lettering on white banner near top .... 200.00 | 250.00
- ☐ **Pabst Blue Ribbon,** Pabst Brewing, 32 oz., blue and white, brand name in white on blue ribbon, "Snap-cap Full Quart" in blue lettering on white banner near top .... 200.00 | 250.00
- ☐ **Pabst Blue Ribbon,** Pabst Brewing, 32 oz., blue, red and white, red diagonal stripe runs through the blue ribbon .... 250.00 | 350.00
- ☐ **Pacific Lager,** Rainier Brewing, 12 oz., blue and white, very plain can with logo of sailboat on waves .... 550.00 | 650.00
- ☐ **Peerless,** LaCrosse Brewing, 12 oz., white and red 60.00 | 80.00
- ☐ **Peerless Extra Premium,** LaCrosse Brewing, 12 oz., white and green .... 70.00 | 95.00
- ☐ **Phoenix Lager,** Phoenix Brewing, 12 oz., red, black and gold .... 350.00 | 425.00
- ☐ **Pickwick Ale,** Haffenreffer Brewing, 12 oz., white can with gold lettering, label resembles coat of arms with a lion and a deer, name of brewer in gold along bottom .... 400.00 | 550.00
- ☐ **Pickwick Ale,** Haffenreffer Brewing, 32 oz., same design as the 12 oz. with coat of arms .... 600.00 | 750.00
- ☐ **Pickwick Light Ale,** Haffenreffer Brewing, 12 oz., white and gold, "light" in blue .... 145.00 | 185.00
- ☐ **Piel's Special Light,** Piel Brothers, 12 oz., dark pink and cream, "special light" in red script lettering .... 150.00 | 180.00
- ☐ **Pilsener Light Lager,** Frederick's Brewing, 12 oz., white and red .... 170.00 | 210.00
- ☐ **Pilser's Original Export Half and Half,** Pilser Brewing, yellow and red, brand name in blue, a mixture of ale and porter .... RARE
- ☐ **Pilser's Original Extra Dry Pilsener,** Metropolis, 12 oz., blue and gold .... 170.00 | 210.00
- ☐ **Pilser's Original Extra Dry Pilsener,** Metropolis, 32 oz., same design as the 12 oz. .... 600.00 | 750.00

Price Range

☐ **Pilser's Original Extra Dry Pilsener,** Pilser Brewing, 12 oz., silver and yellow–CROWNTAINER ..   300.00   400.00

☐ **Pilser's Original Extra Dry Pilsener Light,** Pilser Brewing, 32 oz., cream and blue ....   **RARE**

☐ **Pilser's Original Pale Ale,** Pilser Brewing, 12 oz., silver and yellow–CROWNTAINER 160.00   190.00

☐ **Pilser's Original XXXX Pale Ale,** Pilser Brewing, 12 oz., pale green and yellow ....   **RARE**

☐ **P.O.C.,** Pilsener Brewing, 12 oz., black and gold, shield at upper left 95.00   115.00

☐ **P.O.C. Extra Dry,** Pilsener Brewing, 12 oz., gold, blue and red, shield at lower center 120.00   150.00

☐ **P.O.S. Lager,** Philadelphia Brewing, 12 oz., yellowish green and red, logo of shield supported by pair of lions at upper center 350.00   450.00

☐ **P.O.S. Lager,** Philadelphia Brewing, 12 oz., red and white 150.00   190.00

☐ **Potosi,** Potosi, 12 oz., blue and cream, reads "good old Potosi" 70.00   95.00

☐ **Potosi Pilsener,** Potosi, 12 oz., white, red and gold 110.00   145.00

☐ **Prima,** Prima Brewing, 32 oz., blue and silver ...   450.00   525.00

☐ **Prima Ale,** Prima Brewing, 12 oz., blue and white   150.00   200.00

☐ **Prima Ale,** Prima Brewing, 32 oz., blue and silver   475.00   550.00

☐ **Progress Select,** Progress Brewing, 12 oz., gold and red, brand name in white lettering on red background 140.00   170.00

☐ **R & H Light Beer,** Rubsam & Hortmann, 12 oz., red and gold, brand name in red 700.00   850.00

☐ **Rahr's,** Rahr Brewing, 12 oz., white and violet–CROWNTAINER 100.00   130.00

☐ **Rainier,** Rainier Brewing, 12 oz., gold and red, vignette of snow-capped mountain peak against blue background (the first Rainier cone top) 230.00   285.00
(The mountain was, of course, Mt. Rainier in Washington, not too far from the brewery's San Francisco headquarters.)

☐ **Rainier Club,** Rainier Brewing, 12 oz., black, red and silver 180.00   220.00

☐ **Rainier Extra Pale,** Rainier Brewing, 12 oz., red and blue, brand name horizontal 65.00   80.00

☐ **Rainier Extra Pale,** Rainier Brewing, 12 oz., red and blue, brand name slightly diagonal 60.00   70.00

☐ **Rainier Old Stock Ale,** Rainier Brewing, 12 oz., green and white, brand name horizontal 75.00   100.00

Price Range

☐ **Rainier Old Stock Ale,** Rainier Brewing, 12 oz.,
green and white, brand name slightly diagonal ..   **75.00**   **100.00**
(It has not been determined whether this or the
horizontal version came first.)

☐ **Rainier Special Export,** Rainier Brewing, 12 oz.,
cream, red and gold, sketch of mountain at lower
center **80.00**   **105.00**

☐ **Rainier Special Export,** Rainier Brewing, 12 oz.,
white and red, no mountain **100.00**   **130.00**

☐ **Red Fox Ale,** Largay Brewing, 12 oz., red and
white, cartoon illustration of fox carrying tray ...   **600.00**   **750.00**

☐ **Red Fox Light,** Largay Brewing, 12 oz., red and
gold, small cartoon illustration of fox carrying tray
at upper center **400.00**   **500.00**

☐ **Red Fox Premium,** Largay, 12 oz., red and yellow,
brand name in red, illustration of fox carrying two
glasses on tray **475.00**   **600.00**

☐ **Red Ribbon,** Mathie Ruder Brewing, 12 oz., white,
red and gold **140.00**   **170.00**

☐ **Red Top Ale,** Red Top Brewing, 12 oz., yellow and
red, gold bands at top and bottom **75.00**   **100.00**

☐ **Red Top Extra Dry,** Red Top Brewing, 12 oz.,
white, red and violet **75.00**   **100.00**
(Easy to identify as it is the only Red Top cone top
reading "extra dry.")

☐ **Red Top Extra Pale,** Red Top Brewing, 12 oz.,
white and red **60.00**   **75.00**

☐ **Regal Light Lager,** American Brewing, 12 oz.,
white, yellow and gold, multicolored portrait of
man in seventeenth-century dress holding glass   **300.00**   **350.00**

☐ **Regal Premium,** American Brewing, 12 oz., white,
yellow and gold, multicolored portrait of man in
seventeenth-century dress holding glass **105.00**   **140.00**

☐ **Regal Supreme,** People's Brewing, 12 oz., tan
with gold trim, name in brown **75.00**   **100.00**

☐ **Regal Supreme Strong,** People's Brewing, 12
oz., cream and gold **75.00**   **100.00**

☐ **Regal Supreme,** People's Brewing, 12 oz., cream
and gold, silver top **75.00**   **100.00**
(In addition to the silver top this can is also identifi-
able by the fact that the gold bands, at top and bottom, are fairly pale.)

☐ **Regent Premium,** Century, 32 oz., pink and red,
slogan "Brewery Fresh" **350.00**   **425.00**

☐ **Reisch Gold Top,** Reisch Brewing, 12 oz., gold
and white **65.00**   **80.00**

Top, Left to Right: **Old Topper Snappy Ale,** *12 oz.,* **$40–$50;** *Ortlieb's Premium Lager,* *12 oz.,* **$60–$80.** *Bottom, Left to Right:* **Rainier Old Stock Ale,** *12 oz.,* **$55–$70;** *Regal Light Lager,* *12 oz.,* **$275–$325.**

Price Range

☐ **Renner Premium,** Renner Brewing, 12 oz., red and white, "premium" in white on red banner ..   140.00   170.00

☐ **Renner Premium,** Renner Brewing, 12 oz., brown, gold and cream, "Youngstown" in large letters (Youngstown, Ohio, was the location of the brewery.)   170.00   210.00

☐ **Rex Imperial Dry,** Fitger Brewing, 12 oz., cream and red 75.00   100.00

☐ **Rex Imperial Dry Strong,** Fitger Brewing, 12 oz., cream and red 75.00   100.00

☐ **Rheingold,** Liebmann Brewing, 32 oz., yellow and white, 32 oz. 450.00   550.00

☐ **Rhinelander,** Rhinelander, 12 oz., gray 60.00   70.00

☐ **Rhinelander Export,** Rhinelander, 12 oz., dark green 65.00   80.00

☐ **Rhinelander Export,** Rhinelander, 12 oz., gray, brand name in white on green banner 60.00   70.00

☐ **Richbrau,** Home Brewing, 12 oz., white, blue and red–CROWNTAINER 110.00   150.00

☐ **Ritz Extra Dry,** Edelweiss Brewing, 12 oz., blue and white, brand name in gold 225.00   300.00

☐ **Rocky Mountain Beer,** Anaconda Brewing, 12 oz., brand name in white lettering on red banner, illustration of mountain in upper center 100.00   130.00

☐ **Rolling Rock,** Latrobe Brewing, 12 oz., green and white 160.00   200.00

☐ **Ronz Beer,** Columbus Brewing, 12 oz., white, red and blue, "Light, Dry, Refreshing" appear in blue in upper right, "Beer" also in blue in lower right   **RARE**

☐ **Royal,** Reno Brewing, 12 oz., white and red, hand holding playing cards, slogan, "It can't be beat"   275.00   350.00

☐ **Royal Amber,** Wiedemann, 12 oz., salmon, black and gold 130.00   160.00

☐ **Royal Amber,** Wiedemann Brewing, 12 oz., cream white with gold lettering–CROWNTAINER 225.00   300.00

☐ **Royal Bohemian Style,** Duluth Brewing, 12 oz., white, brown and gold, shield with lions at either side 75.00   100.00

☐ **Royal Bru,** Union, 12 oz., purple and white, large eagle, brand name in white, "Beer" in purple ...   475.00   575.00

☐ **Royal Pilsener,** Koller Brewing, 12 oz., orange and yellow 200.00   275.00

☐ **Royal Pilsener,** Koller Brewing, 12 oz., silver and blue–CROWNTAINER 100.00   125.00

☐ **S.B.,** Southern Brewing, 12 oz., gold and red ...   200.00   250.00

☐ **Scheidt Ram's Head Ale,** Scheidt, 32 oz. 240.00   300.00

Price Range

☐ **Schell's Deer Brand,** Schell, 12 oz., white, yellow
and dark brown–CROWNTAINER 80.00   100.00

☐ **Schlitz,** Schlitz, 12 oz., copper with name in white
on brown rhomboid 30.00   40.00

☐ **Schlitz,** Schlitz Brewing, 12 oz., brown and white,
"Sunshine Vitamin D" appears in lower center . .   90.00   120.00

☐ **Schlitz Lager,** Schlitz, 12 oz., blue and white, slogan "The Beer That Made Milwaukee Famous,"
word "Beer" in larger lettering than rest of slogan   450.00   550.00

☐ **Schlitz Sunshine Vitamin D,** Schlitz, 12 oz.,
brown and white 50.00   65.00

☐ **Schmidt's Cream Ale,** Schmidt, 12 oz., silver and
cream white, illustration of tiger 170.00   210.00

☐ **Schmidt's First Premium,** K.G. Schmidt, 12 oz.,
green with multicolor scene, blue ribbon with
name in white 90.00   115.00

☐ **Schmidt's Old Style Bock,** Schmidt, 12 oz., silver
and red–CROWNTAINER . . . .   **RARE**

☐ **Schmidt's Old Style Bock,** Schmidt, 32 oz., white
and red, ram's head at upper center, 1939 copy-
right date . . . .   **RARE**

☐ **Schmidt's First Premium Lager Beer,** Schmidt
Brewing, 12 oz., green, blue and red, brand name
in white lettering on blue banner near top, illustration of elderly man sitting and holding the can . .   90.00   115.00

☐ **Scotch Highland Genuine Ale,** New Philadelphia
Brewing, 12 oz., red plaid and white, illustration of
bagpiper at upper center 400.00   500.00

☐ **Select Twenty Grand Ale,** Red Top Brewing, 12
oz., green and cream 130.00   170.00

☐ **Seven Eleven,** Altes Brewing, 12 oz., white, red
and gold 225.00   275.00

☐ **Sheridan Lager,** Sheridan Brewing, 12 oz., silver   375.00   475.00

☐ **Sierra,** Reno Brewing, 12 oz., blue, silver and gold,
horizontal bands near top 140.00   170.00

☐ **Silver Bar Sparkling Ale,** Southern Brewing, 12
oz., silver and black 160.00   200.00

☐ **Silver Cream,** Menominee Brewing, 12 oz., silver
and blue 150.00   180.00

☐ **Silver Dime Premium,** Chester, 12 oz., dark blue
and light blue, "Premium" in red . . . .   **RARE**

☐ **Silver Fox,** Fox Deluxe Brewing, 12 oz., white . .   135.00   175.00

☐ **Silver Fox Beer,** Fox Deluxe Brewing, 32 oz.,
same design as the 12 oz.   600.00   700.00

☐ **Silver State Lager,** Schneider Brewing, 12 oz.,
purple and white with gold top . . . .   **RARE**

Price Range

☐ **Silver Stock Lager,** Robert Graupner, Inc., 12 oz.,
red and blue, brand name in red gothic lettering,
no design . . . . **RARE**

☐ **Southern Select,** Galveston Brewing, 12 oz., silver and brown–CROWNTAINER . . . . **RARE**

☐ **Souvenir Light Bright Dry,** Renner, 12 oz., gold
and white 100.00   140.00

☐ **Souvenir Premium,** Renner Brewing, 12 oz., sil-
ver–CROWNTAINER 50.00   60.00

☐ **Spearman Ale,** Spearman Brewing, 12 oz., green
and red 275.00   350.00

☐ **Spearman English Type Ale,** Spearman Brewing,
12 oz., black and red 300.00   350.00
(The other Spearman Ale cone top, which is al-
most identical in design and colors, does not read
"English type.")

☐ **Spearman's Straight Eight,** Spearman Brewing,
12 oz., white and yellow, "8" in dark blue 225.00   285.00

☐ **Stag Extra Dry Pilsener,** Griesedieck, 12 oz., blue
and white 32.50   42.50

☐ **Stag Premium Dry Pilsener,** Griesedieck, 12 oz.,
blue and white 32.50   42.50

☐ **Standard Light Ale,** Standard Brewing, 12 oz., sil-
ver and red–CROWNTAINER 175.00   250.00

☐ **Standard Sparkling Ale,** Standard, 12 oz., orange
with brand name in white on black banner 250.00   325.00

☐ **Star Banner Ale,** Star Brewing, 12 oz., salmon
and red, five-pointed star with letter S in white   **RARE**

☐ **Star Stock Ale,** Star Brewing, 12 oz., red 325.00   400.00

☐ **Stegmaier's Ale,** Stegmaier Brewing, 12 oz., dark
green and red 200.00   250.00

☐ **Stegmaier's Gold Medal,** Stegmaier Brewing, 12
oz., gold and white, brand name in white, initial
shield at center 75.00   100.00

☐ **Stegmaier's Gold Medal,** Stegmaier Brewing, 12
oz., gold and white, "Stegmaier" in red lettering
at center, top reads "Quality since 1857" 90.00   110.00

☐ **Stegmaier's Gold Medal,** Stegmaier Brewing, 12
oz., red and white, tiny gold shields arranged into
pattern at top and bottom 75.00   100.00

☐ **Steinerbru Royal Pale,** Atlantic Brewing, 12 oz.,
red, gold and black . . . . **RARE**

☐ **Stoney's Pilsener,** Jones Brewing, 12 oz., white
and red, cartoon illustration of waiter beckoning   100.00   130.00

Top, Left to Right: **Schlitz,** *12 oz.,* **$30–$40;** *Schlitz Lager, 12 oz.,* **$450–$550.** *Bottom, Left to Right:* **Schmidt's First Premium,** *12 oz.,* **$90–$115;** *333 Pilsener Brand Beer, 12 oz.,* **$85–$110.**

Price Range

☐ **Straight Eight Beer,** Spearman Brewing, 12 oz.,
blue, white and yellow, brand name in blue, large
number in blue against blue background . . . .　　**RARE**

☐ **Sunshine,** Barbey, 12 oz., gold and brown, brand
name in white lettering against brown band, slogan "Since 1861" near top with sunburst–
CROWNTAINER . . . . 　**350.00**　**450.00**

☐ **Sunshine Extra Light,** Sunshine Brewing, 32 oz.,
gold and brown, same design as the 12
oz.–CROWNTAINER . . . . 　**600.00**　**750.00**

☐ **Sunshine Extra Light,** Sunshine Brewing, 12 oz.,
gold and brown–CROWNTAINER . . . . 　**225.00**　**300.00**

☐ **Sunshine Extra Light,** Sunshine Brewing, 12 oz.,
gold, white and brown, brand name in white on
brown banner in upper center, "Premium" in
brown script in lower right . . . . 　**200.00**　**265.00**

☐ **Sunshine Extra Light,** Sunshine Brewing, 32 oz.,
gold, white and brown, same design as 12 oz. . . 　　**RARE**

☐ **Sun Valley Beer,** East Idaho Brewing, 12 oz., blue,
white and yellow, illustration of small town underneath mountains, brand name in yellow in upper
center . . . . 　**110.00**　**140.00**

☐ **Supreme Light,** South Bethlehem Brewing, 12
oz., gold, brand name in blue . . . . 　**200.00**　**275.00**

☐ **Supreme Light,** South Bethlehem Brewing, 32
oz., gold . . . . 　**700.00**　**850.00**

☐ **Tacoma Pale,** Rainier Brewing, 12 oz., blue and
white . . . . 　**200.00**　**275.00**

☐ **Tacoma Pale,** Tacoma Brewing, 12 oz., blue,
white and yellow . . . . 　**300.00**　**400.00**

☐ **Tahoe,** Carson Brewing, 12 oz., black and red, slo-
gan, "Famous as the lake" . . . . 　**300.00**　**400.00**

☐ **Tally-Ho,** City Brewing, 12 oz., white and yellow
with illustration of fox hunters in horse drawn car-
riage . . . . 　**500.00**　**625.00**

☐ **Tam O'Shanter Ale,** American Brewing, 12 oz.,
white and red with Scotch plaid design . . . . 　**225.00**　**300.00**
(Tam O'Shanter was a poem by Robert Burns.)

☐ **Tam O'Shanter Dry Hopped Ale,** American
Brewing, 12 oz., white and red with Scotch plaid
design, brand name in black on white background,
"dry hopped ale" in red . . . . 　**275.00**　**350.00**

☐ **Tavern,** Lafayette Brewing, 12 oz., multicolored
with scene of revelers in horse drawn carriage
pulling up to colonial-style tavern . . . . 　**250.00**　**325.00**

Price Range

- ☐ **Three Thirty-Three Pilsener Brand,** Harold C. Johnson, 12 oz., white with maroon and gold trim   85.00   110.00
- ☐ **Time Lager,** Time Brewing, 12 oz., red and gold, "lager" in yellow 875.00   975.00
- ☐ **Topaz,** Koller, 12 oz., silver, red stripes near bottom—CROWNTAINER 90.00   115.00
- ☐ **Tornberg's Old German Lager,** El Rey Brewing, 12 oz., yellow and red, color illustration of castle at upper center ....   **RARE**
- ☐ **Travis Dark,** Sabinas Brewing, 12 oz., red, yellow and blue, logo of intertwined initials surmounted by large spreadwing eagle ....   **RARE**
- ☐ **Travis Extra Pale,** Sabinas Brewing, 12 oz., red, yellow and blue, logo of intertwined initials surmounted by large spreadwing eagle ....   **RARE**
- ☐ **Trenton Old Stock,** People's Brewing, 12 oz., grayish blue and cream with brand name in red, logo at upper center ....   **RARE**
  (In the very early days of "bottled" beer, when it could be obtained only at taverns, some customers asked for the tavernkeeper's "old stock" in the belief that the extra aging added body and flavor.)
- ☐ **Trenton Old Stock,** People's Brewing, 32 oz., grayish-blue, cream and red, same design as 12 oz. ....   **RARE**
- ☐ **Trenton Old Stock,** People's Brewing, 12 oz., silver and yellow—CROWNTAINER 300.00   375.00
- ☐ **Trophy,** Birk Brewing, 12 oz., white, gold and red   130.00   170.00
- ☐ **Tropical Ale,** Tampa Brewing, 12 oz., white and gold, "ale" in green, wide gold bands at top and bottom (the first version of Tropical Ale's cone top)   250.00   325.00
- ☐ **Tropical Extra Fine Ale,** Tampa Brewing, 12 oz., white and green, "ale" in gold 175.00   250.00
- ☐ **Tropical Extra Fine Ale,** Tampa Brewing, 12 oz., white and green, "ale" in red 200.00   260.00
- ☐ **Tropical Premium,** Florida, 12 oz., brown and white, slogan "Taste Tells" 425.00   525.00
- ☐ **Tru Blu White Seal Pilsener,** Northampton Brewing, 12 oz., silver, red and blue—CROWNTAINER   300.00   375.00
- ☐ **Tube City Beer,** Tube City Brewing, 12 oz., red, white and gold, brand name in white on red background, logo appears between "Tube City" and "Beer" 75.00   100.00
  (The brewer's headquarters, McKeesport, Pennsylvania, was once known as Tube City because of tire manufacturing.)

Price Range

☐ **Tube City Beer,** Tube City Brewing, 32 oz., red, white and gold, colors are the same as the 12 oz., but design is different, brand name appears diagonally, logo appears on top of brand name . . . . . .   **RARE**

☐ **Twenty Grand Ale,** Twenty Grand, 12 oz., red top with metallic green, yellow oval, green band with name in white **90.00**   **115.00**

☐ **Uchtorff Golden Harvest Pilsener,** Uchtorff Brewing, 12 oz., white, brown and gold **200.00**   **265.00**

☐ **Utica Club Pale Cream Ale,** West End Brewing, 12 oz., red **120.00**   **160.00**

☐ **Utica Club Pilsener Lager,** West End Brewing, 12 oz., white with red lettering **60.00**   **80.00**

☐ **Utica Club Pilsener,** West End Brewing, 12 oz., white, does not say "lager" **55.00**   **65.00**

☐ **Utica Club Sparkling Ale,** West End Brewing, 12 oz., blue **160.00**   **200.00**

☐ **Valley Brew,** El Dorado Brewing, 12 oz., silver   **200.00**   **265.00**

☐ **Van Bek Light Lager,** Miami Valley Brewing, 12 oz., silver and brown–CROWNTAINER **215.00**   **250.00**

☐ **Van Merritt,** Burlington Brewing, 12 oz., dark green and white **130.00**   **170.00**

☐ **Van Merritt,** Burlington Brewing, 12 oz., green and white, brand name in blue, no vignette, reads "fully pasteurized" at bottom **110.00**   **140.00**

☐ **Vat Reserve Light Mellow,** B.M. Brewing, 12 oz., silver and cream **550.00**   **650.00**

☐ **Vat Reserve Light Mellow,** B.M. Brewing, 12 oz.,–CROWNTAINER **800.00**   **900.00**

☐ **Vernon Creme,** Vernon Brewing, 12 oz., orange   **250.00**   **300.00**

☐ **Virginia's Famous Lager,** Virginia Brewing, 12 oz., white with red and blue lettering **200.00**   **250.00**

☐ **W,** Wiedemann Brewing, 12 oz., white and red with spreadwing eagle perched atop large "W" –CROWNTAINER **90.00**   **115.00**
(Shortest brand name in the history of brewing.)

☐ **Wacker Premium,** Wacker Brewing, 12 oz., silver, blue and red–CROWNTAINER **800.00**   **950.00**

☐ **Walter's Pilsener,** Walter Brewing, 12 oz., white, green and gold **65.00**   **80.00**

☐ **Washington's XX Pale,** Washington Brewing, 12 oz., silver, blue and white–CROWNTAINER **200.00**   **265.00**

☐ **Washington XX Pale Pilsener,** Washington Brewing, 12 oz., white and gold, spreadwing eagle at upper center **160.00**   **190.00**

Top, Left to Right: **Sunshine** (Crowntainer), 12 oz., **$275–$325**; **Tube City**, 12 oz., **$75–$100**. Bottom, Left to Right: **Walter's Pilsener**, 12 oz., **$65–$80**; **Webber's Old Lager Beer**, 12 oz. **$180–$225**.

Price Range

☐ **Webber's Old Lager,** Webb, 12 oz., white with red
and mustard yellow trim **180.00**   **225.00**

☐ **Weber Waukesha,** Weber Waukesha, 12 oz., yel-
low with green trim, name in red **55.00**   **70.00**

☐ **West Virginia Special Export,** Fesenmeir, 12 oz.,
white and pink, "Special" in blue **175.00**   **250.00**

☐ **White Cap,** Largay Brewing, 12 oz., two shades
of blue, illustration of snow-capped mountain peak   **RARE**

☐ **White Cap,** Largay Brewing, 32 oz., two shades
of blue ....   **RARE**

☐ **White Cap,** Two Rivers Brewing, 12 oz., white and
blue, brand name within ship's wheel **180.00**   **220.00**

☐ **White Horse Pilsener,** Westminster Brewing, 12
oz., red, white and black, sculptured head of horse   **RARE**

☐ **White Seal,** Keiwel Brewing, 12 oz., gold and
white **90.00**   **115.00**

☐ **Wiedemann,** Wiedemann, 12 oz.,–CROWN-
TAINER **75.00**   **100.00**

☐ **Wieland's Extra Pale Lager,** Pacific Brewing, 12
oz., wine red and pale gold **100.00**   **140.00**

☐ **Wolf's,** Fernwood Brewing, 12 oz., gold and red   **375.00**   **450.00**

☐ **Wolf's,** Fernwood Brewing, 32 oz., gold and red
with wolf's head at upper center ....   **RARE**

☐ **Wooden Shoe Lager,** Wooden Shoe Brewing, 12
oz., white, blue and red, view of Dutchmen raising
steins in toast, windmill in background **30.00**   **40.00**

☐ **Yoerg's Cave Aged,** Yoerg Brewing, 12 oz., silver
and red–CROWNTAINER **170.00**   **210.00**

☐ **Yuengling's,** D.G. Yuengling, 12 oz., red with gold
shield, name in white script lettering **40.00**   **55.00**

☐ **Yuengling's Olde Oxford Cream Ale,** Yuengling,
12 oz., yellow and brown, brand name in yellow,
"Cream Ale" in brown **600.00**   **750.00**

☐ **Ziegler's Premium Lager,** Ziegler Brewing, 12
oz., cream and brown, illustration of tavernkeeper
in Tyrolean dress running forward with six steins   **200.00**   **275.00**

FLAT TOPS

Flat top beer cans were introduced in 1935, the same year as cone tops,
but beat the cone tops to the market by several months. So they have the distinction of being the first beer cans. They also lasted longer than cone tops.
After the demise of cone tops in the 1950's, flat tops were the only beer cans
made, until pull tabs came along in the 1960's. Many thousands of flat tops
exist, ranging from common to very rare.

Top, Left to Right: **Wiedemann Bohemian,** *12 oz.,* **$75–$100; Wiedemann's Union Made,** *12 oz.,* **$170–$200.** *Bottom:* **Yuengling's Beer,** *12 oz.,* **$40–$55.**

The definition of a flat top can is one which must be punctured with a tool or instrument. In the traditional practice of beer can collecting, flat tops carry full market value *only* when opened from the bottom. If the can has been punctured at the top, it will be worth considerably less than the values shown here. Of course, other condition factors enter the picture, too.

Most of the cans listed here are readily available on the market and in trading among hobbyists. Some "ultra rarities" have been included in the listings, too. As actual sales of these rare cans occur very infrequently, it is impossible to establish fair market values. Hence, prices are omitted from these specimens.

	Price Range	
☐ **A-1 Pilsner,** Arizona, 12 oz., white with "A-1" in block characters within gold frame	35.00	45.00
☐ **A-1 Pilsner,** Arizona, 12 oz., white and red, oval medallion with white lettering on red background	55.00	65.00
☐ **A-1 Pilsner,** Arizona Brewing, 16 oz., white and red	195.00	230.00
☐ **ABC Beer,** ABC Brewing, red, white and black, brand name in white letters on black banner, "Select Pilsener Type" in white against red background in lower right	100.00	140.00
☐ **ABC Extra Pale Dry,** ABC, 12 oz., blue with "A" in pyramid, "B" in square, "C" in circle	50.00	60.00
☐ **ABC Extra Pale Dry,** Maier, 12 oz., red, white and blue with small stars	20.00	25.00
☐ **Ace Hi,** Ace, 8 oz., squat, white with name in gold-bordered red diamond	40.00	50.00
☐ **Ace Hi Malt Liquor,** Ace, 7 oz., squat, red with name in gold-bordered white diamond	80.00	95.00
☐ **Ace Hi,** Ace Hi Brewing, 12 oz., similar to 8 oz., illustrations of playing card king and queen on can, brand name in white lettering in red or green diamond	40.00	50.00
☐ **Ace Premium Beer,** Sioux City Brewing, 12 oz., black, white, red and gold, brand name in white on black banner in center of can, small squares border brand name, each showing a different playing card suit	90.00	120.00
☐ **Ace Beer,** Sioux City Brewing, 12 oz., white, yellow and blue, brand name in blue against white background, yellow bands beneath and above brand name with white symbols of playing card suit ...	60.00	85.00
☐ **Acme,** Acme, 12 oz., dull gold with brown lettering	575.00	675.00
☐ **Acme,** Acme, 12 oz., black, red and silver, "Acme" in large letters, "Beer" in silver block letters	32.00	42.00
☐ **Acme,** Acme, 12 oz., black and white, "Beer" on banner in gothic letters	17.50	22.50

Price Range

☐ **Acme,** Cerial, 12 oz., black, red and silver, "Acme" in large letters, "Beer" in silver block letters ... 40.00 47.50

☐ **Acme Bock,** Acme, 12 oz., white with caricature of goat in circular medallion 125.00 165.00

☐ **Acme Gold Label,** Acme, 12 oz., gold and white with horizontal gold bands 35.00 45.00

☐ **Acme Light Dry,** Acme, 12 oz., yellow with white at top (designed to resemble glass of beer with head) 20.00 25.00

☐ **Adler Brau,** George Walter, 12 oz., gold and white with brand name on red ribbon 15.00 20.00

☐ **Adler Brau,** George Walter, 15 oz., silver and white with brand name on red ribbon 15.00 20.00

☐ **Albion Old Stock Ale,** Southern, 12 oz., green, yellow and red 250.00 300.00

☐ **All-American Extra Dry Beer,** Atlas Brewing, 12 oz., orange, white and blue, brand name in orange, illustration of sports figures, "extra dry" in blue 60.00 80.00

☐ **All Grain,** Storz, 12 oz., red, blue and white, illustration of man wearing cowboy hat, extremely rare 700.00 825.00

☐ **All Grain,** Storz, 12 oz., white with brand name in red frame 15.00 20.00

☐ **Alpen Glen,** Burgermeister, 12 oz., white with red lettering and artwork, house with Alps in background, gold band at top and bottom 32.00 42.00

☐ **Alpen Glow Ale,** Central, 12 oz. 400.00 500.00

☐ **Alpine,** Fox DeLuxe, 12 oz., white, gold and green 300.00 325.00

☐ **Alpine Lager,** Alpine, 12 oz., white and blue, outlines of peaks of Alpine mountains 7.00 10.00

☐ **Alps Brau,** Centlivre, 12 oz., blue and white, mountain peak against blue sky 4.75 6.75

☐ **Alps Brau,** Grace, 12 oz., blue and white, Alpine mountain scene 75.00 100.00

☐ **Alps Brau,** Old Crown, 12 oz., blue and white, mountain peak against blue sky 3.00 5.00

☐ **Alt Heidelberg,** "Old Heidelberg," Columbia, 12 oz., white gold and blue lettering, small portrait in medallion near top 100.00 140.00

☐ **Altes Golden Lager,** National, 12 oz., red and very pale beige, brand name in script lettering .. 40.00 50.00

☐ **Altes Golden Lager "Fassbier,"** National, 12 oz., white and red 5.00 7.50

☐ **Amberlin,** Gipp's, 12 oz., white and blue 25.00 35.00

☐ **American,** American, 12 oz., white, gold and red, brand name in white on red background 15.00 20.00

Price Range

☐ **Ambassador,** Krueger, 12 oz., beige and white, illustration of polka dancers 32.50 42.50

☐ **Amber Brau Fully Aged Lager,** Maier, 12 oz., brown, white and gold 20.00 25.00

☐ **American Dry,** Eastern, 12 oz., gold, red, white and blue, large eagle near top 10.00 15.00

☐ **American Dry,** Five Star, 16 oz., gold, red, white and blue 20.00 25.00

☐ **Aristocrat,** Tivoli, 12 oz., gold and cream, brand name in oval 75.00 100.00

☐ **Armanetti's Holiday,** Holiday, 12 oz., white, blue and yellow 45.00 55.00

☐ **Arrow,** Globe, 12 oz., gold, black and red, lettering in black with red "depth dimension" 115.00 145.00

☐ **Arrow 77,** Globe, 12 oz., red, white, black and silver 15.00 20.00

☐ **Arrow 200th Anniversary,** Globe, 12 oz., gold, black and red, lettering in black with red "depth dimension" 200.00 265.00

☐ **Astro,** Pilsner, 12 oz., white, blue and black 22.50 27.50

☐ **Astro Stout Malt Liquor,** Maier, 16 oz., blue, white and gold, illustration of spaceship 150.00 190.00

☐ **Atlantic Sparkling Ale,** Atlantic, 12 oz., red and white, illustration of black servant with tray 300.00 325.00

☐ **Atlantic, the Beer of the South,** Atlantic, 12 oz., red, white and gray, illustration of old-time Southern street scene 600.00 725.00

☐ **Atlas Prager,** Atlas, 12 oz., black, gold and red, lettering in gold against black background, circular medallion above lettering 52.00 63.00

☐ **Atlas Prager Bock,** Atlas, 12 oz., gold with name in white on red 65.00 85.00

☐ **Atlas Prager Bohemian,** Atlas, 12 oz., white and red, illustration of musicians and man dancing .. 10.00 14.00

☐ **Atlas Yorkshire Ale,** Atlas Brewers, 12 oz., green, red, brown and white, brand name in white on red banner...................................... 200.00 275.00

☐ **Augustiner,** Wagner, 12 oz., white and gold, large lettering (first version of design) 12.50 17.50

☐ **Balboa Export,** Southern, 12 oz., yellow, red and black 130.00 165.00

☐ **Ballantine,** Ballantine, 16 oz., gold, white and red, three-ring sign in gold 12.50 17.50

Price Range

☐ **Ballantine Ale,** Ballantine, 12 oz., gold, red and white, oval medallion with three-ring sign and "XXX," maker's name in oval frame (this style was introduced in 1935) solid 20.00   25.00

☐ **Ballantine Ale,** Ballantine Brewing, 12 oz., same as above with "Brewed with Brewer's Gold" in red on the side 6.00   8.00

☐ **Ballantine Ale,** Ballantine, 12 oz., gold, red and white, three-ring sign below "XXX," brand name in red, against yellow-tinged background 6.00   8.00

☐ **Ballantine Bock,** Ballantine, 12 oz., gold with ram's head in red circle 60.00   75.00

☐ **Ballantine Draft,** Ballantine, 12 oz., white with "Draft" in large red letters, "Genuine" in red letters at top, three-ring sign in gold 5.00   7.00

☐ **Ballantine Draught Ale,** Ballantine, gallon, green, brown and gold, illustration of glasses being filled from keg 125.00   150.00

☐ **Ballantine Extra Fine,** Ballantine, 12 oz., gold and cream white, "Very Fine" in pale gold letters near bottom of medallion 15.00   20.00

☐ **Ballantine King Size Ale,** Ballantine, 16 oz., gold, cream white and red 20.00   25.00

☐ **Ballantine New York World's Fair (1939/40),** Ballantine, 12 oz., gold and black, narrow medallion, three-ring sign touches sides 45.00   55.00

☐ **Ballantine 100th Anniversary,** Ballantine, 12 oz., gold and black, narrow medallion, three-ring sign touches sides 27.50   37.50

☐ **Ballantine Light Lager,** Ballantine Brewing, 12 oz., gold, yellow and red, brand name in gold against yellow background, "Light Lager" in yellow in red banner in bottom center 17.50   22.50

☐ **Ballantine Light Lager,** Ballantine Brewing, 12 oz., similar to the above, "Light Lager" appears in red banner in *top* center 20.00   25.00

☐ **Ballantine 1952 Republican Convention Can,** Falstaff Brewing, 12 oz., red, white and blue, blue elephant holding a banner reading "I LIKE IKE"   50.00   65.00

☐ **Banner Extra Dry,** Best, 12 oz., white and red, "Premium Beer" in blue 17.50   25.00

☐ **Banner Extra Dry,** Burkhardts, 12 oz., white and red, "Premium Beer" in blue 15.00   20.00

☐ **Banner Extra Dry,** Cumberland, 12 oz., white and red, "Premium Beer" in blue 8.00   10.00

Top, Left to Right: **A-1 Beer** *(Carling), 12 oz.,* **$35–$45;** **All Grain,** *12 oz.,* **$13–$18.**
Bottom, Left to Right: **American,** *12 oz.,* **$27.50–$35;** **Arrow Imperial Lagered Beer,** *12 oz.,* **$65–$85.**

Price Range

☐ **Bantam,** Goebel, 8 oz., squat, white and dark green 26.00 33.00

☐ **Bantam Ale,** Goebel, 8 oz., squat, white and light green 35.00 45.00

☐ **Bartels Pure,** Lion, 12 oz., white and red, illustration of man with long beard 65.00 80.00

☐ **Bavarian Jay Vee,** Grace, 12 oz., blue and white 90.00 115.00

☐ **Bay State,** 12 oz. This Commonwealth Brewing can has the same design as that for Bay State Ale. A ship's helmsman wearing a helmet is pictured at a wheel to the upper left of the brand name. The can is olive green with the center panel in orange. The words "Commonwealth Brewing Corp." are in orange. This can was found in quantity this year. The value has dropped considerably. 600.00 750.00

☐ **Bay State Ale,** Commonwealth, 12 oz., dark green with blue lettering, illustration (upper left) of helmsman at wheel 450.00 575.00

☐ **Becker's Best,** Becker, 12 oz., silver with black lettering 125.00 140.00

☐ **Becker's Mellow,** Becker, 12 oz., cream white with black lettering 2.00 3.00

☐ **Bergheim,** Old Reading, 12 oz., white and straw with pictorial landscape, lettering in red 2.50 4.00

☐ **Berghoff 1887,** Berghoff, 12 oz., white with brand name in black, date "1887" in large white numerals with red borders 15.00 20.00

☐ **Berghoff 1887,** Tennessee, 12 oz., white with brand name in black, date "1887" in large white numerals with red borders 20.00 30.00

☐ **Berghoff 1887,** Tennessee Brewing, 12 oz., brown, yellow and white can is wood-grained to resemble a keg, brand name in white script (diagonal), "1887" in yellow in bottom center 20.00 30.00

☐ **Best,** Best, 12 oz., white, purple and gold, stalks of wheat beside glass 37.50 47.50

☐ **Best,** Best, 12 oz., red and white, letter "B" near top 18.00 23.00

☐ **Best,** Empire, 12 oz., red and white, letter "B" near top 16.00 21.00

☐ **Best,** Spearman, 12 oz., red and white, letter "B" near top 30.00 40.00

☐ **Best,** United States Brewing Co., 12 oz., red and white, letter "B" near top 20.00 25.00

☐ **Best Ale,** Best, 12 oz., white and green, lettering in white 57.50 67.50

Top, Left to Right: **Atlantic Ale,** 12 oz., **$300–$325; Atlantic Beer,** 12 oz., **$600–$725.**
Bottom, Left to Right: **Atlas Prager Bock,** 12 oz., **$65–$85; Ballantine Bock,** 12 oz.,
$60–$75.

Price Range

☐ **Best Ale,** Cumberland, 12 oz., white and green, lettering white 37.50   47.50

☐ **Best's Hapsburg,** 12 oz., silver and blue, "Best's" in blue lettering at top, "Cool Before Serving" at bottom 100.00   135.00

☐ **Best's Hapsburg,** Best, 12 oz., silver and blue, "Best's" in blue lettering at top 75.00   100.00

☐ **Better Foods Markets,** ULTRA RARITY, 12 oz. This one had limited West Coast distribution. It was a product of Pacific Brewing of Oakland. The can is blue with a gold design along the center. The brand name is in pale gold, with the words "Lager" and "Beer" in red. There is a thin gold stripe near the top and bottom. .... **RARE**

☐ **Betts Beer,** Gretz Brewing, 12 oz., red, white and black, brand name in black 400.00   500.00

☐ **Beverwyck,** Beverwyck, 12 oz., gold with white shamrock, name in black 175.00   250.00

☐ **Beverwyck Cream Ale,** Beverwyck, 12 oz., green, white and gold, large green shamrock ... 100.00   130.00

☐ **B.F.C. Export,** Fischbach, 12 oz., white and red, brand name in script lettering 10.00   15.00

☐ **Biermann,** Fox Head, 12 oz., cream background with tavern interior, "Beer" in red 200.00   265.00

☐ **Big Apple,** Waukee, 12 oz., red, white and blue, "Premium" in white lettering on red banner 80.00   100.00
Note: The expression "big apple" referred to New York City. This brand was brewed not far away, in Hammonton, New Jersey.

☐ **Big Cat Malt Liquor,** Pabst, 12 oz., white, red and gold, jumping leopard on vertically striped background 4.00   6.00

☐ **Big Mac,** Menominee-Marinette, 12 oz., white and red, illustration of bridge 105.00   135.00

☐ **Big State,** Tivoli, 12 oz., white, brown and red, white star near top 32.50   42.50

☐ **Bismarck Premium,** Bismarck, 12 oz., white, red and green, brand name in German gothic lettering 20.00   25.00

☐ **Bismarck Premium Export,** Bismarck, 12 oz., white, red and green, brand name in German gothic lettering 25.00   30.00

☐ **Blackhawk Premium,** Cumberland, 12 oz., blue and red, portrait profile of Indian in red, thin red band at top and bottom 38.00   47.00

Price Range

☐ **Blackhawk Premium,** Terre Haute, 12 oz., blue and red, portrait profile of Indian in red, thin red band at top and bottom 30.00 40.00

☐ **Blackhawk Premium,** Uchtorff, 12 oz., blue and red, with white lettering against profile portrait of Indian 125.00 150.00

☐ **Black Dallas Malt Liquor,** Atlantic, 12 oz., blue and black, evening skyline 60.00 70.00

☐ **Black Dallas Malt Liquor,** Leisy, 12 oz., blue and black, evening skyline 60.00 70.00

☐ **Black Label,** Carling, B.C. of America, 12 oz., black, white and red, red cross atop brand name 21.00 28.00

☐ **Black Label,** Carling, B.C. of America, 12 oz., black, white and red, thick white banding at top and bottom, red cross atop brand name 16.00 21.00
Note: Revised version of the original label, in which the amount of black coloring has been reduced—probably because the black can looked smaller than brightly-colored cans.

☐ **Black Label,** Carling, 12 oz., red and black, brand name within tilted medallion, "Carling" in small red letters inside medallion 4.00 6.00

☐ **Blatz,** Pabst, 12 oz., dark brown and beige, brand name in pyramid, white trim within pyramid, phrase "Milwaukee's Finest Beer" in dark brown lettering against white background 2.00 3.25

☐ **Blatz,** Blatz, 12 oz., white, phrase "Milwaukee's First Bottled Beer" has "First" in red, brand name in thick lettering, gold band at top and bottom . . 10.00 15.00

☐ **Blatz,** Blatz, 12 oz., dark brown and beige, brand name in pyramid, white trim within pyramid, phrase "The Finest Beer Brewed in Milwaukee" in dark brown lettering against white background 2.50 4.25

☐ **Blatz Beer,** Blatz Brewing, 12 oz., dark brown and beige, brand name in pyramid, caramel-brown trim within pyramid, phrase "Milwaukee's Finest Beer" in dark brown letters against caramel-brown background 6.00 8.00

☐ **Blatz Pilsener,** Blatz, 12 oz., white and black, "Pilsener" in white on red band, gold at top and bottom 20.00 25.00

☐ **Blitz Weinhard,** Blitz, 12 oz., white, red and gold, brand name against large geometrical design in dark gold 12.50 17.50

☐ **Blue and Gold Premium Lager,** Grace, 12 oz., pale blue and pale gold, "Cool Before Serving" 185.00 235.00

Price Range

☐ **Blue Boar Ale,** Regal Amper, 12 oz., blue and white (non-pictorial) 320.00 420.00

☐ **Blue 'N Gold,** Southern, 12 oz., white, blue and gold, brand name in blue against white medallion 125.00 165.00

☐ **Blue Ribbon Bock,** Pabst, 12 oz., yellow and blue, illustration of ram 60.00 80.00

☐ **Blue Ribbon Bock,** Pabst, 12 oz., gold cream and blue, no illustration of ram 80.00 100.00

☐ **Boh Bohemian Lager,** Enterprise, 12 oz., yellow, red and white, illustration of hat with long feather 32.00 40.00

☐ **Bohemian Club,** Bohemian, 12 oz., white and yellow, illustration of man in Alpine costume holding beer bottle, brand name in yellow, horizontal black banding at bottom 90.00 120.00

☐ **Bohemian Club,** Bohemian, 12 oz., black and red, brand name in white, red band at top 10.00 13.00

☐ **Bohemian Club,** Potosi, 12 oz., black and red, brand name in white, red band at top 3.00 4.25

☐ **Bosch,** Bosch, 12 oz., dark gold and white, without words "Premium Beer" in gold beneath brand name 7.50 11.50

☐ **Braumeister,** Heileman, 12 oz., white and brown, brand name in white on brown ribbon, furls of ribbon prominent at each side 2.75 4.50

☐ **Braumeister,** Independent, 12 oz., light gray, gold and white, imprint reads Sheboygan, Wisconsin instead of Milwaukee 7.00 11.00

☐ **Braumeister,** Independent, 12 oz., light gray, gold and white 8.50 11.50

☐ **Breunig's,** Rice Lake, 12 oz., blue, white and gold, brand name in blue 6.50 8.50

☐ **Brewer's Best,** Grace, 12 oz., white, red, blue and gold, brand name in white on red banner, surmounted by gold crown, lions at either side 27.50 37.50

☐ **Brew 52,** Grace, 12 oz., tomato red with white lettering 75.00 100.00

☐ **Brew 52,** North Bay, 12 oz., tomato red with white lettering 75.00 100.00

☐ **Brew 82,** Brew, 12 oz., red, white and blue, brand name in white on blue background, slogan "Extra Select" ....:.... 100.00 130.00

☐ **Brew 82,** Leisy, 12 oz., red, white and blue, brand name in white on blue background, slogan "Extra Select" 75.00 100.00

*Top, Left to Right: **Banner,** 12 oz., **$12–$16; Becker's,** 11 oz., **$4–$6.** Bottom, Left to Right: **Blatz Bock,** 12 oz., **$13–$18; Bohemian Club,** 11 oz., **$25–$35.***

Price Range

☐ **Brew 82,** Uchtoff, 12 oz., red, white and blue, brand name in white on blue background, slogan "Extra Select" 75.00   100.00

☐ **Brewer's Choice Premium Pale Dry,** Beckers, 12 oz., light brown and white, "Premium Pale Dry" in red script lettering 225.00   300.00

☐ **Brown Derby,** Best, 12 oz., white and brown, S-work border enclosing brand name and derby hat (no cane) 12.50   17.50

☐ **Brown Derby,** Eastern, 12 oz., white and brown, S-work border enclosing brand name and derby hat (no cane) 12.50   17.50

☐ **Brown Derby,** Los Angeles Brewing, 12 oz., pale beige, derby and cane set in very small green shield, word "Pilsener" in red script lettering ... 65.00   75.00

☐ **Brown Derby,** Los Angeles Brewing, 12 oz., silver, brown and blue, derby hat and cane 80.00   100.00

☐ **Brown Derby,** Maier, 12 oz., white and brown, S-work border enclosing brand name and derby hat (no cane) 12.00   16.75

☐ **Brown Derby,** Rainier, 12 oz., pale beige, derby and cane set in very small green shield, word "Pilsener" in red script lettering 65.00   85.00

☐ **Brown Derby,** Rainier, 12 oz., silver, brown and blue, derby hat and cane 80.00   100.00

☐ **Brownie Beer,** Monarch Brewing, 12 oz., black, yellow and brown, brand name in black against yellow background, "Pilsner" in yellow script, illustration on side of can showing oddly dressed, bearded man holding frothy mug of beer .... **RARE**

☐ **Bub's,** Bub's, 12 oz., white and gold, first letter of brand name in red superimposed on stein 4.75   6.75

☐ **Buccaneer,** Gulf, 12 oz., gold with illustration of pirate 560.00   700.00

☐ **Buccaneer Stout,** Pacific, 12 oz., dark green, red and gold 800.00   1000.00

☐ **Buccaneer Stout Malt Liquor,** Pacific, 8 oz., ... 600.00   750.00

☐ **Buckeye,** Buckeye, 12 oz., white, with brand name in red 22.50   27.50

☐ **Buckeye,** Buckeye, 12 oz., red, white and black, brand name in black on white background 25.00   30.00

☐ **Buckeye,** Burgermeister, 12 oz., white and red, brand name in white against red background (dark wine-red) 10.00   15.00

Price Range

☐ **Buckeye,** Meister Brau, 12 oz., white and red, brand name in white against red background (dark wine-red) 10.00   15.00

☐ **Buckingham Ale,** ULTRA RARITY, 12 oz. A very handsome gold can, two royal lions (in black) on either side of a red shield surmounted by a crown. Gothic (old English) lettering on the shield reads, "England's Recipe for New England's Taste." This was a product of the Wehle Brewery of West Haven, Connecticut, and was apparently distributed mainly in the New Haven/Hartford area. . .   RARE

☐ **Budweiser,** Anheuser-Busch, 12 oz., red and white, brand name in blue at middle of can, reading "All Aluminum Can" at bottom 5.75   7.75

☐ **Budweiser,** Anheuser-Busch, 12 oz., red and white, brand name in blue at middle of can, reading "All Aluminum Can" at top 5.75   7.75

☐ **Budweiser,** Anheuser-Busch, 12 oz., gold, red and black, eagle and letter "A" 22.50   32.50

☐ **Budweiser,** Anheuser-Busch, 12 oz., gold, white and red, with white trim on banner reading "Budweiser Lager Beer" near top of can 8.00   12.00

☐ **Budweiser,** Anheuser-Busch, 12 oz., gold, white and red, no white trim on banner reading "Budweiser Lager Beer" near top of can 10.50   15.50

☐ **Budweiser,** Anheuser-Busch, 12 oz., red and white, brand name in blue at middle of can 2.00   4.00

☐ **Budweiser,** Anheuser-Busch, 12 oz., red and white, brand name in white against red background near top of can 1.75   3.25

☐ **Budweiser Big Size,** Anheuser-Busch, 16 oz. . .   9.00   12.00

☐ **Buffalo Pale Beer,** Buffalo Brewing, 12 oz., gold, logo on top of brand name of horseshoe 550.00   700.00

☐ **Bull Dog Ale,** California, 12 oz., white and black, oval medallion with brand name in medium-size red letters, illustration of bulldog against green background 50.00   65.00

☐ **Bulldog Ale,** Grace, 12 oz., green, black and white, brand name in large red lettering, illustration of dog in green on white background 17.50   22.50

☐ **Bulldog Ale,** Grace, 12 oz., white and black, oval medallion with brand name in medium-size red letters, illustration of bulldog against green background 50.00   65.00

Price Range

☐ **Bulldog Lager,** Acme Brewing, 12 oz., black and cream white, oval medallion, small colored portrait of bulldog 50.00 65.00

☐ **Bulldog Malt Liquor,** Grace, 8 oz., squat, white, blue and gold 12.00 16.00

☐ **Bulldog Malt Liquor,** Grace, 12 oz., dark blue, light blue and gold 12.00 16.00

☐ **Bulldog Stout Malt Liquor,** California, 12 oz., white and black, number "14" in red against black oval 27.50 37.50

☐ **Burger,** Burger, 12 oz., white and red, brand name in white against red medallion, no gold banding at top or bottom 22.50 27.50

☐ **Burger,** Burger, 12 oz., white and red, letters in brand name have no black outlines and the red is a strong burgundy-red 10.00 15.00

☐ **Burgemeister Premium,** Warsaw, 12 oz., cream white, red and gold, light gold banding at top and bottom 2.50 4.50

☐ **Burgemeister Pilsener,** Warsaw, 12 oz., cream white, red and gold, "Beer" in black lettering . . . 10.00 14.00

☐ **Burgemeister Premium,** Warsaw, 12 oz., cream white, red and gold, dark gold banding at top and bottom 6.00 9.00

☐ **Burgermeister,** Burgermeister, 12 oz., blue, white and gold, portrait of man holding beer glass (not stein) 10.00 14.00

☐ **Burgermeister,** Burgermeister, 12 oz., blue, white and gold, portrait of man with stein, head and neck only 10.00 14.00

☐ **Burgermeister,** San Francisco, 12 oz., blue and white, ¼" length figure of man in 18th-century costume lofting stein 17.50 22.50

☐ **Burgermeister,** Schlitz, 12 oz., white, blue and gold, brand name in white against pale blue medallion placed high on can, symbol of brew-master in circle attached to ribbon 10.00 14.00

☐ **Burgermeister,** Burgermeister, 16 oz., man holds stein 10.00 14.00

☐ **Burgermeister,** San Francisco, 12 oz., silver, blue and red, illustration of man in late 18th-century costume holding stein, portrait is almost one half length 35.00 45.00

☐ **Burkhardt's Ale,** Burkhardt's Brewing, 12 oz., yellow and brownish-red, "Mug Ale" in red-brown lettering on yellow background 60.00 75.00

Price Range

☐ **Burkhardt's Master Blended,** Burkhardt, 12 oz., red, white and yellow, without "Custom Blended" — 75.00 · 100.00

☐ **Busch Bavarian,** Anheuser-Busch, 12 oz., white and blue, snow-covered mountains, clouds in background .... — 10.00 · 14.00

☐ **Busch Bavarian,** Anheuser-Busch, 12 oz., white and blue, snow-covered mountains, no clouds in background .... — 7.50 · 10.00

☐ **Busch Lager,** Anheuser-Busch, 12 oz., red, white and gold .... — 65.00 · 80.00

☐ **Butte Special,** Butte, 12 oz., white, red and gold, brand name in white lettering against red background, word "Beer" in black, wording "Quality Controlled" in red script lettering .... — 60.00 · 70.00

☐ **Butte Special,** Butte, 12 oz., white, red and gold, brand name in red against white background, word "Beer" in red lettering, "Special" in script lettering — 37.50 · 47.50

☐ **California Gold Label,** California, 12 oz., white and gold, illustration of Conestoga wagon ...... — 30.00 · 40.00

☐ **Canadian Ace Ale,** Canadian Ace, 12 oz., beige, silver and white .... — 15.00 · 20.00

☐ **Canadian Ace Draft,** Canadian Ace, 12 oz., beige, silver and white .... — 25.00 · 35.00

☐ **Canadian Ace King Size,** Canadian Ace, 16 oz., brown and pale blue, "King Size" in red .... — 22.50 · 30.00

☐ **Canadian Ace Malt Liquor,** Canadian Ace, 7 oz., squat, red with name in gold-bordered white diamond .... — 160.00 · 200.00

☐ **Canadian Ace Premium,** Canadian Ace, 12 oz., beige, silver and white .... — 7.50 · 10.00

☐ **Canandaigua Extra Dry,** Stein, 12 oz., light brown, red and blue .... — 110.00 · 140.00

☐ **Cape Cod Beer,** Enterprise Brewing, 12 oz., brand name in white on white background, illustrations of boats and fish .... — 500.00 · 650.00

☐ **Cardinal,** Cardinal, 12 oz., red and white, brand name in white, illustration of cardinal (bird) in bright red .... — 9.00 · 12.00

☐ **Cardinal,** E & B, 12 oz., red and white, brand name in red, small illustration of cardinal (bird) within "C" of brand name .... — 70.00 · 85.00

☐ **Carling's Black Label,** Carling, 12 oz., red and black, brand name within tilted medallion, "Carling" in small red letters inside medallion ...... — 4.00 · 6.00

Price Range

☐ **Carling's Black Label,** B.C. of America, 12 oz.,
black, white and red, red cross atop brand name   15.00   20.00
☐ **Carling's Black Label,** B.C. of America, 12 oz.,
black, white and red 15.00   20.00
☐ **Carling's Black Label,** B.C. of America, 12 oz.,
black, white and red, thick white banding at top
and bottom, red cross atop brand name   16.00   21.00
*Note: Revised version of original label, in which
the amount of black coloring has been reduced.*
☐ **Carling Red Cap Ale,** Carling, 12 oz., black and
very pale brown, "Red Cap" in thick black letters,
medium-size profile portrait of man wearing red
cap 12.00   16.00
☐ **Carling Red Cap Ale,** Carling, 12 oz., green and
very pale brown, "Red Cap" in red script lettering,
small profile portrait of man wearing red cap ...   25.00   32.00
☐ **Cee Bee,** Colonial, 12 oz., white and red 13.00   17.00
☐ **Centilivre Beer,** Centilivre Brewing, 12 oz., red,
black and gold, brand name in white on red banner
in center, "Since 1862" in small shield-like logo
in upper center 250.00   325.00
☐ **Champale Malt Liquor,** Century, 12 oz., green
and white 10.00   14.00
☐ **Champale Malt Liquor,** Metropolis, 12 oz., green
and white 10.00   14.00
☐ **Champagne Velvet,** Atlantic, 12 oz., pale blue
and gold, brand name in blue lettering with red ini-
tial letters, can design forms champagne glass   5.00   7.00
☐ **Champagne Velvet,** B.C. of Oregon, 12 oz., red,
white and gold, large white champagne glass with
brand name in red lettering 20.00   30.00
☐ **Champagne Velvet,** Terre Haute, 12 oz., white
and gold, brand name in black with red initial let-
ters against white background 17.50   22.50
☐ **Champagne Velvet,** Terre Haute, 12 oz., yellow
and gold, brand name in black script lettering on
yellow 22.50   30.00
☐ **Champagne Velvet King Size,** B.C., 16 oz., red
and gold 80.00   100.00
☐ **Chevy 85 Ale,** Hudepohl Brewing, white, red,
black and gold, brand name in white on red banner
in upper center, "85" in white on gold background   110.00   150.00
☐ **Chief Pilsner Beer,** Monarch Brewing, 12 oz., red,
black and white, illustration of Indian chieftain in
upper center 400.00   500.00

Price Range

☐ **Chief Oshkosh,** Oshkosh, 12 oz., red and gold, brand name in white on red badge against solid gold can 20.00   25.00
☐ **Chief Oshkosh,** Oshkosh, 12 oz., green, blue and red, brand name in white against red badge 12.00   16.00
☐ **Class Pilsner,** Class Nachod, 12 oz., silver and pale yellow, woman holding glass .... **RARE**
☐ **Clear Lake,** Grace, 12 oz., green, blue and red, illustration of fish in lake, brand name in white ... 120.00   150.00
☐ **Club House,** Grace, 12 oz., blue and white 100.00   125.00
☐ **Clyde Lager,** Enterprise, 12 oz., cream white and blue, "Lager" in white on blue background 100.00   135.00
☐ **Coburger,** Horlacher, 12 oz., blue, white and gold   8.00   11.00
☐ **Coburger,** Old Dutch, 12 oz., blue, white and gold   8.00   11.00
☐ **Cold Brau,** Schoenhofer-Edelweiss, 12 oz., blue and white 5.00   6.25
☐ **Cold Spring,** Cold Spring, 12 oz., gold and blue (bright brassy gold) 9.00   12.00
☐ **Cold Spring,** Cold Spring, 12 oz., gold and blue (dark gold) 7.50   10.00
☐ **Colorado Gold Label,** Walter, 12 oz., blue, white and red, illustration of lake and mountain peaks, clouds in background 15.00   20.00
☐ **Columbia Ale,** Heidelburg Brewing, 12 oz., cream, brown and red, "Ale" in large red lettering inside a square made of brand name on all four sides   120.00   170.00
☐ **Columbia Beer,** Heidelburg Brewing, 12 oz., white, gold and red, brand name in white on red banner in upper center, gold stars of varying sizes all over can 60.00   70.00
☐ **Connecticut Yankee Ale,** Merrimack, 12 oz., red, white and blue, illustration of man on horseback   400.00   500.00
☐ **Congress Light Beer,** Haberle Brewing, 12 oz., gold, white and red, brand name in red against cream-white label, gold and white checkerboard design with illustrations of different gambling games 60.00   70.00
☐ **Congress Light Beer,** Haberle Brewing, 12 oz., white and red, same design as can with gambling design except without checkerboard 45.00   55.00
☐ **Cook's,** Cook, 12 oz., white, blue and red, wide vertical blue stripe behind brand name 47.50   62.50
☐ **Coors,** Coors, 7 oz., cream white with gold band at bottom 7.50   10.00
☐ **Coors,** Coors, 7 oz., cream white with silver band at bottom 1.25   2.50

Top, Left to Right: **Bohemian Club,** *12 oz.,* **$12.50–$17.50; Brown Derby,** *12 oz.,* **$12.50–$17.50.** *Bottom, Left to Right:* **Buckeye,** *12 oz.,* **$17.50–$22.50; Budweiser** *(note the large open star around the eagle, rare post WW II type opening instructions), 12 oz.,* **$275–$335.**

Price Range

☐ **Coors,** Coors, 12 oz., yellow and black, lion at either side of medallion .... | 9.00 | 12.00

☐ **Coors,** Coors, 12 oz., pale gold and black, words "Export Lager" in red rectangle beneath brand name .... | 150.00 | 190.00

☐ **Copenhagen Castle,** Edelbrew, 12 oz., black, white and yellow, portrait of king wearing crown and beard above brand name, very rare .... | 600.00 | 750.00

☐ **Corona,** Five Star, 12 oz., white, black and yellow, brand name in black forming vaulting of crown | 75.00 | 90.00

☐ **Country Club,** Goetz, 12 oz., white, red and gold | 17.50 | 22.50

☐ **Country Club Malt Liquor,** Goetz, 8 oz., squat, white with "Country Club" in red, gold band at bottom .... | 20.00 | 30.00

☐ **Country Club Malt Liquor,** Goetz, 8 oz., squat, white with red and blue lettering .... | 15.00 | 20.00

☐ **Country Club Malt Liquor,** Pearl, 12 oz., light blue, red and gold, brand name in red .... | 7.00 | 10.00

☐ **Cremo Beer,** Grace Brothers Brewing, 12 oz., brown, beige and red, brand name in white on brown background .... | | RARE

☐ **Crest,** Crest, 12 oz., white, dark brown and light brown, ornamental flourish beneath brand name | 27.50 | 37.50

☐ **Croft Banquet Ale,** Croft, 12 oz., green, red and gold, insignia cross above brand name .... | 110.00 | 135.00

☐ **Croft Cream Ale,** Croft, 12 oz., green and yellow, brand name in yellow, "Cream" in white .... | 60.00 | 80.00

☐ **Crown Darby,** Westminster, 12 oz., black, white and gold, small illustration of rider and horse in circular medallion above brand name .... | 230.00 | 295.00

☐ **Crystal Colorado,** Walter, 12 oz., white, blue and gold, illustration of Rocky Mountains, brand name in large white lettering .... | 8.00 | 11.00

☐ **Crystal Rock,** Cleveland Sandusky, 12 oz., blue and white .... | 45.00 | 60.00

☐ **Custom Club,** Grace, 12 oz., red and white .... | 85.00 | 110.00

☐ **Dakota,** Dakota, 12 oz., pink and red, brand name in red against pink background .... | 45.00 | 55.00

☐ **Dakota,** Dakota, 12 oz., white and red, brand name in white against red background .... | 52.00 | 65.00

☐ **Dawson's Diamond Ale,** Dawson's, 12 oz., blue and silver in alternating horizontal bands running entire height of can .... | 25.00 | 35.00

☐ **Dawson's Extra Dry Ale,** Dawson's, 12 oz., pale brown, green and white, brand name on curving scroll .... | 52.00 | 64.00

Price Range

☐ **Dawson's Sparkling Ale,** Dawson's, 12 oz., blue
and silver in alternating diagonal bands 5.75   7.75

☐ **Denver,** Tivoli, 12 oz., blue and white, Denver skyline 20.00   25.00

☐ **Deutsche Brau,** Grace, 12 oz., white, gold and
blue, golden shield at center with brand name on
a blue banner 75.00   90.00

☐ **Diamond State,** Diamond State, 12 oz., gold and
white 125.00   160.00

☐ **Dobler,** Hampton-Harvard, 12 oz., white and red,
thin red vertical stripes 17.50   22.50

☐ **Dobler Amber 1865 Ale,** Dobler, 12 oz., green,
white and gold, "1865" in white on red badge .. 140.00   180.00

☐ **Dobler Private Label 1865,** Dobler, 12 oz., white,
red and green, "1865" in white on red badge ..   50.00   60.00

☐ **Dodger Lager,** Maier, 12 oz., red, white and gold   30.00   40.00
*Note: Brewed in Los Angeles, the name was obvi-
ously inspired by the baseball team.*

☐ **Dorf,** Drewry, 12 oz., brown, white and red 12.00   17.00

☐ **Dorf,** Great Lakes, 12 oz., red and white, brand
name in gothic lettering on shield 57.50   67.50

☐ **Dorf,** Schoen Edelweiss, 12 oz., brown, white and
red, wood-grain appearance with illustration of
stein 10.00   14.00

☐ **Dorf,** Schoen Edelweiss, 12 oz., red and white,
brand name in gothic lettering on shield 49.00   62.00

☐ **Dortmunder,** Leisy, 12 oz., red, white and gold,
canned at Chicago, Illinois 65.00   80.00
Note: Dortmund is a town in Germany.

☐ **Dortmunder,** Leisy, 12 oz., red, white and gold,
canned in Cleveland, Ohio 50.00   65.00

☐ **Draft,** Maier, 12 oz., brown and red, designed to
resemble beer keg with pouring spout 65.00   85.00

☐ **Draft,** Maier, 12 oz., gold and white, brand name
in dark brown on shield 155.00   195.00

☐ **Drewry's,** Drewry, 12 oz., red and white, no silver
pyramid rising up from base of can 2.50   4.00

☐ **Drewry's Extra Dry,** Drewry, 12 oz., silver, red
and black, shield with illustration of mounted po-
liceman and horse 16.00   21.00

☐ **Drewry's Extra Dry,** Drewry, 12 oz., white and
red, brand name in red 12.50   16.00

☐ **Drewry's Extra Dry,** Drewry, 12 oz., blue and
white, brand name in white against dark blue background 8.00   12.00

Price Range

☐ **Drewry's Extra Dry,** Drewry, 12 oz., red and white, brand name in black against white background, white banding at top and bottom, balance of can red 3.75   5.25

☐ **Drewry's Extra Dry,** Drewry, 16 oz., blue shield, no crown, brand name in white 16.00   21.00

☐ **Drewry's Lager,** Drewry, 12 oz., silver red and black 20.00   30.00

☐ **Drewry's Malt Liquor,** Drewry, 12 oz., red, green and white, brand name in white lettering on green background, slogan "A Man's Drink" at bottom 235.00   285.00

☐ **Drewry's Oldstock Ale,** Drewry, 12 oz., black and white, thick white bands at top and bottom, brand name in small letters 20.00   25.00

☐ **Drewry's Oldstock Ale,** Drewry, 12 oz., green and gold with black lettering 40.00   50.00

☐ **Drewry's Stout Malt Liquor,** Drewry, 12 oz., red, green and white, brand name in white lettering on green background, slogan "A Man's Drink" at bottom 200.00   250.00

☐ **Drewry's Trophy,** Drewry, 12 oz., orange, white, black and red 50.00   60.00

☐ **Duquesne Can-O-Beer,** Duquesne, 12 oz., white and red, illustration of man holding beer in raised right hand 32.50   42.50

☐ **Duquesne Pilsener,** Duquesne, 12 oz., white, red and gold, man holding beer, white background on can with thin horizontal stripes 17.50   22.50

☐ **Durst,** Atlantic, 12 oz., cream white and blue, canned at Chicago 30.00   40.00

☐ **Durst,** Best, 12 oz., cream white and blue 30.00   40.00

☐ **Dutch Lunch Brand,** Grace, 12 oz., blue and red, caricature illustration of man in three-piece suit holding foaming stein 65.00   75.00

☐ **Dutch Lunch Premium Lager,** Grace, 16 oz. .. 200.00   250.00

☐ **Dutch Lunch Beer,** Grace Brothers Brewing, 12 oz., red and white, illustration of tankard of beer and an open window showing a windmill 270.00   210.00

☐ **Dutch Treat Beer,** Arizona Brewing, 12 oz., cream, white and blue, brand name in blue on white background, small illustration of a windmill 70.00   80.00

☐ **Eastern,** Atlas, 12 oz., white and red, brand name in tall red letters on white background 75.00   85.00

☐ **Eastside,** Los Angeles Brewing, 12 oz., blue, red and gold, illustration of eagle 100.00   135.00

Price Range

☐ **Eastside,** Los Angeles Brewing, 12 oz., light tan and white, illustration of eagle 16.00   21.00

☐ **Eastside Old Tap,** Pabst, 16 oz. 15.00   20.00

☐ **Eastside Old Tap,** Pabst, 12 oz., white, red and silver, eagle in silver 10.00   14.00

☐ **Eastside Old Tap Bock,** Pabst, 12 oz., red, white and gold, ram's head atop brand name 95.00   120.00

☐ **E & B Beer,** E & B Brewing, 12 oz., white, gold, red and blue, brand name in red and blue squares, "BREW 103" in black on white banner diagonally across upper center 50.00   60.00

☐ **Edelweiss,** S. Edelweiss, 12 oz., white, blue and other colors, drawings of steins encircling can, brown band at bottom 7.50   10.00

☐ **Edelweiss,** S. Edelweiss, 12 oz., white, blue and gray, brand name in red, drawings of steins encircling can 10.00   14.00

☐ **Edelweiss Bock,** S. Edelweiss, 12 oz., pink, gold and red, "Bock" in white lettering against red oval medallion 40.00   50.00

☐ **Eighteen K,** Fox, 12 oz., white and gold, brand name in white characters against gold background   45.00   60.00

☐ **Elder Brau,** Arizona Brewing Co., 12 oz., white, red and gold, brand name in white against gold heart 35.00   45.00

☐ **Elder Brau,** Grace, 12 oz., white, red and gold, brand name in white against gold heart 30.00   40.00

☐ **Elder Brau,** Maier, 12 oz., white, red and gold, brand name in white on circular medallion with rope-like frame 25.00   35.00

☐ **El Rey "The King,"** Grace, 12 oz., gold and brown, illustration of beer in tall glass, very rare   400.00   525.00

☐ **Embassy Club,** Best, 12 oz., red and gold 20.00   30.00

☐ **English Lad,** Westminster, 12 oz., green and gold with pictorial design of jockey on horse, encircled by horseshoe. Brand name is inscribed on horseshoe 625.00   750.00

☐ **Erin Brew,** Standard, 12 oz., gold and white, brand name in white lettering against gold circle 35.00   45.00

☐ **Erin Brew,** Standard, 12 oz., white and red, brand name in white lettering against red background   40.00   55.00

☐ **Esslinger's,** Esslinger, 12 oz., gold and white, illustration of bellhop carrying beer 125.00   155.00

☐ **Esslinger Premium,** Esslinger, 12 oz., white, red and gold, brand name in white script letters 75.00   100.00

Price Range

☐ **Eulberg Beer,** Eulberg Brewing, 12 oz., red, white and blue, logo in center of a crown in a bow, "Crown Select" on bow 110.00 150.00

☐ **Eureka Pale Dry Beer,** Pacific Brewing, 12 oz., white, red, gold and black, brand name in red on gold background in upper center, triangular gold section to resemble pilsner glass down front of can, "Beer" lettered vertically on gold section .. 130.00 170.00

☐ **Exeter Beer,** Getz Brewing, 12 oz., gold, blue and white, brand name in light blue on gold background 100.00 140.00

☐ **Extra Select 82,** Atlantic, 12 oz., red and blue .. 120.00 150.00

☐ **Falcon Beer,** Pacific Brewing, 12 oz., gold, cream-white and red, brand name in red on cream-white background, illustration of falcon above the "c" in Falcon 125.00 165.00

☐ **Falls City,** Falls City, 12 oz., red and gold, brand name within device resembling 45 rpm phonograph record, design comes very close to touching bottom of can 11.00 15.00

☐ **Falls City,** Falls City, 12 oz., red and gold, brand name within device resembling 45 rpm record, design does not come close to touching bottom of can 10.00 14.00

☐ **Falls City,** Falls City, 12 oz., red, white and gold, white is the predominant color on the front of the can 9.00 12.00

☐ **Falstaff,** Falstaff, 12 oz., white, yellow and gold, gold band at bottom of can only 6.75 9.00

☐ **Falstaff,** Falstaff Brewing, 12 oz., red, white and blue, illustration of colonial American flag (13 stars) and liberty bell 1.50 3.00

☐ **Falstaff,** Falstaff, 12 oz., white, yellow and gold, thin gold band at top and bottom of can 8.00 11.00

☐ **Famous Black Dallas Malt Liquor,** Atlantic, 12 oz., blue and black, evening skyline 55.00 65.00

☐ **Famous Black Dallas Malt Liquor,** Leisy, 12 oz., blue and black, evening skyline 55.00 65.00

☐ **Fehr's,** Fehr, 12 oz., red, white and blue, brand name in circular frame, pictorial illustration at center 50.00 65.00

☐ **Fehr's,** Fehr, 12 oz., white, red and gold 17.50 22.50

☐ **Fehr's Draft,** Fehr, 12 oz., white, red and gold 17.50 22.50

☐ **Feigenspan XXX Amber Ale,** Feigenspan Brewing, black, white and red, red circular logo in center with "P.O.N." in cream-white lettering 100.00 135.00

Price Range

☐ **Fifty-Two,** Grace, 12 oz., tomato red with white lettering 75.00   100.00

☐ **Finast,** Eastern, 12 oz., white, red and gold, solid gold at top and bottom, "Beer" in red lettering against white background 75.00   100.00

☐ **Finer Flaver Fully Aged Ale,** ULTRA RARITY, 12 oz., that isn't a misprint. The Monarch Brewing Co. of Los Angeles chose to spell it "flaver" instead of "flavor." A gold can, with an illustration of a foaming tall glass at the center, against a red background. "Cool Before Serving" at bottom.   **RARE**

☐ **Fisher's Ale,** Atlantic, 12 oz., white, green and blue, "Light Dry" in white script lettering 27.50   37.50

☐ **Fischer's Ale,** Queen City, 12 oz., white, green and blue, "Light Dry" in white script lettering . . .   28.00   36.00

☐ **Fischer's Light Dry,** Atlantic, 12 oz., red, white and blue, "Light Dry" in white script lettering . . .   22.50   27.50

☐ **Fischer's Light Dry,** Queen City, 12 oz., red, gold and white, can is predominantly gold with brand name in white on large red badge 32.50   42.50

☐ **Fisher,** Fisher, 12 oz., gold and red, brand name in white on red background 30.00   40.00

☐ **Fisher,** Fisher, 12 oz., gold and blue, brand name in white on blue background 290.00   300.00

☐ **Fisher Premium Light,** Lucky Lager, 12 oz., white and gold 10.00   14.00

☐ **Fisher Premium Pilsener,** Fisher, 12 oz., white and gold 10.00   14.00

☐ **Fitger's,** Fitger, 12 oz., white and yellow 8.00   11.00

☐ **Fitger's,** Fitger, 12 oz., white and gold 5.00   6.50

☐ **Fitz,** Fitzgerald, 12 oz., red and white, "Beer" in red 21.00   28.00

☐ **Fitz,** Fitzgerald, 12 oz., red and white, "Beer" in black 20.00   27.50

☐ **Fitzgerald Ale,** Fitzgerald, 12 oz., white and red, "Pale Ale" in white block letters 30.00   40.00

☐ **Five Hundred Ale,** Cook, 12 oz., name appears as "500," brand name refers to the Indianapolis 500 auto race, which is pictured on the can 90.00   120.00

☐ **Fort Pitt,** Ft. Pitt, 12 oz., white, black and gold, waiter running with huge glass on tray (one of the all-time classic beer can illustrations), "Cool Before Serving" 240.00   300.00

☐ **Fort Schuyler,** West End, 12 oz., white, red and gold, "Lager" in red script lettering 42.00   54.00

Price Range

☐ **Forty-Niner,** Atlas, 12 oz., white, red and gold, illustration of totem pole 240.00 300.00

☐ **Forty-Niner Premium Lager,** Pacific, 12 oz., cream white, brown and red 400.00 500.00

☐ **Fox DeLuxe,** Fox, 12 oz., red, white, gold and black, large illustration of fox hunter with trumpet, brand name in white lettering 130.00 170.00

☐ **Fox DeLuxe,** Fox, 12 oz., red, white and gold, brand name in oval, small illustration of fox hunter with trumpet 22.50 27.50

☐ **Fox DeLuxe,** Fox, 12 oz., red, white and gold, brand name in rectangular medallion, illustration of fox hunter with trumpet raised 8.00 11.00

☐ **Fox DeLuxe,** Fox Head, 12 oz., blue, white and red, brand name in red 25.00 35.00

☐ **Fox DeLuxe,** Fox Head, 12 oz., red, white and gold, brand name in rectangular medallion, illustration of fox hunter with trumpet raised 7.00 10.00

☐ **Fox DeLuxe,** Heileman, 12 oz., pale blue, red and gold 3.75 5.00

☐ **Fox Head,** Fox Head, 12 oz., white, gold and black, brand name against white background ... 24.00 32.00

☐ **Fox Head 400,** Fox Head, 12 oz., white, blue and gold, brand name against blue background 15.00 20.00

☐ **Fox Head 400,** Fox Head, 12 oz., white, blue and gold, brand name against blue background, "Brewed only in Wisconsin with Pure Spring Water" 12.00 16.00

☐ **Fox Head 400,** Heileman, 12 oz., white, red and brown, brand name against red background 6.00 9.00

☐ **Fox Head Ale,** Fox Head, 12 oz., green and beige 100.00 130.00

☐ **Fox Head Bock,** Heileman, 12 oz., white, light brown and dark brown, canned at Sheboygan, Wisconsin 15.00 20.00

☐ **Frankenmuth Bock,** Frankenmuth, 12 oz., black and brown, yellow band at bottom 170.00 210.00

☐ **Frankenmuth Mel-O-Dry,** Frankenmuth, 12 oz., black and yellow, illustration of man in top hat .. 35.00 45.00

☐ **Frankenmuth Old English Ale,** Frankenmuth, 12 oz., illustration of man in top hat 45.00 55.00

☐ **Frankenmuth Premium Dry,** Frankenmuth, 12 oz., black and yellow 40.00 50.00

☐ **Friars Ale,** Drewry, 12 oz., white and brown, brand name in block letters, reads "Club Special" directly beneath "Friars" 20.00 25.00

Price Range

☐ **Friars Ale,** Drewry, 12 oz., white and dark brown, reads "Extra Aged" at bottom 20.00   25.00

☐ **G.B.,** Grace, 12 oz., gold, blue and beige, "G" in dark blue on blue background, "B" in beige on blue background, rare 160.00   200.00

☐ **G.B. Dark Bock,** Grace, 12 oz., "Beer" in gold letters 100.00   140.00

☐ **G.B. Lager,** Cleveland Sandusky, 12 oz., gold brown and red 35.00   45.00

☐ **Gam Beer,** Wagner Brewing, 12 oz., gold, white and red, brand name in black on white background, illustration of man (head and shoulders) holding a glass of beer 30.00   40.00

☐ **Gambrinus Beer,** Wagner, 12 oz., white, red and gold 4.50   6.50

☐ **Gamecock Ale,** Croft, 12 oz., green and white, illustration of fighting rooster 375.00   475.00

☐ **Genesee,** Genesee, 12 oz., red and white, "Beer" in white, "Naturally More Refreshing" in red 9.00   12.00

☐ **Genesee,** Genesee, 12 oz., red and white, "Beer" in black, "Naturally More Refreshing" in red 17.50   22.50

☐ **Genesee 12 Horse Ale,** Genesee, 12 oz., gold 65.00   85.00

☐ **Genesee 12 Horse Ale,** Genesee, 12 oz., white and green 15.00   20.00

☐ **Genesee Lager,** Genesee, 12 oz., white, red and gold 30.00   40.00

☐ **Genesee Light Lager,** Genesee, 12 oz., gold and white, dark gold band at top and bottom 16.00   21.00

☐ **Genesee Light Lager,** Genesee, 12 oz., white, red and gold, horizontal stripes running whole height of can 12.50   17.50

☐ **Genesee Light Lager,** Genesee, 12 oz., white, red and gold, horizontal stripes running whole height of can, advertising message in red rectangle at front of can 22.50   27.50

☐ **Genesee Light Lager,** Genesee, 12 oz., gold and white, no banding at top or bottom 15.00   20.00

☐ **Gettelman,** Gettelman, 12 oz., brown and white, brand name in white script lettering against brown flask 20.00   25.00

☐ **Gettelman,** Gettelman, 12 oz., white and green, brand name in red at top, caricature illustration of smiling face 10.00   14.00

☐ **Gettelman,** Gettelman, 12 oz., brown and white with pale horizontal striping 7.00   10.00

Top, Left to Right: **Burgermeister**, *12 oz.,* **$17.50–$22.50;** *Canadian Ace, 12 oz.,* **$14–$19.** *Bottom, Left to Right:* **Continental's New Aluminum** *(early 1960's), 12 oz.,* **$17.50–$22.50; Export BFC,** *12 oz.,* **$4–$6.**

Price Range

☐ **Gettelman,** Miller, 12 oz., brown and white, brand name in white against medium-brown background, silver stripes at top and bottom 7.00   10.00

☐ **Gibbons,** Lion, 12 oz., white, red and gold 20.00   30.00

☐ **Gilt Edge Ale,** Hornell, 12 oz., green and white, with Hornell emblem 60.00   75.00

☐ **Gilt Edge Lager Beer,** Buffalo Brewing, 12 oz., blue and white, logo in center of intertwined "G" and "E," brand name in blue on white background 90.00   120.00

☐ **Gipp's Amberlin,** Gipp's, 12 oz., white and blue 25.00   35.00

☐ **Glacier,** Maier, 12 oz., white, gold and blue 35.00   45.00

☐ **Glacier Premium,** ULTRA RARITY, 12 oz., Glacier Premium was a product of Pacific Brewing of Oakland. The can is blue and white, showing a jagged mountain covered in ice. Near the bottom are the words "Light! Bright!" A very thin gold band is near the top. .... **RARE**

☐ **Glory B Lager,** ULTRA RARITY, 12 oz., the expression "glory be" was much more current in the 1930's than today.In this case, the letter "B" takes the place of "be." The can is red, white and blue, with the brand name in white, set against a red background. Glory B Lager was a product of the Pacific Coast Grocery of San Francisco. .... **RARE**

☐ **Gluek's,** Gluek, 12 oz., red, white and blue, small star above brand name 45.00   60.00

☐ **Gluek's Stite Malt Liquor,** 8 oz., squat, white with gold lettering, rampant lion logo at top in small square 12.50   17.50

☐ **Gluek Stite Malt Liquor,** Gluek, 12 oz., white and gray 8.00   12.00

☐ **Gluek's Stite Malt Liquor,** Gluek, 12 oz., green, white and gold 35.00   45.00

☐ **Goebel,** Goebel, 12 oz., gold and red, large red eagle 40.00   50.00

☐ **Goebel,** Goebel, 12 oz., gold, "Extra Dry" in circle near top 16.00   21.00

☐ **Goebel,** Goebel, 12 oz., blue, white and gold, illustration of rooster 10.00   14.00

☐ **Goebel Bantam,** Goebel, 8 oz., squat, black and red, "Light Lager" at top 25.00   35.00

☐ **Goebel Beer,** Boebel Brewing, 16 oz., gold, red and black, brand name in white on red background, "Goebel–King Size–Half Gallon" in white on red banner across top center, "Private Stock 22" in white on black banner under label 50.00   65.00

Price Range

☐ **Goebel Luxury Light Lager,** Goebel, 12 oz., gold, red and white 15.00   20.00

☐ **Goebel Private Stock 22,** Goebel, 12 oz., blue, white and gold, illustration of rooster 8.00   12.00

☐ **Goebel Private Stock 22,** Goebel, 12 oz., gold, brand name in white 20.00   25.00

☐ **Goebel Private Stock 22,** Goebel, 12 oz., gold and white, brand name in black 15.00   20.00

☐ **Goebel 22,** Goebel, 12 oz., gold and white, brand name is shown as "22" only, not "Private Stock"   10.00   14.00

☐ **Goetz,** Country Tavern, 12 oz., dark blue, white and silver 5.00   7.00

☐ **Gold Bond Special,** Cleveland Sandusky, 12 oz., cream white and brown, seal below "Special," can design made to resemble a bond with dollar signs in corners 160.00   200.00

☐ **Gold Label,** Walter, 12 oz., gold, red and white   8.00   12.00

☐ **Gold Medal,** Stegmaier, 12 oz., gold and white   17.50   22.50

☐ **Gold Medal Select Pennsylvania,** Gold Medal, 12 oz., gold, red and white 32.50   42.50

☐ **Gold Mug,** Lebanon Valley, 12 oz., gold, yellow and green with pair of foxes on heraldic shield, one of the most artistically designed on all cans 225.00   300.00

☐ **Goldcrest,** Queen City, 12 oz., gold, white and blue, brand name in blue 40.00   50.00

☐ **Goldcrest,** Tennessee, 12 oz., gold, white and blue, brand name in blue 45.00   55.00

☐ **Golden Brew Lager,** Grace, 12 oz., red, white and silver 30.00   40.00

☐ **Golden Brew, Premium Beer,** Grace Brothers Brewing, 12 oz., red, white and gold, brand name in white on red background, logo at top center of "G" and "B" in a gold and red shield, a golden wheat-stalk on either side of label 15.00   20.00

☐ **Golden Crown Extra Pale Dry,** Maier, 12 oz., gold, white and red 10.00   14.00

☐ **Golden Crown Beer,** Grace Brothers Brewing, 12 oz., black, cream-white, red and blue, brand name in black lettering on cream-white background, "Beer" in white on red banner in lower center . .   RARE

☐ **Golden Gate,** Maier, 12 oz., blue and silver, illustration of Golden Gate bridge 75.00   100.00

☐ **Golden Glow,** Pacific, 12 oz., white, red and gold, extremely rare 200.00   275.00

☐ **Golden Glow Ale,** Golden West, 12 oz., yellow and green, "XXX" above "Ale" 155.00   195.00

Price Range

Note: This was the second version of the Golden Glow Ale can design. It was apparently produced in greater numbers than the first, but still short-lived on the market.

☐ **Golden Glow Ale,** Golden West, 12 oz., yellow and bluish green, "Ale" in white lettering, word "Export" appears beneath "Ale", extremely rare   275.00   350.00

☐ **Golden Lager Premium,** Maier, 12 oz., red and white 20.00   27.50

☐ **Golden Pilsener,** Becker, 12 oz., gold and red   22.50   30.00

☐ **Golden Stein,** Drewry, 12 oz., white, brown and gold 50.00   60.00

☐ **Golden Stein,** S. Edelweiss, 12 oz., white, brown and gold 50.00   65.00

☐ **Golden Velvet,** Maier, 12 oz., white and brown, stalks of barley in brown 75.00   100.00

☐ **Goldenrod Ale,** ULTRA RARITY, 12 oz. Sometimes you'll find this brand's name spelled as two words: Golden Rod. Collectors have picked up that practice because the name was placed on two lines on the can—it was too long to fit on one. However, it was not intended by the manufacturer (Edelbrau of Brooklyn, New York) to be read as two words. A green and white can, with no pictorial work. There is a companion can for Goldenrod Beer, of the same design but of gold and white. It, too, is in the ultra rarity class. . . . .   **RARE**

☐ **Grace Brothers Bavarian,** Grace, 8 oz., squat, white with horizontal banding, white lettering on brown banner 60.00   75.00

☐ **Grace Bros. Bavarian,** Grace, 12 oz., burgundy and white, revised name "Bavarian" instead of "Bavarian Type" 20.00   27.50

☐ **Grain Belt,** Minneapolis Brewing, 12 oz., yellow, brown and white, checkerboard pattern 4.00   6.00

☐ **Grain Belt,** Minneapolis Brewing, 12 oz., burgundy and white, brand name in gothic lettering 10.00   14.00

☐ **Grand Lager,** Fishback Brewing, 12 oz., white, gold and orange, brand name in white on orange shield-like label with gold stripe diagonally through it 35.00   45.00

☐ **Grand Prize,** Gulf, 12 oz., gold, white and red, horizontally banded, brand name on white background   30.00   40.00

☐ **Grand Prize,** Gulf, 12 oz., gold and red, brand name in gold on red background 36.00   45.00

Top, Left to Right: **Fox Deluxe** *(opening instructions), 12 oz.,* **$65–$80; Gluek Stite Malt Liquor,** *8 oz.,* **$13–$17.** *Bottom:* **Goebel Private Stock 22,** *12 oz.,* **$9–$12.**

Price Range

☐ **Great Falls Select,** Great Falls, 12 oz., white, light beige and burgundy red, desert scene 13.00   18.00

☐ **Great Falls Select,** Great Falls, 12 oz., white, red and gold, no illustration of factory 7.00   10.00

☐ **Great Falls Select,** Great Falls, 12 oz., white, gray and red, illustration of factory above brand name, words "Quality Product" near bottom 12.50   17.50

☐ **Great Lakes Premium,** Schoen Edelweiss, 16 oz.   40.00   55.00

☐ **Gretz Half And Half,** Gretz, 12 oz., various colors, small illustration of man riding tall 1890's bicycle; the product was a combination of porter and ale (porter was a type of beer that had been popular in England in the 1700's) 400.00   550.00

☐ **Gretz Beer,** Gretz Brewing, 12 oz., cream, silver and black, opposite side features illustrations of different kinds of cars with information on each, front shows brand name in white against cream background, small illustration of automobile in top center 55.00   65.00

☐ **Gretz Premium,** Ruppert, 12 oz., blue, silver and red 40.00   55.00

☐ **Griesedieck,** Griesedieck, 12 oz., gold, red and white 10.00   14.00

☐ **Griesedieck,** Griesedieck, 12 oz., white, red and black, brand name appears as "GB" on heraldic shield, with "Griesedieck Brothers" above 8.00   12.00

☐ **Griesedieck,** Griesedieck, 12 oz., white, red and black, brand name appears as "GB" on heraldic shield, "G" on black background, "B" on red . .   6.50   9.00

☐ **Gunther,** Gunther, 12 oz., salmon with brown lettering 30.00   40.00

☐ **Gunther,** Gunther, 12 oz., gold, white and red, gold background with white dots 12.50   17.50

☐ **Gunther,** Gunther, 16 oz. 55.00   70.00

☐ **Gunther's Extra Dry,** Gunther, 12 oz., salmon with dark brown lettering 30.00   40.00

☐ **Gunther's Premium Dry,** Gunther, 12 oz., beige and yellow 20.00   30.00

☐ **Gunther's Old English Ale,** Gunther, 12 oz., green and white 70.00   90.00

☐ **Half & Half,** Pilsner Brewing, 12 oz., gold, red and cream, brand name in red on cream background and cream on red background 100.00   135.00

☐ **Hamm's,** Hamm, 12 oz., blue, white and silver . .   3.00   4.50

☐ **Hamm's,** Hamm, 12 oz., gold and silver, badge with red ribbons at center 40.00   55.00

	Price Range	

- ☐ **Hamm's,** Hamm, 12 oz., gold, white and blue . . . — 4.00 / 6.00
- ☐ **Hamm's,** Hamm, 16 oz., gold frame around brand name . . . . — 14.00 / 19.00
- ☐ **Hamm's Preferred,** Hamm, 12 oz., gold and blue, brand name in red . . . . — 7.00 / 10.00
- ☐ **Hamm's Preferred Stock,** Hamm, 12 oz., gold and red, medallion at center with red ribbons . . . — 20.00 / 27.50
- ☐ **Hampden,** Hampden Harvard, 12 oz., white and blue, non-aluminum . . . . — 7.00 / 10.00
- ☐ **Hampden,** Hampden Harvard, 12 oz., red, white and black . . . . — 20.00 / 27.50
- ☐ **Hampden Ale,** Hampden Harvard, 12 oz., green and white . . . . — 12.50 / 17.50
- ☐ **Han's Leeber Brew,** Maier, 12 oz., red, white and plain (absolutely plain—looks like a generic can) — 75.00 / 90.00
- ☐ **Hanley Extra Pale Ale,** Hanley, 12 oz., gold, green and white, vertical green stripe on front . . . . — 65.00 / 80.00
- ☐ **Hanley Pilsner,** Hanley, 12 oz., pale beige and gray . . . . — 7.00 / 10.00
- ☐ **Hanley Special Ale,** Hanley, 12 oz., gold, green and white, brand name in white . . . . — 80.00 / 100.00
- ☐ **Happy Hops Lager,** Grace, 12 oz., gold, blue, white and yellow, caricature figure bearing tray with beer, extremely rare . . . . — 375.00 / 450.00
- ☐ **Hapsburg,** Best, 12 oz., silver and blue, "Best's" in blue lettering at top . . . . — 75.00 / 100.00
- ☐ **Hapsburg,** Best, 12 oz., silver and blue, without "Best's" at top . . . . — 30.00 / 40.00
- ☐ **Hapsburg,** Best, 12 oz., silver and blue, "Best's" in blue lettering at top, "Cool Before Serving" at bottom . . . . — 60.00 / 75.00
- ☐ **Hapsburg,** Hapsburg, 12 oz., white and blue . . . — 25.00 / 33.00
- ☐ **Hartz Western Style Pilsener,** Silver Springs, 12 oz., red and white . . . . — 30.00 / 40.00
- ☐ **Harvard Ale,** Harvard, 12 oz., red, white and brown, brand name in red . . . . — 40.00 / 50.00
- ☐ **Harvard Ale,** Harvard, 12 oz., red, white and yellow . . . . — 55.00 / 65.00
- ☐ **Harvard Ale,** Harvard, 12 oz., green and white — 15.00 / 20.00
- ☐ **Harvard Ale,** Harvard, 12 oz., gray with red trim, name in black . . . . — 75.00 / 100.00
- ☐ **Harvard Export Green Label,** Harvard, 12 oz., green, white and red, brand name in red . . . . — 37.50 / 50.00
- ☐ **Harvard Foam Fresh Green Label,** Harvard, 12 oz., green, white and yellow . . . . — 55.00 / 70.00

Price Range

☐ **Heidelberg,** Carling, 12 oz., yellow, white and gold, diamond-shaped medallion of bellhop with stein 12.50   15.75

☐ **Heidelberg,** Heidelberg, 12 oz., white, red and brown, red medallion of bellhop with stein 26.00   30.00

☐ **Heidelbrau Pilsner,** Heidelbrau, 12 oz., white and red, castle turret in brown 12.25   15.25

☐ **Heileman's Lager,** Heileman, 12 oz., bluish-gray and white, snow-covered mountains 20.00   30.00

☐ **Heileman's Sparkling Stite,** Heileman Brewing, 12 oz., white 4.75   6.50

☐ **Heileman's Special Export,** Heileman, 12 oz., green and white, no leafwork at top 8.00   12.00

☐ **Heileman's Special Export,** Heileman, 12 oz., green and white, green and white leafwork at top, brand name in white 10.00   14.00

☐ **Heileman's Special Export Malt Liquor,** Heileman Brewing, 12 oz., gold, red and black, illustration of sailing ship in upper center 50.00   65.00

☐ **Heim Brau Beer,** Heim Brau Brewing, 12 oz., red and white, brand name in red on red background 4.00   6.00

☐ **Hensler,** Hensler, 12 oz., white and red 50.00   65.00

☐ **Heritage Lager,** Schoen Edelweiss, 12 oz., black, red and white................................ 35.00   45.00

☐ **Heritage Lager,** Tivoli, 12 oz., black, red and white 50.00   65.00

☐ **Heurich's Lager,** Heurich, 12 oz., red, brand name in white against red background, gold banding at top and bottom 65.00   75.00

☐ **Hi Brau,** Huber, 12 oz., white, red and black, brand name in black script lettering with initials in red 7.00   10.00

☐ **Hi Brau,** Huber Brewing, 12 oz., brand name in white on brown diamond-shaped label 17.50   25.00

☐ **High Life,** Miller, 12 oz., red, white, black and gold, quarter-moon emblem above brand name 5.00   6.50

☐ **High Life,** Miller, 12 oz., red, white and gold, brand name in small letters 3.00   4.50

☐ **High Life,** Miller, 12 oz., red, white and gold, brand name in large letters 2.25   3.50

☐ **Highlander Premium,** Missoula, 12 oz., red and white, white portion of can has slight grayish tinge (revised version) 13.00   17.00

☐ **Hillman's Export,** Best, 12 oz., brown and black, grained effect 50.00   65.00

☐ **Hillman's Superb,** United States Brewing, 12 oz., blue and gold................................. 60.00   75.00

Top, Left to Right: **Hamm's**, 12 oz., **$4–$5.25; Hamm's**, 16 oz., **$10–$14.** Bottom, Left to Right: **Hamm's**, 16 oz., **$27–$36; Harvard Export Beer**, 12 oz., **$70–$90.**

Price Range

☐ **Hitt's Sangerfest Colorado,** Walter, 12 oz., white and blue 160.00   200.00

☐ **Hofbrau,** Hofbrau, 12 oz., cream white and red, illustration of German village inn 16.00   21.00

☐ **Hoffman House,** Walter, 12 oz., white, brown and red 4.75   6.50

☐ **Holiday Special,** Potosi, 12 oz., white and brown with blue bands at top and bottom 20.00   25.00

☐ **Holihan's Light Ale,** Diamond Springs, green and cream white 55.00   70.00

☐ **Holihan's Pilsener,** Diamond Spring, 12 oz., white, dark brown and gold, brand name at center surrounded by brown and gold circles 16.00   21.00

☐ **Holihan's Pilsener,** Diamond Spring, 12 oz., cream white with brand name in red 32.50   42.50

☐ **Holland,** Eastern, 12 oz., white and brown, designed to resemble beer barrel 40.00   50.00

☐ **Home Ale,** Drewry, 12 oz., green and white 42.50   55.00

☐ **Home Dry Lager,** Atlas, 16 oz. 50.00   65.00

☐ **Hop Gold,** Star, 12 oz., gold with brand name in white lettering within blue star 300.00   375.00

☐ **Hopsburger Beer,** Pacific Brewing, 12 oz., amber, white and gold, brand name in arc across top center, logo in center of coat of arms with lion 90.00   120.00

☐ **Horluck's Vienna Style Pale Export,** ULTRA RARITY, 12 oz. Made by Horluck's of Seattle, Washington. The colors are a combination of orange and yellow, with a few green leaves thrown in. Near the top is an orange ball with the attention-getting words "Fire Brewed" . . . .   **RARE**

☐ **Huber,** Huber, 12 oz., white and burgundy red, gold band at top and bottom 6.00   8.00

☐ **Hudepohl,** Hudepohl, 12 oz., gold and white, green badge reading "14K" above brand name   8.00   12.00

☐ **Hudepohl,** Hudepohl, 12 oz., gold and white, red symbol above medallion containing brand name, "Golden" in red 30.00   40.00

☐ **Hudson House Lager,** Maier, 12 oz., blue and white 25.00   35.00

☐ **Hull's Cream Ale,** Hull, 12 oz., black, yellow and green, brand name in green 50.00   65.00

☐ **Hull's Export,** Hull, 12 oz., yellow, red and black   65.00   80.00

☐ **Humboldt Beer,** Humboldt Brewing, 12 oz., blue and white, brand name in white on blue background in lower center, illustration of eagle with wings spread in center 250.00   350.00

Price Range

☐ **Hyde Park,** Hyde Park, 12 oz., brown and red ..   45.00   60.00

☐ **Hyde Park Beer,** Hyde Park Brewing, 12 oz., red, white and gold, brand name in gold banner across center, "75" on red ribbon in lower center 40.00   55.00

☐ **Hynne Premium Quality,** Walter, 12 oz., cream white and red with mountain scene 8.00   12.00

☐ **IBC Crown Select,** Indianapolis Brewing, 12 oz., red, white and blue, extremely rare 475.00   600.00

☐ **International Franken Muth,** International, 12 oz., red and white 25.00   32.50

☐ **Iron City,** Pittsburgh, 12 oz., white and red, "It's Real Beer" in red script lettering at bottom 35.00   45.00

☐ **Iroquois Ale,** International Brewing, 12 oz., green and white, logo of Indian's head on top of label   40.00   55.00

☐ **Iroquois,** Iroquois, 12 oz., red, gold and black, check pattern, brand name in white 55.00   65.00

☐ **Jacob Ruppert Bock,** ULTRA RARITY, 12 oz. This was the first effort by Jacob Ruppert at canned bock beer—quite possibly the first effort by anybody at canned bock beer. Can dates from 1937. At that time Col. Jacob Ruppert himself was still alive and was by far the most famous brewer in the world (he owned the N.Y. Yankees baseball team). A strikingly attractive silver can with a large drawing of a mountain goat's head ....   **RARE**

☐ **Jacob Ruppert Ale,** Ruppert Brewing, 12 oz., green and white, brand name in white on diagonal green banner across center 60.00   70.00

☐ **Jax,** Jackson, 12 oz., pink, red and gold, black horse 20.00   25.00

☐ **Jay Vee Bavarian,** Grace, 12 oz., blue and white   90.00   110.00

☐ **Jester,** Jester, 12 oz., black and white, illustration of court jester 225.00   300.00

☐ **Jet Malt Liquor,** Westminster, 12 oz., white and silver 15.00   20.00

☐ **Jet Non-Alcoholic Near Beer,** United States Brewing, 12 oz., blue and white, statement of contents does not appear directly beneath "Near Beer" 10.00   14.00

☐ **Jet Non-Alcholic Near Beer,** United States Brewing, 12 oz., blue and white, statement of contents appears directly beneath "Near Beer" 12.00   15.00

☐ **Jet Stout Malt Liquor,** Canadian Ace, 12 oz., white and silver 20.00   30.00

☐ **J.F. Lanser's A-1,** Arizona, 12 oz., white, red, blue and green, blue stripe at top, "Full 12 Ounces"   50.00   60.00

Price Range

☐ **Karl's,** Grace, 12 oz., red, white and blue	125.00	140.00
☐ **Karlsbrau,** Duluth, 12 oz., red, reads "Old Time Beer"	12.00	16.00
☐ **Katz,** Drewry, 12 oz., red and white, very large red medallion with brand name, surmounted by carica- ture of cat	8.00	12.00
☐ **Katz,** Drewry, 16 oz.........................	160.00	200.00
☐ **KC's Best Premium Pilsener,** United States Brewing, 12 oz., white and brown	20.00	27.50
☐ **Keeley Ale,** Best, 12 oz., green, white and silver	37.50	45.00
☐ **Keeley Ale,** Cumberland, 12 oz., green, white and silver	37.50	45.00
☐ **Keg Natural Flavor,** Maier, 12 oz., pink, red and white	16.00	21.00
☐ **Keglet,** Esslinger, 12 oz., brown, designed to re- semble beer keg	32.50	42.50
☐ **Keglet,** Ruppert, 12 oz., brown, designed to re- semble beer keg	30.00	40.00
☐ **Keller's Holiday,** Holiday, 12 oz., white, blue and yellow, "Keller's" in gold lettering at top	40.00	55.00
☐ **Kentucky Malt Liquor,** Fehr, 12 oz., white and gold, slogan "Extra Good"	32.50	45.00
☐ **Kentucky Malt Liquor,** Fehr, 12 oz., white and gold, slogan "Man Size"	30.00	40.00
☐ **Kings Beer,** Kings Brewing, 12 oz., blue, red and white, "Fit for a King" in blue on orange banner across top, "rich Old Lager" in blue in shield-like logo in lower center		**RARE**
☐ **Kings' Taste,** Grace Brothers Brewing, 12 oz., gold, blue and white, brand name in blue on white banners on top and bottom, large blue crown in center of can	120.00	160.00
☐ **Kingsbury Bock,** Kingsbury, 12 oz., yellow and brown, silhouette of ram's head in yellow	44.00	57.00
☐ **Kingsbury Brew Near Beer,** Kingsbury, 12 oz., pale buff, red and gold	2.75	4.00
☐ **Kingsbury Real Draft,** Kingsbury, 12 oz., white, brown and red, lower portion of can has wood- grain finish	12.00	16.00
☐ **Knickerbocker,** Jacob Ruppert, 12 oz., gold, red, white and blue, wording in bottom in white against gold background	6.00	8.00
☐ **Koch's Golden Anniversary,** Koch, 12 oz., white, red and gold	8.00	12.00
☐ **Koenig Brau,** Bismarck, 12 oz., gold and white	12.00	16.00

Price Range

☐ **Koenig Brau,** Canadian Ace, 12 oz., gold and white 9.25 12.75

☐ **Koenig Brau,** Koenig Brau, 12 oz., gold and white, brand name in red 8.00 12.00

☐ **Kol,** Wisconsin, 12 oz., blue and white 36.00 47.00

☐ **Kold Brau,** -choen Edelweiss, 12 oz., blue, white and silver 50.00 65.00

☐ **Krueger,** Krueger, 12 oz., pink, dark red and silver, without traditional company symbol (pictorial letter "K") 25.00 35.00

☐ **Krueger,** Krueger, 12 oz., yellow, red and white, "Light Lager" in black 40.00 55.00

☐ **Krueger,** Krueger, 12 oz., brown, gold and red, "Finest" in white 30.00 40.00

☐ **Krueger,** Krueger, 12 oz., red, gold and black, large trademark (pictorial letter "K"), 1930's 225.00 300.00

☐ **Krueger Ale,** Krueger, 12 oz., white, black and gold, without usual trademark (pictorial letter "K") 20.00 30.00

☐ **Krueger Bock Beer,** Krueger Brewing, 12 oz., gold and red, illustration of ram's head, "Cool Before Serving" in bottom center .... RARE

☐ **Krueger Cream Ale,** Krueger, 12 oz., green, blue and red, trademark (pictorial letter "K") in red near top 35.00 44.00

☐ **Krueger Cream Ale,** Krueger, 12 oz., green and gold, trademark (pictorial letter "K") in black within gold rectangle 160.00 200.00

☐ **Krug Beer,** Rainier Brewing, 12 oz., blue, silver and red, brand name in silver diagonally across center, illustration of frothy tankard of beer in upper center .... RARE

☐ **Krueger Pilsner,** Krueger, 12 oz., white, gray and red 8.00 12.00

☐ **L and M,** Maier, 12 oz., brown and yellow 50.00 65.00

☐ **L and M,** Maier, 16 oz. 140.00 180.00

☐ **Lassen,** Grace, 12 oz., very dark blue and white, illustration of mountains 150.00 200.00

☐ **Lebanon Valley,** Lebanon Valley, 12 oz., white, blue and gold, wide gold band near bottoms ... 90.00 120.00

☐ **Leinenkugel's,** Leinenkugel, 12 oz., yellow and dark gold, horizontal bands, "Beer" in block letters (red) 13.00 17.00

☐ **Leinenkugel's,** Leinenkugel, 12 oz., white, red and gold 6.00 9.00

☐ **Leisy's Dortmunder,** Leisy, 12 oz., red, white and gold, canned at Cleveland, Ohio 50.00 60.00

Price Range

☐ **Leisy's Dortmunder,** Leisy, 12 oz., red, white and
gold, canned at Chicago, Illinois 60.00   75.00
☐ **Leisy's Light,** Leisy, 12 oz., blue, yellow and gold   42.50   53.50
☐ **Leisy's Pilsner,** Leisy, 12 oz., light brown, dark
brown and white 110.00   140.00
☐ **Liebmann's XXX Cream Ale,** ULTRA RARITY, 12
oz., You'll also find this one referred to as "Triple
X." The Liebmann Brewing Co. was located in the
Harlem district of New York City in the 1930's. It
was not a small organization by any means, which
shows that the rarity of a can is not determined
by the size of its manufacturer. Bright green can
with a large cream-white oval at the front and
black lettering—except for the X's, which are in
red. . . . .   **RARE**
☐ **Light And Mellow,** 12 oz., brown and yellow . . .   50.00   65.00
☐ **Linden Light,** Colonial, 12 oz., white with name in
black, word "beer" in red 75.00   100.00
☐ **Little Imp Extra Dry Pale,** ULTRA RARITY, 12
oz., Little Imp was a devil, who (on this can) has
a flowing red cape and brandishes a pitchfork. The
central portion of the can is silver, the surrounding
area gold, while the word "Imp" is printed in large
red letters. Little Imp Extra Dry Pale Beer was a
product of the Southern Brewing Co. of Los Ange-
les. . . . .   **RARE**
☐ **Little King Premium Beer,** Horlacher Brewing, 12
oz., white, red and black, brand name in red on
white background, illustration of a imp-like king in
upper center 75.00   85.00
☐ **Lone Star,** Lone Star, 12 oz., red, white and blue,
blue medallion at top with star 30.00   38.00
☐ **Lubeck,** Lubeck, 12 oz., white and black 60.00   75.00
☐ **Lubeck Premium,** Canadian Ace, 12 oz., green,
yellow and gold 27.00   34.00
☐ **Lubeck Premium,** Lubeck, 12 oz., green, yellow
and gold 23.00   30.00
☐ **Lucky Lager,** Lucky Lager, 12 oz., red, gold and
white, large crossed bands (red and dark red),
brand name reads straight across, not curved . .   10.00   14.00
☐ **Lucky Lager,** Lucky Lager, 12 oz., gold and red,
horizontal banding, medallion at center reads
"Age Dated Beer" 12.00   16.00
☐ **Lucky Lager,** Lucky Lager, 12 oz., gold, yellow
and red, diamond banding, does not read "Age
Dated Beer" 10.00   14.00

Top, Left to Right: **Highlander,** 12 oz., **$8–$12; Jax,** 12 oz., **$20–$30.** Bottom, Left to Right: **Karlsbrau,** 12 oz., **$20–$30; Kingsbury,** 12 oz., **$14–$19.**

Price Range

☐ **Maier Select,** Maier, 12 oz., red, white and blue, blue leaf near top 10.00   14.00

☐ **Malt Marrow,** Best Brewing, 12 oz., gold, red and white, brand name diagonal across center in red, "The Pure Malt" in blue diagonally beneath brand name 600.00   750.00

☐ **Manhattan Premium Bock,** ULTRA RARITY, 12 oz. This beer was made by Manhattan Brewing, which was located in Chicago. The can is gold and dark black, with a ram's head near the top and a silhouette skyline of Manhattan at the bottom. "Bock" is in large white letters. None are known of in excellent condition. . . . .   **RARE**

☐ **Mann-Chester Beer,** Maier Brewing, 12 oz., white, red and black, brand name in white on red banner in center, "Extra Pale" and "Extra Dry" in black above and below the label 30.00   40.00

☐ **Matts,** West End, 12 oz., white and pale green, "Premium" in white lettering on red ribbon 30.00   40.00

☐ **Medallion Beer,** Maier Brewing, 12 oz., gold and cream-white, brand name in gold at center, logo of a medallion with the world on it at upper center, "The Experts Choice" in black script at bottom center 100.00   135.00

☐ **Meister Brau,** Peter Hand, 12 oz., red, gold and white 25.00   33.00

☐ **Meister Brau,** Peter Hand, 12 oz., blue, white and silver 23.00   31.00

☐ **Meister Brau,** Peter Hand, 12 oz., gold and white, no red band at top 17.50   22.50

☐ **Meister Brau,** Peter Hand Brewing, 12 oz., white, gold and red, brand name in white on red background, brewer's logo in bottom center of a hand holding a capital "P" 50.00   60.00

☐ **Meister Brau Bock,** Peter Hand, 12 oz., white, brown and red, small ram's head, brand name in brown 20.00   25.00

☐ **Meister Brau Bock,** Peter Hand, 12 oz., white and brown, gold bands at top and bottom 75.00   90.00

☐ **Meister Brau Bock,** Peter Hand, 12 oz., white, red and orange, large ram's head, brand name in orange, does not state "Real Draft Beer" above ram's head 20.00   25.00

Price Range

☐ **Meister Brau Draft,** Peter Hand, 12 oz., light brown, dark brown and black, textured to resemble beer keg, words "Real Draft Beer" in white on red ribbon 7.00   10.00

☐ **Metz,** Metz, 12 oz., green, does not state "Extra Dry" 35.00   45.00

☐ **Metz Extra Dry,** Metz, 12 oz., white and red . . .   25.00   35.00

☐ **Metz Premium,** Metz, 12 oz., white, red and gold   20.00   25.00

☐ **Metz Premium,** Metz, 12 oz., white and red, brand name outlined in red 12.75   16.75

☐ **Mickey Malt Liquor,** Sterling, 8 oz., squat, dark green with coat-of-arms and shamrocks 40.00   55.00

☐ **Mile Hi,** Tivoli, 12 oz., red, white and blue, illustration of Colorado mountain 45.00   55.00

☐ **Mile Hi,** Tivoli, 12 oz., red, white and blue, illustration of Colorado mountain, reads "Light Premium Quality" in bands at bottom, mountain illustration has dark blue background 35.00   50.00

☐ **Miller,** Miller, 10 oz., white with gold-bordered white medallion 12.75   16.75

☐ **Miller High Life,** Miller, 12 oz., red, white, black and gold, quarter-moon emblem above brand name 5.00   6.50

☐ **Miller High Life,** Miller, 12 oz., white and gold, brand name in large letters 2.25   3.25

☐ **Miller High Life,** Miller, 12 oz., red, white and gold, brand name in small letters 3.00   4.00

☐ **Miller Select,** Miller, 12 oz., red, white and blue, quarter-moon emblem in blue medallion 50.00   65.00

☐ **Milwaukee Premium,** Waukee, 12 oz., white, red and gold 13.00   15.00

☐ **Mitchell's Premium,** Mitchell, 12 oz., red, white and blue 75.00   90.00

☐ **Modern Growler Ale,** ULTRA RARITY, 12 oz. Also known as Eigenbrot's Ale. Brewed by Globe of Baltimore. This 1930's can has a dark green front panel; the rest of the can is a light yellowish green. The letters "G.B." appear on a shield at the center with a bird on each side. "Ale" is in very large letters . . . .   RARE

☐ **Monarch,** Monarch, 12 oz., red, white and gold   20.00   30.00

☐ **Mr. Lager, For Men Only,** Fox Head, 12 oz., black, gray and red, spotlight effect 240.00   300.00

☐ **Munich Light Lager,** Feigenspan, 12 oz., white, blue and gold 5.25   6.50

Price Range

☐ **My,** Metz, 12 oz., gold and white 55.00 65.00
☐ **My,** Walter, 12 oz., gold and white 55.00 65.00
☐ **Narragansett,** Narragansett, 12 oz., white and
gold 40.00 50.00
☐ **Narragansett,** Narragansett, 12 oz., white, red
and gold, "Lager" in red above brand name ... 17.50 22.50
☐ **Narragansett,** Narragansett, 12 oz., gray and
white, no red band at bottom 8.00 12.00
☐ **Narragansett,** Narragansett, 12 oz., red, gold and
black, "Ale" in large red letters 115.00 145.00
☐ **Narragansett Ale,** Narragansett, 12 oz., gold, red
and white, "Ale" in white lettering 52.50 65.00
☐ **Narragansett Ale,** Narragansett, 12 oz., grey,
white and red 7.00 10.00
☐ **National Bohemian,** National, 7 oz., white, lettering within gold frame on black background 20.00 27.50
☐ **National Bohemian,** National, 12 oz., red and
white, silver and gold bands at top and bottom 10.00 14.00
☐ **National Bohemian Light,** National, 12 oz., red,
white and black, gold band at top and bottom .. 12.00 15.00
☐ **National Bohemian Light,** National, 12 oz., red,
white and black 10.00 14.00
☐ **National Bohemian Pale,** National, 12 oz., red,
white and black 20.00 25.00
☐ **National Pale Dry Premium,** National, 12 oz.,
white, violet and red 37.50 47.50
☐ **Near Beer,** Goetz, 12 oz., white, red and yellow 5.00 6.50
☐ **Neuweiler Light Lager,** Neuweiler, 8 oz., squat,
white with gold trim at top and bottom 20.00 30.00
☐ **Neuweiler Light Lager,** Neuweiler, 12 oz., blue
and gold 12.50 16.50
☐ **New York Special Brew (Near Beer),** Cleveland
Sandusky, 12 oz., red, white and blue, illustration
of Statute of Liberty 150.00 180.00
☐ **Nine-O-Five,** Drewry, 12 oz., red and white, blue
bands near bottom 5.00 6.50
☐ **Nine-O-Five (905),** Drewry, 12 oz., white and red,
shield and ribbon at bottom 5.25 6.75
☐ **Nine-O-Five (905),** Drewry 16 oz. 25.00 35.00
☐ **Nine-O-Five (905),** Nine-O-Five, 12 oz., white and
red, shield and ribbon at bottom 6.00 8.00
☐ **Nine-O-Five (905),** Nine-O-Five, 12 oz., red and
white, blue bands near bottom 6.00 8.00
☐ **Nine-O-Five (905),** Nine-O-Five, 12 oz., red and
white, black bands near bottom 7.00 10.00
☐ **Northern,** Northern, 12 oz., blue, white and gold 6.50 8.50

Price Range

☐ **Northern,** Northern, 12 oz., yellow and brown .. | 10.00 | 14.00
☐ **North Star,** Associated, 12 oz., red, white and blue | 7.00 | 10.00
☐ **North Star,** Schmidt, 12 oz., red, white and blue | 9.00 | 12.00
☐ **Norvic,** Regional, 12 oz., white and gold, brand name in red .... | 35.00 | 45.00
☐ **Nu-Deal,** Grace, 12 oz., white, blue and orange | 825.00 | 950.00
☐ **Oconto,** Oconto, 12 oz., blue, white and gold .. | 17.50 | 22.50
☐ **Oertel's '92,** Oertel, 12 oz., red, white and gold, read "Beer" beneath brand name (not "Lager Beer"), and "Premium Quality" .... | 12.00 | 16.00
☐ **Oertel's '92,** Ortel, 12 oz., white and red, gold band at top and bottom .... | 10.00 | 14.00
☐ **Oertel's '92 Lager,** Oertel, 12 oz., red, white and gold, five yellow bands at top and bottom ...... | 16.00 | 20.00
☐ **Old Bohemian Cream Ale,** Eastern, 12 oz., white, green and black, word "Old" in green lettering | 100.00 | 125.00
☐ **Old Bohemian Light,** Eastern, 12 oz., red, yellow and black .... | 35.00 | 45.00
☐ **Old Bohemian Light,** Eastern, 12 oz., white, red and black, world "Light" in black lettering ...... | 7.00 | 10.00
☐ **Old Bohemian Light,** Eastern, 12 oz., white, red and silver .... | 2.75 | 4.25
☐ **Old Bohemian Light,** Harvard, 12 oz., red, yellow and black .... | 55.00 | 65.00
☐ **Old Craft Brew,** Oconto, 12 oz., red, white and blue .... | 30.00 | 40.00
☐ **Old Crown Ale,** Centlivre, 12 oz., brown and yellow, "Lazy Aged" over brand name .... | 65.00 | 80.00
☐ **Old Crown Bock,** Centlivre, 12 oz., brown and white, illustration of ram's head .... | 8.00 | 12.00
☐ **Old Crown Premium Quality Ale,** Centlivre, 12 oz., brown and white, "Ale" in black lettering ... | 20.00 | 25.00
☐ **Old Dutch,** Krantz, 12 oz., multicolored pictorial, scene of people dining at table, yellow background, wide black bands at top and bottom ... | 17.50 | 22.50
☐ **Old Dutch Beer,** Eagle Brewing, silver, red and cream-white, illustration in upper center of a bearded man drinking a frothy mug of beer .... | 110.00 | 150.00
☐ **Old Dutch Bock,** 12 oz., Old Dutch Bock was brewed by the Old Dutch Brewing Co. of Brooklyn, New York. It was one of the first bock beers to be sold in cans. The can is gold with gold lettering against a blue medallion background. But the main attraction is the large illustration of a ram's head, looking directly outward from the can .... | 475.00 | 600.00

Top, Left to Right: **Leinenkugel's**, 12 oz., **$17.50–22.50**; **Lucky Lager**, 12 oz., **$8–$12**. Bottom, Left to Right: **Meister Brau**, 12 oz., **$30–$40**; **Metz**, 12 oz., **$17.50–$22.50**.

Price Range

☐ **Old Dutch Lager,** Maier, 12 oz., white, red and black, illustration (small) of Dutch countryside with windmill etc. 30.00   40.00

☐ **Old Dutch Lager,** Old Dutch, 12 oz., silver, red and blue, illustration of windmill in red 135.00   160.00

☐ **Old Dutch Premium Lager,** Eagle, 12 oz., white and gold 35.00   45.00

☐ **Old England Beer,** Fox Head Brewing, 12 oz., white, black and red, brand name in white on black label, illustration of sailing ship on top of label . . 300.00   400.00

☐ **Old Export,** Cumberland, 12 oz., red, white and black 5.00   6.50

☐ **Old Frisco Extra Pale Lager,** General, 12 oz., copper with name in black on white shield 350.00   450.00

☐ **Old Georgetown,** Heurich, 12 oz., pale brown, street map of the Georgetown section of Washington, D.C. printed on can 225.00   300.00

☐ **Old Georgetown,** Heurich, 12 oz., yellow and white 60.00   80.00

☐ **Old German,** Colonial, 12 oz., red, white and black 5.00   6.50

☐ **Old German Premium Lager,** Queen City, 12 oz., red and white, symbol of world globe at upper left 6.00   8.00

☐ **Old Gold Lager,** Manhattan, 12 oz., gold, brown and white 375.00   475.00

☐ **Old India Pale Ale,** Hull Brewing, 12 oz., green, red and white, "Old" in red, rest of brand name in white, two bands—one red and one green—make up label 80.00   95.00

☐ **Old Milwaukee,** Schlitz, 12 oz., gold and red, scene within rectangular frame 25.00   35.00

☐ **Old Milwaukee,** Schlitz, 12 oz., red and white, dark printing on shield symbol 5.00   7.00

☐ **Old Tankard Ale,** Pabst Brewing, 12 oz., gray, red and black, brand name in red in upper center, illustration of swashbuckler holding a mug of ale in center 100.00   135.00

☐ **Old Tankard Ale,** Pabst Brewing, 12 oz., gray red and black, identical to above can except that "Pabst" appears on this can where the brand name appears on the other, in the top center . . 80.00   90.00

☐ **Orbit Premium,** Orbit, 12 oz., white with blue rocks and planet, name in gold 50.00   65.00

☐ **Pabst Blue Ribbon,** Pabst, 12 oz., gold, white and blue, slogan above gold band at bottom 7.00   10.00

☐ **Pabst Blue Ribbon,** Pabst, 12 oz., gold, white and blue, slogan on gold band at bottom 7.00   10.00

	Price Range	
☐ **Pabst Blue Ribbon,** Pabst, 12 oz., blue and white	8.00	12.00
☐ **Pabst Blue Ribbon,** Pabst, 16 oz., gold at top and bottom, "TapaCan" slogan at bottom	25.00	35.00
☐ **Pabst Blue Ribbon Ale,** Pabst, 12 oz., white, silver and red	100.00	150.00
☐ **Pabst Blue Ribbon Bock,** Pabst, 12 oz., yellow and blue, illustration of ram	55.00	70.00
☐ **Pabst Blue Ribbon Bock,** Pabst, 12 oz., silver, red and white, illustration of ram's head, extremely rare	200.00	265.00
☐ **Pabst Blue Ribbon Bock,** Pabst, 12 oz., gold, cream and blue, illustration of ram	75.00	100.00
☐ **Pabst Blue Ribbon Export,** Pabst, 12 oz., silver, blue and red	22.50	30.00
☐ **Pabst Blue Ribbon Export,** Pabst, 12 oz., silver, blue and red	22.50	30.00
☐ **Pabst Bock,** Pabst, 12 oz., silver, red and white, illustration of ram's head, extremely rare, does not state "Blue Ribbon"	200.00	265.00
☐ **Pabst Export,** Pabst, 12 oz., silver, blue and red	30.00	40.00
☐ **Pabst Old Tankard Ale,** Pabst, 12 oz., gold, cream and red, illustration of man with shield and stein	100.00	135.00
☐ **Pacific Beer,** Rainier Brewing, 12 oz., light blue and white, brand name in white, illustration of sailboat in lower center	100.00	135.00
☐ **Padre Pale Lager,** Maier, 12 oz., various shades of brown, illustration of padre mission	13.00	17.00
☐ **Palomar Pilsner,** Monarch, 12 oz., red and black		RARE
☐ **Pathmark Premium Lager,** Hofbrau, 12 oz., white and blue	3.25	4.50
☐ **Patrick Henry Malt Liquor,** Fox Deluxe, 12 oz., green and white, small profile portrait	120.00	155.00
☐ **Paul Bunyon,** Wisconsin, 12 oz., red, white and blue, illustration of Paul Bunyon with axe	75.00	85.00
☐ **PB,** Horlacher, 12 oz., gold, red and white	2.75	4.25
☐ **Pearl Lager,** Pearl, 12 oz., cream white, red and white, with sunbeams radiating from behind brand name	35.00	45.00
☐ **Pearl Lager,** Pearl, 12 oz., cream white, red and white, without sunbeams radiating from behind brand name	25.00	35.00
☐ **Pearl Lager,** Pearl, 12 oz., gold, red and white	30.00	40.00
☐ **Perfection Premium,** Horlacher, 12 oz., white and red, illustration of penguin	20.00	25.00

Price Range

☐ **Peter Hand's Extra Pale,** Peter Hand, 12 oz., gold
and brown 275.00   350.00

☐ **Pfeiffer,** Pfeiffer, 12 oz., red, white and blue, fanciful illustration of a frothy mug of beer with a smiling
face on it 14.00   19.00

☐ **Pfeiffer's,** Pfeiffer, 12 oz., gold, white and red, no
striping at top, brand name in white lettering ... 7.50   10.00

☐ **Pfeiffer's,** Pfeiffer, 12 oz., gold, white and red, horizontal striping 8.00   12.00

☐ **Pfeiffer's Beer,** Pfeiffer Brewing, 12 oz., brand
name in white on red label, small illustration at top
of label of strutting fife player, several different illustrations on front of can are possible—mostly
sporting scenes (fishing, skiing or boating) or wildlife scenes (ducks, geese or deer) 50.00   65.00

☐ **Pfeiffer Party Keg Draught,** Associated, gallon,
brown. Probably the handsomest of the gallon
cans—a perfect replica of a keg with very authen-
tic wood graining effect 150.00   200.00

☐ **Pickwick Ale,** Haffenreffer, 12 oz., gold, black and
white 65.00   80.00

☐ **Piel's Light,** Piel, 12 oz., cream and gold, brand
name in blue 20.00   30.00

☐ **Piels Light Lager,** Piel, 16 oz., "King Size" on red
ribbon at top, gold bands top and bottom 15.00   20.00

☐ **Pike's Peak Malt Liquor,** Walter, 8 oz., squat,
white with red and gold ribbon, sketch of Pike's
Peak 35.00   45.00

☐ **Pike's Peak Malt Liquor,** Walter Brewing, 12 oz.,
red, yellow, blue and white, brand name in red
arching over upper center of can, very attractive
illustration of Pike's peak in center of can, yellow
bands at top and bottom "Brewed in the Heart of
the Rockies" in bottom band 150.00   190.00

☐ **Pilgrim Ale,** ULTRA RARITY. 12 oz. The Croft
Brewing Co. of Boston produced Pilgrim Ale—very
briefly. It's a gray can showing a man in pilgrim
costume standing atop a rock (intended Plymouth
Rock). The pilgrim figure is in green, the lettering
is red, and there is horizontal striping along the
can. .... **RARE**

☐ **Pilsengold,** San Francisco, 12 oz., gold and silver,
emblem of eagle 125.00   165.00

☐ **Pioneer,** Pioneer, 12 oz., red, white and blue,
brand name in red, illustration of powder horn .. 25.00   35.00

Price Range

☐ **Pioneer,** Pioneer, 12 oz., red, white and brown, illustration of buffalo	27.50	37.50
☐ **P.O.C.,** Pilsener, 12 oz., gold and tomato red, brand name in red	75.00	100.00
☐ **P.O.C.,** Pilsener, 12 oz., white, gold and red, no statement of contents on front above gold band at bottom	8.00	12.00
☐ **Point,** Stevens Point, 12 oz., blue, red and white, medium dark red, wide red frame above logo at top	15.00	22.50
☐ **Point,** Stevens Point, 12 oz., blue, red and white, very dark red	10.00	14.00
☐ **Prager,** Atlas, red and white, white lettering in red medallion	16.00	21.00
☐ **Prager,** Atlas, 12 oz., black, gold and red, lettering in gold against black background, circular medallion above lettering	50.00	65.00
☐ **Prager,** Atlas, 12 oz., gold and red, white lettering against red background	17.50	22.50
☐ **Prager Bohemian,** Atlas, 12 oz., white and red, illustration of musician and man dancing	8.00	12.00
☐ **Prima,** Prima, 12 oz., blue and white, very dark blue (almost violet), does not state "Gold Medal Beer"	25.00	35.00
☐ **Prima,** Prima, 12 oz., blue and white	13.00	17.00
☐ **Prima Gold Medal,** Prima, 12 oz., dark blue, white and gold	65.00	80.00
☐ **Primo,** Hawaii Brewing, 12 oz., silver with blue trim, name in white with red shading, paper label	175.00	225.00
Note: The paper label is a major contributing factor in the price of this can, as most specimens have lost their label over the years or had it badly damaged.		
☐ **Prizer Extra Dry,** Reading, 12 oz., white, red and gold illustration of stein	3.25	4.75
☐ **Prost Eastern Premium,** Edelwiss, 12 oz., white, red and gold, illustration of stein	45.00	60.00
☐ **Rahr's,** Rahr, 12 oz., dark reddish gold and white, does not state "All Star"	16.00	21.00
☐ **Rahr's All Star,** Rahr, 12 oz., reddish gold and white, speckled background	27.00	37.00
☐ **Rainier,** Sicks, 12 oz., white and red	40.00	50.00
☐ **Rainier Ale,** Sicks, 12 oz., dark silver and white, "Ale" in black lettering	20.00	30.00

Price Range

☐ **Rainier Ale,** Sicks, 12 oz., yellow and black 10.00   14.00

☐ **Rainier's Extra Pale,** Sicks, 12 oz., white, red and gold 30.00   40.00

☐ **Reading Premium,** Reading, 12 oz., blue, gold and white 6.00   8.00

☐ **Red Cap Ale,** Carling, 12 oz., green and very pale brown, "Red Cap" in red script lettering, small profile portrait of man wearing red cap 12.00   16.00

☐ **Red Cap Ale,** Carling, 12 oz., black and very pale brown, "Red Cap" in thick black letters, medium-size profile portrait of man wearing red cap 13.00   17.00

☐ **Red Fox,** Best Brewing, 12 oz., white and red, illustration of fox 35.00   45.00

☐ **Red Fox,** Cumberland, 12 oz., white and red, illustration of fox 30.00   40.00

☐ **Red Fox,** Jacob Ruppert, 12 oz., white and red, illustration of fox 90.00   120.00

☐ **Redtop,** Atlantic, 12 oz., red, gold and white ...   20.00   30.00

☐ **Redtop Extra Dry,** Red Top, 12 oz., white, red and gold 40.00   50.00

☐ **Regal,** American, 12 oz., cream white and red ..   12.50   15.50

☐ **Regal Ale,** Anheuser-Busch, 12 oz., green and white, illustration of three mugs 80.00   105.00

☐ **Regal Ale,** Regal, 12 oz., green and white, illustration of three mugs 75.00   100.00

☐ **Regal Amber,** Regal Amber, 12 oz., red and white, extremely rare 400.00   500.00

☐ **Regal Bock,** Maier, 12 oz., white, blue and gold, brand name in small script letters 100.00   135.00

☐ **Regal Pale,** Regal, 12 oz., white, blue and gold, brand name against white background 12.00   16.00

☐ **Regal Pale Beer,** Regal Amber Brewing, 12 oz., blue, gold and white, brand name in white on blue banners......................................   50.00   65.00

☐ **Regency,** Maier, 12 oz., yellow and white, brand name in white on red ribbon 30.00   40.00

☐ **Reidenbach,** Canadian Ace, 12 oz., gold, white and blue 30.00   40.00

☐ **Reisch,** Reisch, 12 oz., white and gold, gold flecked background 30.00   40.00

☐ **Reserve,** Peter Hand, 12 oz., blue and silver, back of can had illustration of "upper crust" people holding a glass of beer, above illustration was "There's so much in RESERVE for you" 30.00   40.00

☐ **Reserve of Wisconsin,** Wisconsin, 12 oz., red and white 35.00   45.00

Price Range

☐ **Rex Pale Lager,** Maier, 12 oz., red, white and blue	25.00	35.00
☐ **R & H Light,** Rubsam Horrmann, 12 oz., gold, red and white	150.00	190.00

☐ **R & H Special XXX Ale.** Ultra Rarity. 12 oz. The R & H Brewing Co. was located in Staten Island, New York—in direct competition with the giant breweries of New York, Brooklyn and New Jersey. Its Special XXX Ale was apparently not a top seller, and the can has become one of the hobby's foremost rarities. It's chiefly green with the lettering in white. A red central medallion is placed behind the letters "R & H." Incidentally, R & H stood for Rubsam and Horrmann. . . . . **RARE**

☐ **Rheingold Ale,** Liebman, 12 oz., green, red and white	90.00	120.00
☐ **Rheingold Extra Dry Giant,** Liebman, 16 oz. . . .	17.50	22.50
☐ **Rheingold Extra Dry Giant,** Rheingold, 16 oz.	12.00	16.00
☐ **Rheingold Extra Dry Lager,** Liebmann, 12 oz., brown woodgrain with name in black on tan background.	325.00	400.00
☐ **Rheingold Extra Dry Lager,** Rheingold, 12 oz., red and white	7.00	10.00
☐ **Rheingold Extra Pale,** United States, 12 oz., gold, white and black	52.00	65.00

☐ **Rheingold McSorley's Ale,** Liebmann Brewing, 12 oz., gold, white and red, illustration of a bust of man with long handlebar moustache . . . . **RARE**

☐ **Rheingold Scotch Ale,** Liebman, 12 oz., gold and cream with Scotch plaid	25.00	35.00
☐ **Rheinlander,** Rheinlander, 12 oz., silver, white and orange, illustration of snow-laden field with trees, speckled effect on can to give appearance of falling snow	20.00	30.00

☐ **Rishwain Special.** Ultra Rarity. 12 oz. It was made by the San Francisco Brewing Co. This very rare can is a bright banana yellow with the brand name in white letters outlined in red. The word "Special" is in script lettering, above a small medallion picturing a tall glass. At the top is a decorative letter "R" supported by a pair of lions. . . . . **RARE**

☐ **Riviera Dark,** Atlantic, 12 oz., blue and yellow . .	145.00	185.00
☐ **Rolling Rock,** Latrobe, 12 oz., dark green and white	12.50	16.50
☐ **Royal Award,** Maier, 12 oz., white, gold and blue	95.00	125.00
☐ **Royal Farms Premium,** Sunshine, 12 oz., red, white and blue	170.00	210.00

Top, Left to Right: **Mile Hi**, 12 oz., **$40–$50; Mule Head Stock Ale**, 12 oz., **$275–$325.**
Bottom, Left to Right: **Narragansett Ale**, 12 oz., **$75–$110; Rheingold Extra Dry Lager**,
12 oz., **$320–$380.**

Price Range

☐ **Royal 58,** Duluth, 12 oz., white and gold 11.00   15.00

☐ **Royal Pale Dry,** Maier, 12 oz., yellow, brown and white, shield illustration 45.00   55.00

☐ **Royal Premium,** Royal, 12 oz., light blue and dark blue 50.00   60.00

☐ **Ruhstaller's Gilt Edge.** Ultra Rarity, 12 oz., Ruhstaller's was made by the Buffalo Brewing Co.—which was not in Buffalo, New York, but in Sacramento, California. It seems to have been distributed only in California and probably far from state-wide even at that. The can is white with "Gilt Edge" in red letters. . . . .   **RARE**

☐ **Ruppert,** Jacob Ruppert, 12 oz., yellowish brown with reddish brown lettering 42.50   52.50

☐ **Ruppert Ale,** Jacob Ruppert, 12 oz., beige, green and white 225.00   300.00

☐ **Ruppert Knickerbocker,** Jacob Ruppert, 12 oz., light brown and dark brown, brand name in white, ribbon above 40.00   50.00

☐ **Ruppert Knickerbocker,** Jacob Ruppert, 12 oz., white, red and gold, standing figure of "Father Knickerbocker," wording and barley-stalk motifs within gold frame, brand name in red on white background 12.00   16.00

☐ **Ruppert Knickerbocker,** Jacob Ruppert, 12 oz., gold, red, white and blue, wording in bottom in white against gold background 6.00   8.00

☐ **Ruppert Knickerbocker Beer,** Jacob Ruppert Brewing, 12 oz., white, red and gold, standing figure of "Father Knickerbocker," the white background has a slightly bluish tinge, there is no lettering within the gold frame 16.00   21.00

☐ **Ruppert Knickerbocker,** Jacob Ruppert, 12 oz., white and gold, standing figure of "Father Knickerbocker," wording and barley-stalk motifs within gold frame, brand name in white on red banner   10.00   14.00

☐ **Ruppert Knickerbocker,** Jacob Ruppert, 12 oz., white and red, half length figure of "Father Knickerbocker" hoisting glass 8.00   12.00

☐ **Ruppert Knickerbocker Bock,** Jacob Ruppert, 12 oz., white, brown and gold 40.00   52.50

☐ **Ruppert Knickerbocker King Size,** Jacob Ruppert, 16 oz., Father Knickerbocker lower right holding glass 30.00   40.00

Price Range

☐ **Ruppiner Dark Beer,** Jacob Ruppert Brewing, 12 oz., tan, brown and light blue, small illustration of a Dutch girl in center 80.00 95.00

☐ **Ruser,** Arizona Brewing, 12 oz., blue and yellow with illustration of Alpine mountain peak 125.00 155.00

☐ **Ruser,** Grace, 12 oz., blue and yellow with illustrations of Alpine mountain peak 135.00 165.00

☐ **Salzburg,** S. Edelweiss, 12 oz., white, blue and red. 60.00 80.00

☐ **Schaefer,** Schaefer, 12 oz., white, red and gold, brand name repeated in balloons around can, reads "Established 1842" at upper right 8.00 12.00

☐ **Schaefer,** Schaefer, 12 oz., cream white, red and gold, does not state "Full 12 Ounces" near bottom 16.00 21.00

☐ **Schaefer,** Schaefer, 12 oz., cream white, red and gold, "Full 12 Ounces" in script lettering near bottom 16.00 21.00

☐ **Schaefer,** Schaefer, 12 oz., brown, black and red, textured to resemble beer keg 25.00 35.00

☐ **Schaefer Irish Cream Ale,** Schaefer, 12 oz., cream white and green, large shamrock 45.00 55.00

☐ **Schell's,** Schell, 12 oz., white, light brown and dark brown 16.00 21.00

☐ **Schlitz,** Schlitz, 12 oz., white and brown, in slogan "The Beer That Made Milwaukee Famous," the word "Beer" is in larger lettering than the other words, and the entire slogan is printed in dark gray 5.00 7.00

☐ **Schlitz,** Schlitz, 12 oz., white and brown, in slogan "The Beer That Made Milwaukee Famous," the word "Beer" is in the same size lettering as the other words 8.00 12.00

☐ **Schlitz,** Schlitz, 12 oz., white and brown, in slogan "The Beer That Made Milwaukee Famous," and word "Beer" is in larger lettering than the other words, and the entire slogan is printed in brown; does not read "12 Fluid Ounces at Top" 3.50 4.75

☐ **Schlitz,** Schlitz, 12 oz., white and brown, in slogan "The Beer That Made Milwaukee Famous," the word "Beer" is in larger lettering than the other words, and the entire slogan is printed in brown; reads "12 Fluid Ounces at Top" 5.00 7.00

☐ **Schlitz,** Schlitz, 12 oz., white and brown, no brown trim at top and bottom 2.00 3.25

☐ **Schlitz,** Schlitz, 12 oz., white and brown, no brown trim at top and bottom, reads "Softop" in blue to left of and above brand name 3.00 4.25

Price Range

☐ **Schlitz,** Schlitz, 16 oz., brown bands at top and bottom . . . . : 10.00 13.25

☐ **Schmidt's,** E and B, 12 oz., red, white and silver, brand name in slanted lettering 25.00 33.00

☐ **Schmidt's,** E and B, 12 oz., red, white and gold, brand name in slanted lettering 20.00 30.00

☐ **Schmidt's,** E & B Brewing, gold, black and red, brand name in white on black banner in center of can, "Since 1873" and "Premium Quality Beer" both appear in white lettering on red banners on top and beneath brand name 30.00 40.00

☐ **Schmidt's,** E and B, 12 oz., gold and white 40.00 50.00

☐ **Schmidt's,** Schmidt, 12 oz., gold, cream and red 8.00 12.00

☐ **Schmidt's,** Schmidt, 12 oz., silver and cream white, illustration of tiger 40.00 50.00

☐ **Schmidt's Ale,** Schmidt Brewing, 12 oz., green and gold, illustration of a tiger at top of label, beside illustration reads "Tiger Brand" in green . . . 35.00 45.00

☐ **Schmidt's Bock,** Schmidt, 12 oz., red, white and gold, illustration of ram's head 55.00 70.00

☐ **Schmidt's City Club,** Schmidt, 12 oz., gold, red and black, circle at center with 5-pointed star .. 20.00 30.00

☐ **Schmidt Extra Special,** Pfeiffer, 12 oz., white, black and red, "Beer" in white lettering 6.50 8.50

☐ **Schmidt's Extra Special,** Schmidt, 12 oz., gold, white and red 8.00 12.00

☐ **Schmidt's Light,** Schmidt, 12 oz., gold, red and white 20.00 30.00

☐ **Schoen's Old Lager,** Wausau, 12 oz., red and white 25.00 35.00

☐ **Schoenling Lager,** Schoenling, 12 oz., red, white and gold 12.00 16.00

☐ **Schoenling Old Time Bock Beer,** Schoenling Brewing, 12 oz., red, blue and white, brand name in red diagonally across upper center of can, illustration of ram near water pump and glass of beer **RARE**

☐ **Sebewaing,** Sebewaing, 12 oz., pale beige and red, uncolored illustration of bird in flight 27.50 37.50

☐ **Sebewaing,** Sebewaing, 12 oz., blue, colored illustration of bird in flight 35.00 45.00

☐ **Select Pennsylvania,** Gold Medal, 16 oz., gold, red and white 35.00 45.00

☐ **Senate Ale,** Heurich, 12 oz., brown with gold trim, red banner with name in white . . . . : 300.00 425.00

☐ **Sheridan,** Walter, 12 oz., gold, white and red, illustration of bucking bronco 16.00 21.00

Price Range

☐ **Sheridan Export,** Sheridan, 12 oz., yellow with red lettering, slogan "Famous for Flavor" 25.00   35.00

☐ **Sierra,** Reno, 12 oz., blue and white, gold horizontal stripes 75.00   100.00

☐ **Silver Bar Beer,** International Brewing, 12 oz., white and green, brand name in white on green background, circular illustration of a bearded man laughing and holding a glass 90.00   120.00

☐ **Silver Bar Sparkling Ale,** Southern, 12 oz., very dark green and white 115.00   145.00

☐ **Silver Spring,** Star, 12 oz., blue and silver, extremely rare (one of the rarest flat tops) ....   **RARE**

☐ **Silver Top Premium,** Duquesene, 12 oz., red, white and blue 65.00   80.00

☐ **Skol Eastern Premium,** Drewry, 12 oz., white with illustrations of color steins 50.00   65.00

☐ **Skol Eastern Premium,** Atlas. 16 oz. 27.50   37.50

☐ **Skol Premium,** Jax Ice and Cold Storage, 12 oz., white with red shield, name in white 175.00   210.00

☐ **Snowcrest,** Grace, 16 oz. 350.00   450.00

☐ **Southern Select,** Galveston, 12 oz., gold and white 65.00   80.00

☐ **Sparkling Stite,** Heileman, 8 oz., squat, white with red band near top 4.00   6.00

☐ **Sparkling Stite,** Heileman, 12 oz., white 5.00   7.00

☐ **Spearman Ale,** Spearman, 12 oz., metallic green with red brand, name in white 160.00   200.00

☐ **Special Brew,** Southern, 12 oz., silver, brand name in gothic lettering 100.00   130.00

☐ **Special Export,** Heileman, 12 oz., green and white, green and white leafwork at top, brand name in white 10.00   14.00

☐ **Special Export Malt Liquor,** Heileman, 8 oz., squat, white with beige medallion, red lettering   35.00   45.00

☐ **Special Export Old Style Lager,** Heileman, 12 oz., green, yellow and white, leafwork at top in yellow 35.00   45.00

☐ **Special Export Stout Malt Liquor,** Heileman, 8 oz., squat, white with beige medallion, red lettering   40.00   50.00

☐ **Sportsman,** Grace, 12 oz., gold, white and red   25.00   35.00

☐ **Sportsman,** Maier, 12 oz., gold, white and red ..   20.00   25.00

☐ **Spring,** Maier, 12 oz., light blue and dark blue ..   15.00   22.50

☐ **Stag Premium Dry Pilsener,** Carling, 12 oz., gold, yellow and red 8.00   12.00

☐ **Stag Premium Dry Pilsener,** Griesedieck, 12 oz., gold, yellow and red 10.50   14.00

FLAT TOPS / 135

Price Range

- **Standard Beer,** Standard Brewing, 12 oz., gold, yellow and brown, brand name in yellow, label is made to look like wood grain, illustration of mug of beer 20.00 25.00
- **Standard Dry Ale,** Standard Rochester, 12 oz., blue and white 25.00 35.00
- **Star Model Premium Quality,** Star Union, 12 oz., white and red 15.00 20.00
- **Steinbeck Lager Beer,** Grace Brothers Brewing, 12 oz., red, blue and white, brand name in red across top, illustration of a beer stein ornately carved with a man standing by a house 40.00 50.00
- **Stegmaier Gold Medal,** Stegmaier, 12 oz., white, read and gold 37.50 47.50
- **Stegmaier Gold Medal,** Stegmaier, 12 oz., gold and white 17.50 25.00
- **Stein's Canandaigua Extra Dry,** Stein, 12 oz., light brown, red and blue 65.00 75.00
- **Steinbrau Pale Dry Lager,** Maier, 12 oz., white and red 8.00 12.00
- **Sterling Pilsener,** Sterling, 12 oz., silver, blue and red, brand name in white on very dark blue ribbon, "Pilsener" in small blue letters, "Beer" in white letters 12.00 16.00
- **Sterling Premium Pilsener,** Sterling, 12 oz., silver, blue and red, reads "Premium" above brand name, red oval behind brand name is narrow ... 4.50 6.00
- **Sterling Premium Pilsener,** Sterling, 12 oz., silver, blue and red, reads "Premium" above brand name, red oval behind brand name is wide 6.00 8.00
- **Stolz Premium,** International, 12 oz., white and red 45.00 60.00
- **Storz,** Storz, 12 oz., white, red, blue and gold, logo in red circle against beneath brand name 10.00 13.25
- **Storz All Grain,** Storz, 12 oz., red, blue and white, illustration of man wearing cowboy hat 700.00 825.00
- **Storzette,** Storz, 8 oz., squat, white with brand name in blue 35.00 45.00
- **Storz Premium,** Storz, 12 oz., white, red, gold and blue, brand name on flag against blue background (fades to white at bottom) 7.00 9.00
- **Storz Premium,** Storz, 12 oz., white, red and gold, does not read "The Orchid of Beer" at bottom 8.00 12.00
- **Storz Premium Dry,** Storz, 12 oz., white and red, does not state "Select" 11.00 15.00

Top, Left to Right: **Silver Bar Ale,** *12 oz.,* **$115–$145;** **Simon Pure,** *12 oz.,* **$25–$30.**
Bottom, Left to Right: **Skol Premium Beer,** *12 oz.,* **$175–$210;** **Spearman Ale,** *12 oz.,*
$160–$200, *Courtesy of Rogalski Brothers, Gainesville, FL.*

Price Range

☐ **Storz Premium Dry Select,** Storz, 12 oz., white and red, reads "Premium Dry Select" beneath brand name 15.00   20.00

☐ **Stroh's Bohemian Style,** Stroh, 12 oz., white, dark brown and gold, no statement of contents at bottom of can front 6.00   8.00

☐ **Strong White Bear,** White Bear, 12 oz., red and white, illustration of Polar bear standing. New and old cans both exist with this design. Value listed is for old cans, new cans worth only about $1.   220.00   260.00

☐ **Super X Pale Dry,** Lucky Lager, 12 oz., red and white 100.00   130.00

☐ **Super X Pale Dry,** Maier, 12 oz., red and white   90.00   115.00

☐ **Superior Premium,** Superior, 12 oz., red, white and gold 25.00   35.00

☐ **Tahoe Lager,** Maier, 12 oz., black, white and yellow, illustration of brimming glass 140.00   180.00

☐ **Tavern Pale Bar,** Atlantic, 12 oz., cream and tomato red 20.00   26.00

☐ **Tavern Pale Dry,** Atlantic, 16 oz., red, silver and white 5.00   7.00

☐ **Tavern Pale Vintage,** Atlantic, silver and red ...   30.00   40.00

☐ **Tempo Beer,** Blatz Brewing, 12 oz., gold, red, white and black, brand name in white on black banner across center of can, "Lightest Beer Ever" in black script on red background, gold bands at top and bottom 135.00   165.00

☐ **Three Thirty Three Pilsener,** Gold Brau, 12 oz., cream and gold 35.00   45.00

☐ **Thousand Dollar Beer,** Gettelman Brewing, 12 oz., yellow, gold and red, brand name diagonally across center, logo in upper center of a hand holding a beer glass 40.00   50.00

☐ **Tivoli,** Tivoli, 12 oz., red and white, brand name in white lettering within red diamond 30.00   40.00

☐ **Topper Light Dry Pilsener,** Standard Rochester, 12 oz., white and red 5.00   7.00

☐ **Topper Light Dry Pilsener,** Standard Rochester, 12 oz., gold, white and red, gold bands at top and bottom, trademark (silhouette of top-hatted man) above brand name 30.00   40.00

☐ **Trommer's Bock Beer,** Trommer's Brewing, 12 oz., gold, red, black and blue, brand name in black across top center, blue illustration of a ram's head   **RARE**

☐ **Trophy,** Drewry, 12 oz., orange, white, black and red 45.00   60.00

Price Range

- [ ] **Trophy,** Edelweiss, 16 oz., orange, white, black and red 50.00   62.50
- [ ] **Trumps Ale.** Ultra Rarity. 12 oz. The can shows a hand holding a fan of playing cards, and near the edge of the can are tiny playing card symbols—hearts, diamonds, clubs and spades. The overall color is a bright copper, with the brand name in white ....   **RARE**
- [ ] **Tudor,** Best Brewing, 12 oz., red, blue and white, illustration of headpiece from suit of armor 17.50   22.50
- [ ] **Tudor Bock,** Metropolis, 12 oz., yellowish with brown shield 160.00   200.00
- [ ] **Tudor Cream Ale,** Best Brewing, 12 oz., white and green, illustration of headpiece from suit of armor.   22.50   30.00
- [ ] **Tudor Cream Ale,** Cumberland, 12 oz., white and green, illustration of headpiece from suit of armor   20.00   25.00
- [ ] **Tudor Cream Ale,** Tudor, 12 oz., green and white, small red "A & P" logo above brand name 8.00   12.00
- [ ] **Tudor Cream Ale,** Tudor, 16 oz. 140.00   180.00
- [ ] **Twenty (20) Grand Select Ale,** Red Top Brewing, 12 oz., green, gold and white, brand name in white on green banner diagonally across can, "Constant Quality Control" in green script lettering in lower center of can, green and white checkerboard design on lower half of can 70.00   80.00
- [ ] **Uinta Club,** Becker, 12 oz., gold, blue and red ..   100.00   130.00
  Note: You will often find this one listed as "Unita Club" on sale and swap lists, but the correct spelling is "Uinta."
- [ ] **Uinta Club Beer,** Becker Brewing, 12 oz., gold, black and red, "Uinta" in white lettering on red banner, "Club" in white lettering on black banner, logo in center of can shows a bronco-buster in a white oval imposed on a white, black and red "V"   70.00   85.00
- [ ] **University Club Malt Liquor,** Miller, 8 oz., squat, white 15.00   20.00
- [ ] **University Club Stout Malt Liquor,** Miller, 8 oz., squat, white 20.00   25.00
- [ ] **Utica Club Pale Cream Ale,** West End, 12 oz., black and silver, brand name centerized on can, does not state "Extra Dry" 37.50   45.00
- [ ] **Utica Club Pale Cream Ale,** West End, 12 oz., red, white and yellow 50.00   65.00
- [ ] **Utica Club Pilsener Lager,** West End, 12 oz., gold and white, brand name below center of can, medallion centerized above it 16.00   21.00

Top, Left to Right: **Sterling Ale,** *12 oz.,* **$750–$790; Straight Eight Beer,** *12 oz.,* **$115–$140.** *Bottom:* **Tudor Bock,** *12 oz.,* **$150–$200.**

Price Range

☐ **Utica Club Pilsener Lager,** West End, 12 oz., gold and white, brand name centerized on can, medallion to upper left 20.00   30.00

☐ **Utica Club Pilsener Lager,** West End, 12 oz., white, blue and red, brand name in red 50.00   62.00

☐ **Valley Forge,** Valley Forge, 12 oz., red, white and dark blue, word "Beer" in red lettering below shield 17.50   22.50

☐ **Valley Forge,** Scheidt, 12 oz., red, white and blue, word "Beer" appears within shield carrying brand name 20.00   30.00

☐ **Valley Forge,** Scheidt, 12 oz., red, white and blue, brand name in white lettering on red oval flanked by "minutemen" 47.50   60.00

☐ **Van Merritt,** Van Merritt, 12 oz., green and white, multicolor illustration of windmill, thin green band at top and bottom 7.00   10.00

☐ **Van Merritt,** Van Merritt, 12 oz., green, white and red, brand name in white lettering against red banner 40.00   52.50

☐ **Viking Premium,** Sewanee, 12 oz., white with yellow illustrations of Vikings, brand name in red ..   130.00   160.00

☐ **Volksbrau,** Drewry, 12 oz., red, white and blue   35.00   45.00

☐ **Waldorf Red Band,** Forest City Brewers, 12 oz., gold, red and black, brand name in red lettering on gold band at top of can, "Red Band" in gold lettering on red banner in upper center, logo of eagle at bottom center 250.00   190.00

☐ **Waldorf Red Band Beer,** Forest City Brewers, 12 oz., brown, white and red, brand name in white lettering in upper center, "Red Band Beer" appears on three separate red bands around middle of can   60.00   70.00

☐ **Walter's Premium Pilsener,** Walter, 12 oz., red, cream white and gold 27.00   36.00

☐ **Weber,** Weber, 12 oz., black, white and red 35.00   44.00

☐ **Weber Waukesha,** Weber, 12 oz., black, red and gold 25.00   30.00

☐ **Wehle Colonial Ale,** Wehle, 12 oz., orange with silver oval, orange band with name in silver 325.00   400.00

☐ **Wellington Stout,** Walter, 12 oz., pale blue and black, "Stout" in red 40.00   50.00

☐ **Western Style Pilsener,** Silver Springs, 12 oz., red and white 47.50   60.00

☐ **West Virginia Light,** Fesenmeier, 12 oz., white, red and gold 30.00   37.50

Top, Left to Right: **Tudor Cream Ale**, *12 oz.,* **$23–$30;** **Viking Premium Beer**, *12 oz.,* **$200–$250.** *Bottom:* **Wehle Colonial Ale**, *12 oz.,* **$320–$380.**

Price Range

☐ **White Horse,** Westminster Brewing, 12 oz., white, black and red, brand name in white on black background, illustration of white horse head against red background .... **RARE**

☐ **White Label,** Storz, 12 oz., white and gold 5.00 7.00

☐ **Wiedemann,** Wiedemann, 12 oz., red, white and black 8.00 12.00

☐ **Wiesnner's Regal,** Wiessner, 12 oz., gray and red, illustration of castle turret 150.00 190.00

☐ **Winchester Stout,** Walter, 12 oz., cream white and gold 65.00 80.00

☐ **Wisconsin Club Premium Pilsner,** Huber, 12 oz., white and gold, brand name in gold lettering ... 12.50 15.50

☐ **Wisconsin Gold Label Premium,** Huber, 12 oz., gold and white 8.00 12.00

☐ **Wisconsin Premium,** Fox Head, 12 oz., blue, white and gold, brand name set against map of Wisconsin 25.00 35.00

☐ **Wisconsin Premium,** Wisconsin, 12 oz., red, white and black, "Premium" in large script letters 20.00 27.50

☐ **Wisconsin Premium,** Wisconsin, 12 oz., white, red and blue, small map of Wisconsin 4.75 6.50

☐ **Wisconsin's Private Club,** Spring City, 12 oz., white and blue 75.00 100.00

☐ **Wunderbrau,** Wunderbrau, 12 oz., gold, black and red 40.00 50.00

☐ **Yankee Premium,** Yankee, 12 oz., white and blue stripes, red banner with name in white 100.00 140.00

☐ **Ye Old English Style Ale,** Ultra Rarity, 12 oz., the Star Brewing Co. of Vancouver, Washington (right on the Canadian border) made this one; it's also known as "Hop Gold." The name "Hop Gold" is in white lettering on a blue five-pointed star near the bottom of the can. The lower part of the can is orange and the upper part white, with a small illustration of a mug to the left of the words "Ye Old English." .... **RARE**

☐ **York Light,** Colonial, 12 oz., red and white 75.00 90.00

☐ **Yorktown Extra Fine Premium,** Reading, 12 oz., red, white and black 13.00 17.00

☐ **Yusay,** Pilsen, 12 oz., red and white, "Yusay" in large letters, "Oremium Beer" in white, eagle is colored 20.00 30.00

☐ **Yusay,** Pilsen, 12 oz., red and white, "Pilsen" in large white letters, "Premium Beer" in black ... 35.00 45.00

Price Range

☐ **Yusay,** Pilsen, 12 oz., reddish gold and white, large eagle near top 42.50   60.00
☐ **Zing Near Beer,** Kingsburg, 12 oz., white and blue   20.00   25.00
☐ **Zobelein's Eastside,** Los Angeles, 12 oz., blue, cream and white and red, eagle 60.00   70.00
☐ **Zobelein's Eastside Genuine Bock,** Los Angeles, 12 oz., gold, cream and red, illustration of smiling ram 450.00   550.00

PULL TABS

The first pull tab beer cans went on the market in 1962—more than 20 years ago. Like many other good ideas, the pull tab was considered a passing fancy by some observers. However, by 1965 it was obvious that the old flat top can had met its match, and that in time virtually every beer can (not to mention soda can) would be a pull tab. One drawback of the pull tab can was that it encouraged littering. Many people who would not throw a whole can out of their car window would think nothing of tossing out the pull tab ring or tab. An attempt was made to solve this with a push-type can, which could be opened without tearing anything away. Another drawback of the early pull tabs was that the edges were too sharp. A lot of people cut their fingers and mouths on the cans. This problem was corrected quickly, however.

Beginners to the hobby usually start with pull tab cans, as they're the most readily available. You can get them anywhere, and a pull tab collection builds up rapidly. Do not make the assumption that all pull tab cans are less valuable than flat tops. Most of them are, but some pull tabs do have a scarcity factor and sell at rather stiff prices, as the following listings will show. Most of the currently manufactured pull tabs are worth from 40¢ to 60¢. A currently made can could be worth a little more than this, if it has very limited local distribution.

Be sure to open these cans from the bottom, using an opener. A rule of thumb to remember is that the can should retain as much of its original appearance as possible.

Price Range

☐ **A-1 Light Pilsner,** National, 12 oz., cream white and brown 40   .60
☐ **A-1 Premium Beer,** National Brewing, 12 oz., white, blue and gold, brand name in curved lettering, Phoenix Suns (basketball team) emblem in upper center of can (obviously, this can sells particularly well in Arizona) 4.00   5.00
☐ **A-1 Premium Beer,** National Brewing, 12 oz., white, blue and gold, similar to above can, but without basketball emblem 3.00   4.00

Price Range

☐ **ABC Premium,** Garden State, 16 oz., dark red and
white 2.50   3.25

☐ **ABC Premium,** Wagner, 12 oz., red and white,
"AGED" in rectangular frame 1.75   2.50

☐ **ABC Premium Ale,** Eastern, 12 oz., dark green
with "AGED" in rectangular frame 85   1.20

☐ **Acme,** General Brewing, 12 oz., pictorial can with
medieval scene 2.50   3.50

☐ **Adler Brau,** George Walter, 12 oz., tomato red
with circular medallion of black and gold 10.00   14.00

☐ **Alpen Brau,** Alpen Brau, 12 oz., blue, white and
silver with snow-covered Alps 3.00   4.00

☐ **Alpen Glen,** Hamm, 12 oz., white with red lettering, brown and green artwork, house with Alps in
background, green trees 20.00   30.00

☐ **Alpine Lager,** Alpine Brewing, 12 oz., white,
brown and blue, sharply triangular mountains ring
the bottom of the can, brand name in blue on white
background in upper center, "Sparkling Clear" in
red in very top center 3.00   4.00

☐ **Alpine Lager,** Alpine, 12 oz., white and blue, out-
lines of peaks of Alpine mountains 1.50   2.00

☐ **Alpine, "Refreshing As Mountain Air,"** General,
12 oz., white, gold and blue 1.85   2.65

☐ **Alpine, "Refreshing As Mountain Air,"** Maier, 12
oz., white, gold and blue 12.00   16.00

☐ **Alps Brau,** Old Crown, 12 oz., blue and white,
mountain peak against blue sky 1.50   2.25

☐ **Alta,** Blitz-Weinhard, 12 oz., silver and white, blue
lettering 40   .60

☐ **Altes Fassbler,** National, 16 oz., white, red and
gold 4.00   5.50

☐ **Amana,** Cold Spring, 12 oz., jet black and white

☐ **Ambassador,** Krueger, 12 oz., beige and white, il-
lustration of polka dancers 20.00   30.00

☐ **Amber Brau Fully Aged Lager,** General, 12 oz.,
blue and gold (two shades of blue) 2.25   3.25

☐ **American,** American, 12 oz., white, gold and red,
brand name in white on red background, eagle
with spread wings in upper center 10.00   14.00

☐ **American Dry,** Eastern, 12 oz., gold, red, white
and blue, large eagle near top 12.00   16.00

☐ **Anoka Humane,** Walter, 12 oz., be kind to animals
message 1.00   1.35

Top, Left to Right: **ABC Premium**, *12 oz.,* **$1.75–$2.50**; *Alpen Brau, 12 oz.,* **$1.75–$2.50.**
Bottom, Left to Right: **Alta**, *12 oz.,* **$.40–$.60**; *Amana Beer,* **$5–$7.**

Price Range

☐ **Arrow,** Globe, 12 oz., red and white, elongated globe of the world with brand name diagonally across it 3.00   4.00

☐ **Arrow 77,** Globe, 12 oz., red, white, black and silver 12.50   16.50

☐ **Arrowhead,** Cold Spring, 12 oz., blue and white, sawtooth banding at bottom 90   1.40

☐ **Aspen Gold,** Blitz-Weinhard, 12 oz., blue and white, illustration of snow-capped mountain 2.75   3.75

☐ **Aspen Gold,** Tivoli, 12 oz., blue and white, illustration of snow-capped mountain 11.00   15.00
Note: At first glance this can might be mistaken for a Schaefer. It uses a multiple-balloon design similar to Schaefer's.

☐ **Atlas Prager Bohemian,** Associated Breweries, 12 oz., white and red, illustration of musicians and man dancing 1.00   1.65

☐ **Augsburger,** Peter Hand Brewing, 12 oz., cream-yellow and gold, brand name in gold-outlined white lettering, logo in center is like a coat-of-arms . . .   10.00   14.00

☐ **Augustiner,** Wagner, 12 oz., white and gold, large lettering (first version of design) 2.50   3.50

☐ **Augustiner,** Wagner, 12 oz., white and gold, small lettering, artwork (military decoration) in reduced size 1.75   2.50

☐ **Ballantine,** Ballantine, 16 oz., gold, white and red   6.00   8.00

☐ **Ballantine,** Falstaff, 12 oz., red, white and blue (issued for 1976 bicentennial), Liberty Bell against American flag 1.00   1.75

☐ **Ballantine,** Falstaff, 12 oz., gold and white with three-ring sign 40   .65

☐ **Ballantine Ale,** Ballantine, 12 oz., gold, red and white, three-ring sign above "XXX," brand name in red; large-size oval medallion (late version), in which the background is no longer tinged with yellow but has become pure white 85   1.35

☐ **Ballantine Ale,** Falstaff, 16 oz. 1.25   2.00

☐ **Ballantine Bock,** Ballantine, 12 oz., gold with ram's head in red circle 2.00   2.50

☐ **Ballantine Draft Brewed,** Falstaff, 12 oz., white with "Draft" in large red letters, "Genuine" in red letters at top, three-ring sign in gold 40   .65

☐ **Ballantine King Size Ale,** Ballantine, 16 oz., gold, cream white and red, "King Size" in white 8.00   12.00

Price Range

☐ **Ballantine Premium Lager,** Ballantine, 12 oz., gold, white and red, shield-shaped medallion with large red three-ring sign .... .85   1.35

☐ **Ballantine Premium Lager,** Ballantine, 16 oz., gold, white and red 4.00   5.00

☐ **Ballantine Premium Lager,** Flastaff, 16 oz., gold, white and red, brand name in red 1.00   1.75

☐ **Bartels,** Lion Brewing, 12 oz., gold and light-brown, brand name in amber on diagonal light brown banner across center of can 2.50   3.50

☐ **Bartels Pure,** Lion, 12 oz., gold and black, brand name in orange 1.00   1.75

☐ **Bavarian,** Duquesne, 12 oz., blue and white, illustration of landscape with Christmas trees and snow 1.25   2.00

☐ **Bavarian Club,** Huber, 12 oz., white and black with pictorial medallion of man in Alpine costume ... .50   .75

☐ **Bavarian Lager,** Van Lauter, 12 oz., dark blue and light blue with brand name in red .... .90   1.40

☐ **Bavarian Pilsener,** Weiss, 16 oz. 20.00   25.00

☐ **Bavarian Type Premium,** Mount Carbon, 12 oz., white and black with brand name in red .... .40   .65

☐ **Bavarian's Select,** Associated Brewing, 12 oz., light yellow and dark yellow with pennants in navy blue, robin's-egg blue and green 8.00   12.00

☐ **Bavarian's Select,** Bavarian's, 12 oz., light yellow and dark yellow with pennants in red, green and blue 8.00   12.00

☐ **Bean & Bacon Days,** Walter, 12 oz., horseshoe motif 1.00   1.65

☐ **Bergheim,** Bergheim, 12 oz., white and straw with pictorial landscape, lettering in red .... .90   1.35

☐ **Berghoff Draft,** Walter, 12 oz., brown with woodgrain look to resemble keg, lettering in white, date "1887" in yellow 8.00   12.00

☐ **Berghoff 1887 Pale Extra Dry,** Walter, 16 oz. 8.00   10.00

☐ **Big Apple Beer,** Waukee Brewing, 12 oz., brand name in white on blue background, "Premium" in white on red diagonal banner, "Beer" in red lettering in lower center of can 60.00   75.00

☐ **Big Cat Malt Liquor,** Pabst, 12 oz., white, red and gold, jumping leopard on vertically stripe background .... .45   .65

☐ **Big Cat Malt Liquor,** Pabst, 16 oz., white, red and gold, reads "Half Quart" at top 9.00   12.00

Price Range

☐ **Big Cat Stout Malt Liquor,** Pabst, 12 oz., white, red and gold, jumping leopard on vertically stripe background 4.50   6.25

☐ **Big Sky,** Great Falls, 12 oz., white and blue, illustration of glass of beer 30.00   40.00

☐ **Billy Beer,** Cold Spring, 12 oz. 1.00   1.50

☐ **Billy Beer,** Falls City, 12 oz. 90   1.20

☐ **Bilow Garden State,** Garden State, 12 oz., white, black and red, diagonal banding 10.00   14.00

☐ **Blatz,** Heileman, 12 oz., white and dark brown . .   .40   .60

☐ **Blatz Draft,** Heileman, 12 oz., white and dark brown 75   1.00

☐ **Black Dallas Malt Liquor,** Walter, 12 oz., blue and black, evening skyline 24.00   31.00

☐ **Black Horse Ale,** Black Horse, 12 oz., white, red and black, profile protrait of black horse 90   1.20

☐ **Black Label,** Carling, 12 oz., silver, red and black   1.85   2.30

☐ **Black Label,** Carling, 12 oz., red and black, brand name within tilted medallion, "Carling" in red within medallion, coat-of-arms in gold, no thin white band near bottom 80   1.15

☐ **Black Label,** Carling, 12 oz., red and black, brand name within tilted medallion, "Carling" does not appear in medallion, lettering in script but without excessive flourishes, map of U.S. on side opposite to brand name 1.85   2.60

☐ **Black Label,** Carling, 12 oz., red and black, brand name within tilted medallion, "Carling" does not appear in medallion, lettering in script but without excessive flourishes, map of the world on side opposite to brand name 1.85   2.60

☐ **Black Label,** Carling, 12 oz., red and black, brand name within tilted medallion, "Carling" does not appear in medallion, lettering in script but without excessive flourishes, no map 1.25   2.25

☐ **Black Label,** Carling, 12 oz., red and black, brand name within tilted medallion, "Carling" in red within medallion, coat-of-arms in white 50   .70

☐ **Black Label,** Carling, 16 oz., red, black and gold, gold at top bottom 14.00   19.00

☐ **Black Label,** Carling, 16 oz., black, red and white, thick white band at top with wording "King Size, Half Quart" in red 2.25   3.00

☐ **Black Label,** Carling, 16 oz., black, red and white, pale gold coat of arms behind brand name, reads "Fluid 16 Ounces" in black type near bottom . . .   2.00   2.75

Top, Left to Right: **Astor**, 12 oz., **$2–$2.50**; **Ballantine**, 12 oz., **$1–$1.50**. Bottom, Left to Right: **Bergheim**, 12 oz., **$.90–$1.20**; **Berghoff 1887**, 12 oz., **$10–$13**.

Price Range

☐ **Black Label,** Carling, 16 oz., black, red and white, dark gold coat of arms behind brand name, reads "Fluid 16 Ounces" in white near top 1.50 2.25

☐ **Black Label,** Carling, 16 oz., silver black and white, very small brand name 11.00 15.00

☐ **Black Label Draft,** Carling, 16 oz., red, white and black 20.00 30.00

☐ **Black Label Export,** Carling, 16 oz., gold and black 10.00 14.00

☐ **Black Label Malt Liquor,** Carling, 12 oz., black and gold 8.00 12.00

☐ **Black Pride,** West Bend Lithia, 12 oz., gold, black and yellow, illustration of prancing lion 12.00 16.00

☐ **Blanchard's,** Waukee Brewing, 12 oz., white and red, brand name in white on red diagonal banner, illustration of beer stein in lower right 5.00 6.00

☐ **Blatz,** Heileman, 16 oz., light brown and dark brown 2.00 2.50

☐ **Blatz,** Pabst, 12 oz., dark brown and beige, brand name in pyramid, white trim within pyramid, phrase "Milwaukee's Finest Beer" in dark brown lettering against white background, message "No Opener Needed" 3.50 4.50

☐ **Blatz,** Pabst, 16 oz., light brown and dark brown, brand name in white, reads "16 Fl. Ozs." near bottom 8.00 11.25

☐ **Blatz,** Pabst, 16 oz., light brown and dark brown, brand name in white, does not read "16 Fl. Ozs." near bottom 4.00 5.50

☐ **Blatz Bock,** Pabst, 12 oz., dark brown and beige 8.00 12.00

☐ **Blitz Weinhard,** Blitz Weinhard, 12 oz., white, red and gold, brand name against small geometrical design in light gold .... .45 .65

☐ **Blitz Weinhard,** Blitz Weinhard, 12 oz., white, red and gold, brand name against medium-size geometrical design in light gold .... .90 1.20

☐ **Blitz Weinhard,** Blitz Weinhard, 12 oz., white, red and gold, brand name against large geometrical design in light gold 8.00 12.00

☐ **Blitz Weinhard,** Blitz Weinhard, 16 oz., white, red and pale gold, large brand name 4.50 6.00

☐ **Blitz Weinhard,** Slitz Weinhard, 16 oz., white, red and pale gold, small brand name .... .90 1.20

☐ **Blue Ribbon Bock,** Pabst, 12 oz., white, red and blue, ram's head in white, large slogan at bottom .40 .60

Top, Left to Right: **Big Cat Malt Liquor**, *12 oz., $.45–$.65;* **Billow Garden State**, *12 oz.,* **$10–$13.25.** *Bottom, Left to Right:* **Black Horse Ale**, *12 oz., $.90–$1.20;* **Blanchard's**, *12 oz., $.85–$1.15.*

Price Range

☐ **Blue Ribbon Bock,** Pabst, 12 oz., white, red and blue, ram's head in white, small slogan at bottom — 3.00 / 4.00

☐ **Bohack Draft,** Richards, 12 oz., dark brown, gold and red, illustration of foaming glass of beer, brand name in red letters .... — 20.00 / 25.00

☐ **Bohack Draft,** Richards, 12 oz., dark brown, gold and red, illustration of foaming glass of beer, brand name in white on red label .... — 4.00 / 6.00

☐ **Bohack Premium,** Richards, 12 oz., blue, gold and white, illustration of foaming glass of beer, brand name in white lettering .... — 25.00 / 35.00

☐ **Bohack Premium,** Richards, 12 oz., dark blue, gold and white, illustration of foaming glass of beer, brand name in against red label .... — 4.00 / 6.00

☐ **Bohemian Club,** Bohemian Club of Oregon, 12 oz., white, blue and gold, brand name in blue near top, multiple illustration of steins .... — .85 / 1.20

☐ **Bohemian Club,** Huber, 12 oz., black and red, brand name in white, red band at top .... — .45 / .65

☐ **Bohemian Pilsener Light,** Maier, 12 oz., white, blue and red .... — 4.50 / 6.50

☐ **Bohemian Tap,** Burger, 12 oz., dark brown with brand name in white pyramid .... — 5.75 / 7.50

☐ **Bold Malt Liquor,** Rainier, 12 oz., black, white, red and gold .... — 10.00 / 14.00

☐ **Bonanza,** Garden State, 12 oz., blue, brown and white, illustration of steins near bottom .... — 14.00 / 19.00

☐ **Bonanza,** Old Dutch, 12 oz., blue, brown and white, illustration of steins near bottom .... — 15.00 / 20.00

☐ **Bosch,** Bosch, 12 oz., dark gold and white, with "Premium Beer" in gold beneath brand name .. — 2.00 / 3.00

☐ **Bosch,** Houghton Brewing, 12 oz., dark gold and white, with "Premium Beer" in gold beneath brand name .... — .45 / .65

☐ **Brau Haus,** General, 12 oz., yellow, blue and white, coat of arms .... — 10.00 / 14.00

☐ **Brau Haus,** General, 12 oz., blue and silver, coat of arms .... — 2.00 / 3.00

☐ **Braumeister,** Heileman, 12 oz., white and brown, brand name in white on brown ribbon, no furls on ribbon .... — 1.50 / 2.25

☐ **Braumeister,** Peter Hand, 12 oz., white and brown, brand name in white on brown ribbon, no furls on ribbon .... — .40 / .60

Top, Left to Right: **Blitz Weinhard,** *16 oz.,* **$.90–$1.20;** **Blitz Weinhard,** *12 oz.,* **$8–$10.75.** *Bottom, Left to Right:* **Bohemian Club,** *12 oz.,* **$.85–$1.20; Bosch,** *12 oz.,* **$2–$3.**

Price Range

☐ **Breunig's,** Walter, 12 oz., maroon and white, crest with lion, slogan "Superior Quality" in white lettering .... .70   1.00

☐ **Breunig's,** Walter, 12 oz., blue, white and gold, brand name in blue .... .60   .85

☐ **Brew II,** Horlacher, 12 oz., cream white and blue, large "II" beneath brand name in block letters, slogan "Second to None" .... .45   .65

☐ **Brew 102,** Maier Brewing, black, yellow and white, "102" appears in white lettering on background of an illustration of a glass of beer, "New Pale Dry Brew" in black lettering on white background of "head" of beer 2.00   3.00

☐ **Brewer's Best,** Maier, 12 oz., white, red, black and gold, word "Premium" on black frame at center 15.00   20.00

☐ **Brewer's Best Premium Bavarian Type,** Maier, 16 oz. 20.00   25.00

☐ **Brewmaster,** Maier Brewing, 12 oz., brand name in white on oval shaped background surrounding an illustration of a bearded man carrying six steins of beer 15.00   20.00

☐ **Brewmaster,** Maier Brewing, 12 oz., red, white, and blue, brand name in white on diagonal red banner, illustration of two mountains in very top left of can 15.00   20.00

☐ **Brickseller,** Pittsburgh Brewing Co., 12 oz., Endangered Species Series (bald eagle, brown pelican, Florida panther, grizzly bear, leatherback sea turtle, sonoran pronghorn and Texas field wolf) 2.50   3.50

☐ **Brown Derby,** General Brewing, 12 oz., white, red and brown, brand name in white lettering (script), topped by small derby, with dimensional shadowing behind letters .... .40   .60

☐ **Brown Derby,** Huber, 12 oz., white, red and brown, brand name in white lettering (script), topped by small derby, no dimensional shadowing behind letters .... .90   1.20

☐ **Brown Derby,** Maier, 12 oz., brown and white, brand name in white lettering (script) on brown background topped by small derby 10.00   14.00

☐ **Brown Derby,** Maier, 12 oz., white, red and brown, brand name in white lettering (script), topped by small derby, no dimensional shadowing behind letters 2.00   2.75

*Top, Left to Right: **Bosch**, 12 oz., **$.45–$.65**; **Breunig's**, 12 oz., **$.70–$1**. Bottom, Left to Right: **Brown Derby**, 12 oz., **$1.50–$2.25**; **Brown Derby**, 16 oz., **$2.25–$3**.*

Price Range

☐ **Brown Derby,** Pearl, 12 oz., white, red and brown, brand name in white lettering (script), topped by small derby .... .40 .65

☐ **Brown Derby,** Pittsburgh, 12 oz., white, red and brown, large brand name in white lettering (script), topped by small derby .... .40 .65

☐ **Brown Derby,** Queen City, 12 oz., white, red and brown, brand name in white lettering (script), topped by small derby 1.00 1.75

☐ **Brown Derby,** Storz, 12 oz., white, red and brown, brand name in white lettering (script), topped by small derby 2.00 2.75

☐ **Brown Derby,** Storz, 12 oz., brown and white, brand name in white lettering (script), on brown background topped by small derby 10.00 14.00

☐ **Brown Derby,** Walter, 12 oz., white, red and brown, brand name in white lettering (script), topped by small derby, no dimensional shadowing behind letters 1.50 2.50

☐ **Brown Derby,** Grace brothers, 16 oz., brown, gold and white, brand name in gold lettering with brown outline on a white background, actual illustration of a brown derby (later cans have just an outline) 16.00 21.00

☐ **Brown Derby,** Maier Brewing, 16 oz., brown and white, brand name in white on brown label, small outline of derby in upper label 12.00 16.00

☐ **Brown Derby,** General Brewing, 16 oz., amber and white, same design as the Maier Brewing can 4.00 5.00

☐ **Brut,** Lone Star Brewing, 12 oz., gold, amber and red, brand name in white on red background, logo of torch in upper center of label 20.00 27.50

☐ **Buckeye,** Meister Brau, 12 oz., red, white, with brand name in red 20.00 30.00

☐ **Buckhorn,** Buckhorn, 12 oz., light cream white with illustration of antelope head in gold medallion, brand name in grayish silver .... .90 1.45

☐ **Buckhorn,** Buckhorn, 12 oz., red, black and white, stylized drawing of antelope head within white medallion 6.00 8.50

☐ **Buckhorn,** Hamm, 12 oz., medium cream white, black and silver, illustration of antelope head in silver medallion, brand name in silver 1.00 1.75

☐ **Buckhorn,** Hamm, 12 oz., yellowish cream white with illustration of antelope head in gold medallion, brand name in grayish silver .... .90 1.45

Price Range

☐ **Buckhorn,** Hamm, 16 oz., cream white	3.00	4.00
☐ **Buckhorn,** Lone Star, 12 oz., gold and white, illustration of antelope heads encircling lower portion of can	.85	1.40
☐ **Buckhorn,** Olympia, 12 oz., yellow with illustration of antelope head in gold medallion, brand name in silver lettering	.40	.65
☐ **Buckhorn,** Olympia, 12 oz., dark yellow with illustration of antelope head in dark brassy gold medallion, brand name in bluish silver ....:.	.40	.65
☐ **Budweiser,** Anheuser-Busch, 12 oz., white and red, current	.40	.65
☐ **Budweiser,** Anheuser-Busch, 12 oz., red and white, "Tab Top" lettered around base	2.25	3.25
☐ **Budweiser,** Anheuser-Busch, 16 oz., red and white	.90	1.45
☐ **Budweiser,** Anheuser-Busch, 16 oz., "Tab Top"	4.00	5.50
☐ **Budweiser Malt Liquor,** Anheuser-Busch, 12 oz., black, brand name in red	1.75	2.50
☐ **Budweiser Malt Liquor,** Anheuser-Busch, 16 oz.	10.00	14.00
☐ **Budweiser,** Anheuser Busch Brewing, 16 oz., commemorative cans for class reunions, usually incorporated is the university's mascot on the can, "Compliments of Budweiser" is lettered on the bottom on each can	17.50	22.50
☐ **Buffalo,** Blitz Weinhard, 12 oz., light brown with illustration of buffalo	1.00	1.50
☐ **Bulldog Malt Liquor,** Drewys, 12 oz., dark blue, light blue and gold	8.00	12.00
☐ **Bulldog Malt Liquor,** Maier, 16 oz.	12.00	16.00
☐ **Bulldog Stout Malt Liquor,** Grace, 16 oz.	20.00	30.00
☐ **Burgemeister Premium,** Warsau, 16 oz........	15.00	20.00
☐ **Burger,** Burger, 16 oz., brown medallion with brand name in white, "Brewed with Artesian Spring Water"	14.00	19.00
☐ **Burger,** Burger, 16 oz., brown medallion with brand name in white	15.00	20.00
☐ **Burger,** Burger, 12 oz., white, red, blue and gold, brand name white against red medallion	.80	1.25
☐ **Burger,** Burger, 16 oz., red medallion with brand name in white	30.00	40.00
☐ **Burger,** Hudepohl, 12 oz., white, red, blue and gold, brand name in white against red medallion	.70	1.00
☐ **Burger Ale,** Burger, 12 oz., white, green and gold, brand name in white lettering against green medallion	15.00	22.50

Price Range

☐ **Burgermeister,** Burgermeister, 16 oz., white, blue and gold, does not read "Burgie" 8.00   12.00

☐ **Burgermeister,** Peter Hand, 12 oz., white with name reading vertically on red ribbon at side of can 40   .65

☐ **Burgermeister Premium,** Warsaw, 12 oz., cream white, red and gold, light gold banding at top and bottom 2.00   3.00

☐ **Burgermeister,** Burgermeister, 12 oz., white, blue, gold and red, name "Burgie" in large red characters near top 3.00   4.00

☐ **Burgermeister Beer,** Hamm Brewers, 12 oz., white, blue, gold and red, brand name in white on blue background, "Burgie!" in red lettering in upper center 4.00   6.00

☐ **Burgermeister Draft Beer,** Hamm Brewers, 12 oz., white, blue and silver, brand name in white on blue background, "Draft Beer" in blue in upper center 2.50   3.50

☐ **Burgermeister,** Pabst, 12 oz., white, blue, gold and red, name "Burgie" in large red characters near top 40   .65

☐ **Burgermeister,** Schlitz, 12 oz., white, blue and gold, brand name in white against dark blue medallion placed high on can, symbol of brew-master in circle attached to ribbon 8.00   12.00

☐ **Burgermeister Draft,** Schlitz, 12 oz., white, blue and gold, no symbol of brew-master 4.50   6.25

☐ **Burgermeister Draft,** Hamm, 12 oz., white, gold and blue, wording "Draft Beer" in blue characters against white background 85   1.35

☐ **Burgermeister Draft,** Schlitz, 12 oz., white, gold and blue, wording "Draft Beer" in white character against muddy gold background 8.00   12.00

☐ **Burgie,** Pabst, 12 oz., dark yellow, brand name in beige 90   1.35

☐ **Burgie,** 16 oz., pale brown and gold 6.50   8.50

☐ **Busch Bavarian,** Anheuser-Busch, 10 oz., white and blue, Alpine mountains 80   1.15

☐ **Busch Bavarian,** Anheuser-Busch, 12 oz., white and blue, snow-covered mountains, no clouds in background 1.75   2.50

☐ **Busch Bavarian,** Anheuser-Busch, 12 oz., white and blue, snow-covered mountains, no clouds in background, "Tab Top" in white lettering on red band near top of can 8.00   12.00

Price Range

☐ **Busch Bavarian,** Anheuser-Busch, 12 oz., white and blue, snow-covered mountains, no clouds in background, "Tab Top" in white lettering against dark blue band at bottom of can 1.25   2.00

☐ **Busch Bavarian,** Anheuser-Busch, 12 oz., white and blue, snow-covered mountains, no clouds in background, does not read "Tab Top," brand name encircled by thin red frame .... .40   .65

☐ **Busch Bavarian,** Anheuser-Busch, 16 oz., does not read "Half Quart" near top 13.00   17.00

☐ **Busch Bavarian,** Anheuser-Busch, 16 oz., reads "half Quart" near top, "Tab Top" at bottom 5.00   6.50

☐ **Busch Bavarian,** Anheuser-Busch, 16 oz., reads "Half Quart" near top, brand name circled in red, solid blue band at bottom 2.00   2.75

☐ **Calgary Malt Liquor,** Carling Brewing, 12 oz., white, black and red, brand name in white on black background, "Malt Liquor" in black lettering on red banner diagonally across lower center of can, "Export" in white script directly underneath brand name 90.00   120.00

☐ **Calgary Malt Liquor,** Carling Brewing, 16 oz., white, black and red, same design as the 12 oz. 170.00   210.00

☐ **Canadian Ace Premium,** Canadian Ace, 12 oz., gold, silver and white .... .50   2.50

☐ **Canadian Ace Premium,** Canadian Ace, 16 oz., gold, silver and white, same design as the 12 oz. 8.00   12.00

☐ **Cans of the Month Club—Labrador Retriever,** Pickett, 12 oz. 1.25   2.00

☐ **Carling Black Label,** Carling, 16 oz., silver, black and white, very small brand name 12.00   16.00

☐ **Carling Black Label,** Carling, 16 oz., red, black and gold, gold at top and bottom 13.00   17.00

☐ **Carling Black Label,** Carling, 16 oz., black, red and white pale gold coat of arms behind name, reads "Fluid 16 Ounces" in black type near bottom 2.00   2.75

☐ **Carling Black Label,** Carling, 16 oz., black, red and white, dark gold of arms behind brand name, reads "Fluid 16 Ounces" in white near top 1.50   2.25

☐ **Carling Black Label,** Carling, 16 oz., red and white, dark gold coat of arms behind brand name, narrow gold band at top .... .80   1.10

☐ **Carling Black Label Draft,** Carling, 16 oz., orange, white and black 15.00   20.00

*Top, Left to Right: **Bub's**, 12 oz., **$.45–$.65; Budweiser "Tab Top"** (note use of "Tab Top" wording across the bottom. This was used shortly after flat tops were phased out), 12 oz., **$1.50–$2.50**. Bottom, Left to Right: **Burgie** (can shows San Francisco bay), 12 oz., **$1.75–$2.50; Burgermeister**, 12 oz., **$3–$4**.*

Price Range

☐ **Carling Black Label Draft,** Carling, 16 oz., red, white and black **20.00**   **27.50**

☐ **Carling Black Label Export,** Carling, 16 oz., gold and black **10.00**   **14.00**

☐ **Carling Malt Liquor,** Carling, 12 oz., black, white and red, large ornamental initial C, wording "Malt Liquor" in black against red band, brand name in thin white lettering **27.50**   **35.00**

☐ **Carling Red Cap Ale,** Carling, 12 oz., green, very light brown (yellowish brown), and red. "Red Cap" in red letters, portrait of man wearing red cap at lower center, canned at Natick, Massachusetts   **1.25**   **2.00**

☐ **Carling Red Cap Ale,** Carling, 12 oz., black, light beige and white, "Red Cap" in large black letters topped by illustration of a red cap (no portrait of man), "Ale" in very thin red script lettering **6.50**   **8.50**

☐ **Carling Red Cap Ale,** Carling, 12 oz., green, very light brown (yellowish brown) and red, "Red Cap" in red letters, portrait of man wearing red cap at lower center, canned at Baltimore, Maryland ... **1.50**   **2.25**

☐ **Carling's Black Label,** Carling, 12 oz., red and black, brand name within tilted medallion, "Carling" in red within medallion, coat-of-arms in gold, no thin white band near bottom .... **.75**   **1.25**

☐ **Carling's Black Label,** Carling, 12 oz., red and black, brand name within tilted medallion, "Carling" in red within medallion, coat-of-arms in gold   **1.50**   **2.50**

☐ **Carling's Black Label,** Carling, 12 oz., red and black, brand name within tilted medallion, "Carling" does not appear in medallion, lettering in script but without excessive flourishes, map of the world on side opposite to brand name **1.50**   **2.50**

☐ **Carling's Black Label,** Carling, 12 oz., red and black, brand name within tilted medallion, "Carling" does not appear in medallion, lettering in script but without excessive flourishes, map of U.S. on side opposite to brand name **1.50**   **2.50**

☐ **Carling's Black Label,** Carling, 12 oz., red and black, brand name within tilted medallion, "Carling"in red within medallion, coat-of-arms in gold, gold band at top .... **.50**   **.90**

☐ **Carling's Tuborg,** Carling, 12 oz., dark gold and dark red .... **.40**   **.60**

☐ **Cascade,** Blitz Weinhard, 12 oz., blue and white, brand name in white on blue background **1.50**   **2.50**

Top, Left to Right: **Busch Bavarian**, 16 oz., **$2–$2.50**; **Cans of the Month Club-Labrador Retriever**, 12 oz., **$1.50–$1.90**. Bottom, Left to Right: **Carling Black Label**, 16 oz., **$2.25–$3**; **Carling Red Cap Ale**, 12 oz., **$6.50–$8.50**.

Price Range

☐ **Cascade,** Blitz Weinhard, 16 oz., does not state "King Size" 1.50   2.50

☐ **Cascade,** Blitz Weinhard, 16 oz., states "King Size" near top 10.50   15.50

☐ **Cee Bee,** Colonial Brewing, 12 oz., red, white and black, "beer" in white on red background, "Pilsner" in black script on white background 12.00   16.00

☐ **Champale Malt Liquor,** Champale, 12 oz., green and white, canned at Norfolk, Virginia 7.00   10.00

☐ **Champale Malt Liquor,** Champale, 12 oz., large illustration of beer in champagne glass against green background .... .40   .65

☐ **Champale Malt Liquor,** Champale, 12 oz., large illustration of beer in champagne glass against green background, canned at Norfolk, Virginia .. 1.00   1.75

☐ **Champale Malt Liquor,** Champale, 12 oz., green and white, canned at Trenton, New Jersey 5.50   7.50

☐ **Champagne Velvet,** Associated, 12 oz., pale blue and gold, brand name in blue lettering with red initial letters, can design forms champagne glass .90   1.20

☐ **Champagne Velvet,** Heilman, 12 oz., pale blue and gold, brand name in blue lettering with red initial letters, can design forms champagne glass .45   .65

☐ **Champagne Velvet,** Pickett Brewing, 12 oz., same design as can by Heilman Brewing ...... .45   .65

☐ **Champagne Velvet Malt Liquor,** Associated, 12 oz., gold and white, brand name in white lettering 4.00   5.50

☐ **Champagne Velvet King Size,** Associated, 16 oz., blue and gold 12.00   16.00

☐ **Champale,** Champale Brewing, 12 oz., green, white, red and gold, brand name in white on green background, "Sparkling" in red in upper center 7.00   11.00

☐ **Charge,** Little Switzerland, 12 oz., light grayish blue, illustration of horse and rider, wording "The Bold American" in red 3.25   4.25

☐ **Chief Oskhosh,** Oshkosh, 12 oz., green, blue and red, brand name in white against red badge 6.50   8.50

☐ **Chief Oshkosh,** People's Brewing Co., 12 oz., green, blue and red, brand name in white against red badge 6.50   8.50

☐ **Chilympiad,** Spoetzl, 12 oz., "10th Anniversary Republic of Texas State Chili Cook-Off" 2.00   2.50

☐ **Chippewa Pride,** Leinenkugel, 12 oz., yellow, beige and maroon, non-pictorial design 85

☐ **Cloud Nine Malt Lager,** DuBois, 12 oz., green and white, brand name in white 30.00   40.00

Top, Left to Right: **Carling's Red Cap Ale,** *12 oz.,* **$1.85–$2.35; Carling's Black Label,** *12 oz.,* **$ .50–$ .70.** *Bottom, Left to Right:* **Cascade,** *12 oz.,* **$1.85–$2.50; Cascade,** *16 oz.,* **$2–$2.50.**

Price Range

☐ **Cloud Nine Malt Liquor,** DuBois, 12 oz., green and white, brand name in white	**1.75**	**2.50**
☐ **Club Special,** Maier, 12 oz., white and blue, wording "Premium Beer" in orange	**55.00**	**70.00**
☐ **Coburger,** Old Dutch Brewing, 12 oz., white, blue and gold, brand name in blue on gold background, "Extra Dry" in blue script, "Beer" in blue-framed gold letters	**8.00**	**12.00**
☐ **Cold Brau,** Cold Spring, 12 oz., blue and white	**.90**	**1.20**
☐ **Cold Spring,** Cold Spring, 12 oz., gold and blue (dark gold), with wording "Spring Top"	**6.50**	**8.50**
☐ **Cold Spring,** Cold Spring, 12 oz., white, blue and silver, word "beer" in blue lettering, not circle ..	**.85**	**1.10**
☐ **Cold Spring,** Cold Spring, 16 oz.	**8.00**	**11.00**
☐ **Colorado Gold Label,** Walter, 12 oz., blue, white and red, illustration of lake and mountain peaks, clouds in background	**5.50**	**7.25**
☐ **Colorado Gold Label,** Walter, 16 oz.	**7.00**	**10.00**
☐ **Colt,** National, 12 oz., white, blue and gold, brand name in white letters on blue banner running at 45 degree angle upwards	**11.00**	**15.00**
☐ **Colt 45 Malt Lager,** Carling National, 12 oz., blue, white and gold, brand name in blue, illustration of horseshoe with horse leaping fence	**6.25**	**7.75**
☐ **Colt 45 Malt Liquor,** National, 8 oz., white with black lettering	**1.00**	**1.65**
☐ **Colt 45 Malt Liquor,** National, 8 oz., squat, white with black lettering	**.90**	**1.40**
☐ **Colt 45 Malt Liquor,** Carling National, 12 oz., blue, white and gold, illustration of horseshoe with horse leaping fence	**.40**	**.60**
☐ **Colt 45 Malt Liquor,** National, 12 oz., blue, white and gold, brand name in blue, illustration of horseshoe with horse leaping fence	**.40**	**.60**
☐ **Colt 45 Malt Liquor,** National, 16 oz.	**2.00**	**3.00**
☐ **Colt 45 Stout Malt Liquor,** National, 12 oz., blue, white and gold, brand name in blue, illustration of horseshoe with horse leaping fence	**2.00**	**3.00**
☐ **Colt Malt Lager,** National, 16 oz.	**20.00**	**25.00**
☐ **Columbia,** Carling, 12 oz., white, red and gold, illustration of Statute of Liberty, canned at Tacoma, Washington	**1.00**	**1.75**
☐ **Cook's,** Heileman, 12 oz., white and red, reads "Export Beer" at top	**3.00**	**4.00**
☐ **Cook's.** Sterling Brewing, 12 oz., white and red, same design as Heileman can	**3.00**	**4.00**

Price Range

☐ **Cook's,** Associated, 12 oz., white and red, same design as Heileman can 3.00   4.00

☐ **Cook's,** Heileman, 12 oz., white and red, reads "Premium Beer" at top 60   1.00

☐ **Coors,** Coors, 16 oz. 8.00   12.00

☐ **Coor's Light,** Coors, 12 oz., heraldic lions beside emblem 50   .80

☐ **Corona Extra,** General, 12 oz., light blue, dark blue and gold 3.00   4.25

☐ **Country Club,** Pearl, 12 oz., yellow and black, brand name in black lettering 85   1.35

☐ **Country Club Malt Liquor,** Pearl, 8 oz., squat, white with red and blue lettering, "malt liquor" in small letters 10.00   14.00

☐ **Country Club Malt Liquor,** Pearl, 8 oz., squat, white with red and blue lettering, "malt liquor" in large letters 1.60   2.30

☐ **Country Club Malt Liquor,** Pearl, 12 oz., light blue and brown, brand name in brown lettering 40   .65

☐ **Country Club Malt Liquor,** Pearl, 16 oz., gold bands at top and bottom 3.00   4.00

☐ **Country Club Malt Liquor,** Pearl, 12 oz., light blue, red and gold, brand name in red 85   1.35

☐ **Country Club Premium Light,** Pearl, 8 oz., light beige 3.50   5.00

☐ **Country Club Stout Malt Liquor,** Pearl, 8 oz., squat, white with red and blue lettering 4.50   5.50

☐ **Country Club Stout Malt Liquor,** Pearl, 12 oz., light blue, red and gold, brand name in red 8.00   12.00

☐ **Country Club Stout Malt Liquor,** Pearl, 16 oz. 3.50   4.50

☐ **Country Tavern,** Pearl, 12 oz., white, brown and black, brand name in brown, set against white background with woodgrained effect 80   1.15

☐ **Country Tavern,** Pearl, 12 oz., brown and white .80   1.10

☐ **Crystal Colorado,** Walter, 12 oz., white, blue and gold, illustration of Rocky Mountains, brand name in large white lettering 2.75   3.75

☐ **Crystal Colorado,** Walter, 16 oz. 12.50   16.50

☐ **Dart Drug,** Eastern, 12 oz., bright tomato red, white and silver, brand name in white lettering on silver 15.00   20.00

☐ **Davidson Premium Beer,** Colonial Brewing, 12 oz., brand name in white on red background . . . 25.00   32.50

☐ **Dawson's Diamond Ale,** Dawson's, 12 oz., blue and silver in alternating horizontal bands running entire height of can 20.00   25.00

Price Range

☐ **Dawson's Lager,** Dawson's, 12 oz., gold and white in alternating diagonal bands, canned at New Bedford, Massachusetts 8.00   12.00

☐ **Dawson's Lager,** Dawson's, 12 oz., gold and white in alternating diagonal bands, canned at Willimansett, Massachusetts 2.00   3.00

☐ **Dawson's Lager,** Dawson's, 12 oz., gold and white in alternating diagonal bands, canned at Hammonton, New Jersey .... .75   1.25

☐ **Dawson's Sparkling Ale,** Dawson's, 12 oz., blue and silver in alternating diagonal bands 4.50   5.50

☐ **Denver,** Tivoli, 12 oz., blue and white, Denver skyline 20.00   25.00

☐ **Dis-Go Beer,** Eastern, 12 oz., light pink, illustration of man wearing green shirt playing guitar 15.00   20.00

☐ **Dis-Go Near Beer,** Eastern, 12 oz., dark pink, illustration of girl in green dress dancing 15.00   20.00

☐ **Dixie,** Dixie, 12 oz., white and green, no silver bands .... .40   .75

☐ **Dixie,** Dixie, 12 oz., white, green and silver, silver band at top and bottom...................... 1.75   2.50

☐ **Dixie Light,** Dixie Brewing, 12 oz., white, gold and green, "Dixie" in white lettering with gold bordering, "Light" in green on white background ..... .75   1.25

☐ **Dorf,** Schoen Edelweis, 12 oz., brown, white and red, wood-grain appearance with illustration of stein 10.00   14.00

☐ **Drewry's,** Associated, 12 oz., red and white .... .85   1.15

☐ **Drewry's,** Drewry, 12 oz., red and white, small silver pyramid at base of can 1.00   1.50

☐ **Drewry's,** Heileman, 12 oz., red and white, dark gold frame surrounding brand name 1.00   1.50

☐ **Drewry's,** Heileman, 12 oz., red and white, light gold band surrounding brand name .... .50   .75

☐ **Drewry's Draft,** Drewry, 12 oz., brown, yellow and black, illustration of end of beer keg with spigot 7.00   10.00

☐ **Drewry's Draft,** Heileman, 12 oz., blue, white and silver, word "Draft" in large red letters .... .90   1.25

☐ **Drewry's Draft,** Associated, 16 oz. 4.00   5.50

☐ **Drewry's Edelweiss Light,** Drewry, 16 oz. 5.50   7.50

☐ **Drewry's Half Quart,** Drewry, 16 oz., gold crown near top, "Half Quart" in red 5.50   7.50

☐ **Drummond Bros.,** Drummond Brothers, 12 oz., blue, white and gold .... .70   .95

☐ **Drummond Bros.,** Falls City, 12 oz., blue, white and gold .... .50   .70

Top, Left to Right: **Champagne Velvet Malt Liquor,** *12 oz.,* **$2.50–$3.50;** **Cloud Nine Malt Liquor,** *12 oz.,* **$3.50–$5.** *Bottom, Left to Right:* **Colt 45 Malt Liquor,** *16 oz.,* **$2–$2.75;** **Cook's,** *12 oz.,* **$ .60–$ .80.**

Price Range

☐ **DuBois,** DuBois, 12 oz., red, white and black, brand name in tall black letters near top of can   15.00   20.00

☐ **DuBois Premium,** DuBois, 12 oz., white gold, brand name in circular medallion 8.00   12.00

☐ **Dubuque Star,** Pickett, 12 oz., red and white 55   .70

☐ **Duke,** Ducquesne, 12 oz., gold and white, emblem above brand name 11.00   15.00

☐ **Duke,** Duquesne, 12 oz., gold and white, male figure above brand name with upraised glass 5.00   6.50

☐ **Duke,** Duquesne, 12 oz., white and red, illustration of man hoisting beer in right hand 75   1.00

☐ **Duquesne Pilsener,** Duquesne, 12 oz., white, dark blue and red, man holding beer, portrait of man is small version 30.00   40.00

☐ **Dutch Treat,** Dutch Treat, 12 oz., white, blue and silver 1.00   1.75

☐ **Eastside,** Pabst, 12 oz., red and white, "12 Fl. Oz." in gold 2.00   3.00

☐ **Eastside,** Pabst, 16 oz., "Half Quart" in red lettering near bottom 8.00   12.00

☐ **Edelbrau,** General, 12 oz., white, blue and red, brand name in German gothic lettering, illustration of stein 10.00   14.00

☐ **Edelweiss,** Associated, 12 oz., white, blue and other colors, drawings of steins encircling can, brown band at bottom 1.75   2.50

☐ **Edelweiss,** Pickett, 12 oz., white, blue and other colors, drawings of steins encircling can, brown band at bottom 40   .65

☐ **Edelweiss Light,** Associated, 16 oz. 4.50   5.50

☐ **Einbock Bock,** Maier, 12 oz., light beige and green, imprinted "6 for $1.09." 35.00   45.00

☐ **Einbock Bock,** Maier, 12 oz., light beige and green, without "6 for $1.09." 7.00   11.00

☐ **Einbock Bock,** Walter, 12 oz., light beige and green 3.50   5.50

☐ **El Rancho,** Falstaff, 12 oz., red and white, unillustrated 2.50   3.25

☐ **El Rancho,** Maier, 12 oz., yellow, red and green, illustration of cactus plant in desert 20.00   25.00

☐ **Encore,** Schlitz Brewing, 12 oz., white and gold, brand name in black-bordered gold letters on white background, gold fleur-de-lis logo on white circular background in upper center of can, "1849" in black lettering above logo 17.50   22.50

*Top, Left to Right: **Coors**, 16 oz., **$7–$10**; **Country Club Malt Liquor**, 8 oz., **$1.80–$2.25**. Bottom, Left to Right: **Country Club Malt Liquor**, 12 oz., **$ .40–$ .60**; **Drewry's Draft**, 16 oz., **$4–$5.50**.*

Price Range

☐ **Encore,** Schlitz Brewing, 12 oz., white and gold, very similar to above can except brand name lettering doesn't have black bordering 5.00   7.00

☐ **Esquire,** Jones, 12 oz., white, brown and gold, designed to resemble beer keg 75   1.25

☐ **Esslinger,** Ruppert, 12 oz., white and red, illustration of man in 18th-century costume at center of can, brand name in blue 1.00   1.75

☐ **Fabacher Brau,** Jackson, 10 oz., silver with "gothic" lettering 7.00   11.00

☐ **Falls City,** Falls City, 12 oz., red, white and gold, brand name in white script lettering, does not say "Beer" 3.00   4.00

☐ **Falls City,** Falls City, 12 oz., red, white and gold, brand name in white script lettering, "Beer" beneath brand name 3.25   4.50

☐ **Falls City,** Falls City, 12 oz., red, white and gold, shield above brand name, can decorated with vertical striping, "Premium Beer" in white script lettering 70   1.00

☐ **Falls City,** Falls City, 16 oz., red and white 9.50   13.50

☐ **Falstaff,** Falstaff, 12 oz., white, yellow and gold, blue band at bottom of can 3.00   4.00

☐ **Falstaff,** Falstaff, 12 oz., "New Aluminum Can" in blue lettering 8.50   12.00

☐ **Falstaff,** Falstaff, 12 oz., white, yellow and brown, small shield on upper one half of can, large brand name in brown at center, shield is half brown and half yellow 1.00   1.50

☐ **Falstaff,** Falstaff, 12 oz., white, yellow and brown, small shield on upper one half of can, large brand name in brown at center, shield in half black and half yellow 60   .80

☐ **Falstaff,** Falstaff, 12 oz., red, white and blue, American flag and Liberty Bell 70   1.00

☐ **Falstaff,** Falstaff, 16 oz., blue band above "One Pint" 5.00   6.50

☐ **Falstaff,** Falstaff, 16 oz., gold band at bottom with "One Pint" in white lettering 2.00   2.50

☐ **Falstaff,** Falstaff, 16 oz., gold band at bottom with "Half Quart" 3.00   4.00

☐ **Falstaff,** General, 12 oz., white, yellow and brown, small shield on upper one half of can, large brand name in brown at center, shield is half black and half yellow 60   .80

Top, Left to Right: **DuBois**, 12 oz., **$15–$20**; **DuBois Premium**, 12 oz., **$8.–$11**. Bottom, Left to Right: **Eastside**, 16 oz., **$2–$2.75**; **Edelweiss**, 12 oz., **$2.50–$3.75**.

Price Range

☐ **Falstaff Draft,** Falstaff, 12 oz., white, blue, yellow and gold	23.00	31.00
☐ **Falstaff Draft,** Falstaff, 16 oz.	18.00	23.00
☐ **Famous Black Dallas Malt Liquor,** Walter, 12 oz., blue and black, evening skyline	22.50	32.50
☐ **F And S,** Fuhrmann and Schmidt, 12 oz., red and white	3.50	4.25
☐ **Fauerbach,** Fauerbach, 12 oz., dark and light blue	75.00	100.00
☐ **Fehr's X/L (Extra Light),** Fehr, 12 oz., white, red and gold	12.00	16.00
☐ **Finast,** Eastern, 12 oz., white, red and yellow, "Beer" in black lettering against yellow background	1.75	2.30
☐ **Fischer's,** Fischer, red, white and gold, "Old German Style" in white lettering, 12 oz.	2.00	2.65
☐ **Fischer's,** Fischer, 12 oz., red, white and gold, "Old German Style" in white lettering, canned at Auburndale, Florida	.70	1.10
☐ **Fisher,** General, 12 oz., red, white and blue, "6 for 99¢"	3.00	4.00
☐ **Fisher,** General, 16 oz., gold band at top and bottom, no indication of price	4.00	5.25
☐ **Fisher,** General, 16 oz., gold band at top and bottom, "6 for $1.29," c. 1970	8.00	12.00
☐ **Fisher,** General, 16 oz., red, white and blue, "6 for $1.29," c. 1970	5.50	6.50
☐ **Fisher,** General, 16 oz., red, white and blue, "6 for $1.54," c. 1974	4.50	5.50
☐ **Fisher Lager,** General, 12 oz., "6 for $1.09" . . .	2.00	3.00
☐ **Fisher Light,** General, 12 oz., red, white and blue, "6 for $1.29"	.90	1.45
☐ **Fisher Light,** General, 12 oz., red, white and blue, no price stated on can	.40	.65
☐ **Fisher Light,** General, 12 oz., white and gold . .	2.00	2.50
☐ **Fisher Light,** Lucky, 12 oz., white and gold	2.00	3.00
☐ **Fisher Premium Light,** Lucky, 12 oz., reads "6 for 99¢"	8.00	12.00
☐ **Fischer's Ale,** Fischer, 12 oz., white, green and yellow, "Old German Style" in white lettering against green background, canned at Auburndale, Florida	.90	1.45
☐ **Fischer's Ale,** Fischer, 12 oz., white, green and yellow, "Old German Style" in white lettering against green background	2.00	2.50

Top, Left to Right: **Falls City,** *12 oz.,* **$3.25–$4.50;** **Falls City,** *16 oz.,* **$9.75–$13.**
Bottom, Left to Right: **Falstaff,** *12 oz.,* **$3–$4;** **Falstaff,** *16 oz.,* **$3–$4.**

Price Range

☐ **Fitger's,** Fitger, 12 oz., white and gold 6.00 8.00
☐ **Fitger's,** Fitger, 12 oz., white and gold, red band
at bottom 6.00 8.00
☐ **Foodtown,** Old Dutch, 12 oz., red and gold 25.00 35.00
☐ **Fort Pitt,** Fort Pitt, 12 oz., red, white and pale
gold 15.00 20.00
☐ **Forty-Niner (49'er) Premium,** Atlas Brewing, 12
oz., white, red and blue, brand name in large red
lettering at top center of can, illustration of Indian
totem pole underneath 90.00 125.00
☐ **Fox DeLuxe,** Cold Spring, 12 oz., pale blue, red
and gold 85 1.10
☐ **Fox DeLuxe,** Heileman, 12 oz., pale blue, red and
gold 2.00 2.65
☐ **Fox Head Bock,** Heileman, 12 oz., white, light
brown and dark brown, canned at Newport, Ken-
tucky 8.00 12.00
☐ **Fox Head 400,** Heileman, 12 oz., white, red and
brown, brand name against red background 3.50 4.75
☐ **Fox Head 400 Draft,** Heileman, 12 oz., red,
white and blue, brand name against blue back-
ground 85 1.10
☐ **Fox Head Malt Liquor,** Heileman, 12 oz.,
white 10.00 14.00
☐ **Frankenmuth Bavarian Dark,** Geyer, 12 oz.,
black and yellow, Prussian shield 15.00 20.00
☐ **Frankenmuth Bavarian Light,** Geyer, 12 oz.,
black and white, Prussian shield 3.00 5.00
☐ **Frankenmuth Bock,** Frankenmuth, 12 oz., light
brown and dark brown 20.00 25.00
☐ **French 76 Malt Liquor,** National, 8 oz., squat,
white with script lettering, Eiffel tower 32.50 40.00
☐ **Friendship Lounge, Winger,** Schell, 12 oz., illus-
tration of snow scene (from a set) 80 1.35
☐ **Fyfe and Drum,** Genesee, 12 oz., silver and
brown 1.00 1.75
☐ **Gablinger's,** Forrest, 12 oz., gold, white and grey,
large portrait of Gablinger 10.00 14.00
☐ **Gablinger's,** Forrest, 12 oz., gold, white and grey,
large portrait of Gablinger, canned at Orange, New
Jersey 8.00 12.00
☐ **Gablinger's,** Forrest, 12 oz., dark gold and white,
small portrait of Gablinger, "Doesn't Fill You Up"
directly beneath portrait 4.00 5.25

Price Range

☐ **Gablinger's,** Forrest, 12 oz., dark gold and white, small portrait of Gablinger, does not read "Doesn't Fill You Up" directly beneath portrait, has small letters around top of can 1.00   1.75

☐ **Gablinger's,** Forrest, 12 oz., dark gold and white, small portrait of Gablinger, does not read "Doesn't Fill You Up" directly beneath portrait, no lettering around top of can .... .85   1.10

☐ **Gablinger's,** Forrest, 16 oz. 8.00   12.00

☐ **Gablinger's Extra Light,** Forrest, 12 oz., red and white .... .40   .60

☐ **Gackle,** Schell, 12 oz., illustration of duck in flight, words "North Dakota's Duck Hunting Capital" .. 2.00   3.00

☐ **Gambrinus,** Pittsburgh, 12 oz., white, red and gold .... .90   1.45

☐ **Gambrinus,** Wagner, 12 oz., white, red and gold .... .90   1.45

☐ **Gambrinus Gold Beer,** Pittsburgh Brewers, 12 oz., gold and yellow, brand name in yellow on gold background, very plain can 1.00   2.00

☐ **Gambrinus Golden Highlights,** Pittsburgh, 12 oz., white and gold 4.50   5.50

☐ **Gamecock Ale,** Cumberland, 12 oz., white, red and apple green 27.50   35.00

☐ **Garten Brau,** Brau, 12 oz., gold and white 7.00   10.00

☐ **G.B. Dark Bock,** Maier, 12 oz., "Beer" in white letters 75.00   100.00

☐ **GBX Malt Liquor,** Fuhrmann and Schmidt, 12 oz., blue 4.00   6.00

☐ **GBX,** Grain Belt, 16 oz. 3.00   5.00

☐ **Gemeinde Brau,** Cold Spring, 12 oz., green and white .... .90   1.25

☐ **Generic Beer,** all types .... .75   1.25

☐ **Genesee,** Genesee, 12 oz., red and white, "Beer" in white, "Naturally More Refreshing" in red 11.00   15.00

☐ **Genesse,** Genesse Brewing, 12 oz., white and red, brand name in white on red background, "Cold Aged" in black lettering across lower center .... .75   1.25

☐ **Genesee Cream Ale,** Genesee, 12 oz., white and green 10.00   14.00

☐ **Genesee Cream Ale,** Genesee, 12 oz., white and green with stalk of barley 2.50   3.50

☐ **Genesee Light Cream Ale,** Genesee, 12 oz., white and green 12.00   16.00

Price Range

☐ **Genesse Light Beer,** Genesse Brewing, 12 oz., green and white, brand name in green on white background .... .40 .65

☐ **Gettelman,** Miller, 12 oz., brown and white, brand name in white against medium-brown background, silver stripes at top and bottom 5.00 7.00

☐ **Gettelman Bock,** Miller, 12 oz., light brown, dark brown and white 7.00 10.00

☐ **Geyer's Lager,** Geyer, 12 oz., red, white and yellow 35.00 44.00

☐ **Giant Food,** Eastern, 12 oz., red, yellow and white, "Beer" in white lettering 15.00 20.00
Note: "Giant Food" was the name of a supermarket chain in which this brand was sold.

☐ **Giant Food,** Eastern, 12 oz., red, yellow and white, "Beer" in yellow 1.25 2.75

☐ **Giant Food,** Lion, 12 oz., red and white .... .40 .60

☐ **Gibbons,** Lion, 12 oz., gold, white and red, no stripes 1.25 1.65

☐ **Gibbons,** Lion, 12 oz., silver, white and red, no staples .... .90 1.45

☐ **Gibbons,** Lion, 12 oz., white, red and gold, with slogan "It's Good" repeated around lower portion of can 15.00 20.00

☐ **Gilley's,** Spoetzel, 12 oz., close-up portrait of Mickey Gilley .... .90 1.45

☐ **Gilley's,** Spoetzel, 12 oz., portrait of Mickey Gilley against outline of State of Texas 2.50 3.50

☐ **Gilt Edge,** Bosch, 12 oz., yellow, red and white, wavy pattern all over can 15.00 20.00

☐ **Gilt Edge,** Bosch, 12 oz., white and gold 4.00 5.00

☐ **Glacier,** Maier, 12 oz., white, gold and blue 30.00 40.00

☐ **Gluckliches,** Pickett Brewing, 12 oz. 1.25 2.25

☐ **Gluek,** Cold Spring, 12 oz., brown and yellow ... .70 1.15

☐ **Goebel Light Lager,** Goebel, 12 oz., blue, white and gold, brand name in blue on white background 1.75 2.50

☐ **Goebel Real Draft,** Goebel, 12 oz., blue, white and gold 8.00 12.00

☐ **Goebel Draft,** Goebel Brewing, 12 oz., blue, white and gold, brand name in blue on white background, the word "Real" does not appear 8.00 12.00

☐ **Goetz,** Pearl, 12 oz., blue, white and brown .... .40 .60

☐ **Goetz,** Pearl, 12 oz., dark blue, white and silver .90 1.20

☐ **Gold Medal,** Stegmaier, 12 oz., gold and white .90 1.20

Top, Left to Right: **Gablinger's**, *16 oz.,* **$9–$12; Grain Belt Bock,** *12 oz.,* **$1–$2.** *Bottom, Left to Right:* **Heritage House,** *12 oz.,* **$1.50–$2.25; Holiday Bock,** *12 oz.,* **$6–$9.**

Price Range

☐ **Gold Medal, Dart Drug,** Eastern, 12 oz., maroon and white, words "Premium Beer" in maroon near bottom	12.00	16.00
☐ **Golden Brew Premium,** General, 12 oz., blue, white and yellow	1.75	2.25
☐ **Golden Brew Premium,** General, 12 oz., red, white and yellow	2.50	3.25
☐ **Golden Crown Draft,** General, 12 oz., blue and white, illustration of foaming glass of beer	14.00	19.00
☐ **Golden Crown Draft,** Maier, 12 oz., blue and white, illustration of foaming glass of beer	17.00	20.00
☐ **Golden Crown Extra Pale Dry,** General, 12 oz., gold and white, "Beer" in red	2.00	2.50
☐ **Golden Crown Extra Pale Dry,** General, 12 oz., gold and white, "Beer" in blue	.45	.65
☐ **Golden Crown Extra Pale Dry,** Maier, 12 oz., gold, white and red	4.75	6.25
☐ **Golden Harvest,** General, 12 oz., pale blue, dark blue and gold	9.75	13.25
☐ **Golden Lager,** Burgermeister, 12 oz., white and gold, heraldic lions at either side of foaming glass of beer	35.00	45.00
☐ **Golden Lager,** Hamm, 12 oz., white and gold, heraldic lions at either side of foaming glass beer	25.00	33.00
☐ **Golden 16,** Schell, 16 oz., moose head against white background	4.25	5.50
☐ **Golden Velvet,** Blitz-Weinhard, 12 oz., blue and white	2.25	3.25
☐ **Goodwill From Good People, Iron City Christmas Issue,** Pittsburgh, 16 oz.	42.50	52.50
☐ **Gorilla,** Schell, 12 oz., caricature of gorilla	1.00	1.35
☐ **Grace Brothers Bavarian,** Maier, 16 oz.	30.00	40.00
☐ **Grain Belt,** Grain Belt, 16 oz.	1.60	2.10
☐ **Grain Belt,** Grain Belt, 12 oz., gold, silver and white, "Beer" in black lettering	1.75	2.35
☐ **Grain Belt,** Grain Belt, 12 oz., gold, silver and white, dark red lozenge at center with brand name, yellow ornament above	.65	.85
☐ **Grain Belt,** Grain Belt, 12 oz., gold, silver and white, light red lozenge at center with brand name, white ornament above	.45	.65
☐ **Grain Belt,** Heileman, 16 oz.	1.00	1.50
☐ **Grain Belt,** Heileman, 12 oz., gold, silver and white, light red lozenge at center with brand name, white ornament above	.40	.65

Price Range

☐ **Grain Belt Bock,** Grain Belt, 12 oz., light brown and dark brown	.80	1.25
☐ **Grain Belt Premium,** Grain Belt, 12 oz., gold and white	1.00	1.50
☐ **Grain Belt Premium,** Heileman, 12 oz., white and red	.45	.65
☐ **Grand Union,** Eastern, 12 oz., gold and red	1.00	1.55
☐ **Grand Union,** Eastern, 12 oz., white and gold with large illustration of glass of beer	10.00	14.00
☐ **Grand Falls Select,** Glitz Weinhard, 12 oz., white and red	.90	1.30
☐ **Grand Falls Select,** Great Falls, 12 oz., white, grey and red	17.00	22.00
☐ **Grand Lager,** Grand Lager, 12 oz., white and red	5.00	6.50
☐ **Great Lakes,** Associated, 12 oz., blue, red and silver	7.00	10.00
☐ **Great Lakes,** Great Lakes, 12 oz., blue, red and silver	12.00	16.00
☐ **Great Lakes,** Heileman, 12 oz., blue, red and silver	8.00	12.00
☐ **Griesedieck Malt Liquor,** Falstaff, 16 oz.	8.00	12.00
☐ **Griesedieck Malt Liquor,** Griesedieck, 12 oz., pale gold and white, brand name spelled out in full, along with lengthy message in old-style script lettering	3.00	4.00
☐ **Gunther,** Gunther, 12 oz., red and white, gold band at top and bottom, red shows beneath bottom band	.65	.85
☐ **Gunther,** Gunther, 12 oz., red and white, gold band at top and bottom, red does not show beneath bottom band	1.00	1.50
☐ **Gunther,** Gunther, 12 oz., gold, white and red, gold background with white dots	8.25	11.50
☐ **Haentjens Ale,** Yuengling, 12 oz., multicolored with medieval castle on mountain	.80	1.10
☐ **Haffenreffer Private Stock Malt Liquor,** Narragansett, 12 oz., red, white and gold	40.00	50.00
☐ **Hamm's,** Hamm, 12 oz., blue, white and silver	1.50	2.25
☐ **Hamms's,** Hamm, 12 oz., gray, white and blue, "Beer" in red under brand name	.65	.85
☐ **Hamm's,** Olympia, 12 oz., beige, white and blue	.40	.60
☐ **Hamm's Draft,** Hamm, 12 oz., white, blue and gold, "Real" over "Draft"	4.50	6.25
☐ **Hamm's Draft,** Hamm, 12 oz., light blue and dark blue, "Draft" in block letters	1.35	1.65

Price Range

☐ **Hamm's Draft,** Hamm, 12 oz., silver, can is shaped as beer keg with ribbing 1.85 2.50

☐ **Hamm's Preferred Stock,** Hamm, 12 oz., white and black, illustration of city scene 1.85 2.50

☐ **Hamm's Preferred stock,** Olympia, 12 oz., white and black, illustration of city scene 1.00 1.75

☐ **Hampden,** Hampden Harvard, 12 oz., white and blue .... .75 1.25

☐ **Hampden Ale,** Hampden Harvard, 12 oz., green and white .... .85 1.15

☐ **Handy Keg Lone Star Draft,** Lone Star, 12 oz., silver, "Charcoal Filtered" directly above "Draft" .40 .65

☐ **Handy Keg Lone Star Draft,** Lone Star, 12 oz., silver, with green star over emblem, reads "Pasteurized" at bottom 5.00 7.00

☐ **Handy Keg Lone Star Draft,** Lone Star, 12 oz., silver "Honest to Goodness" directly above "Draft" 3.00 4.00

☐ **Handy Keg Lone Star Draft,** Lone Star, 12 oz., gold, red and black.......................... 200.00 250.00

☐ **Hanley Lager Beer,** Hanley Brewing, 12 oz., grey, white and silver, brand name in white on blue background, logo in upper center of a white letter "H" on red circle .... .75 1.25

☐ **Happy Birthday Beer from Bilow,** Garden State, 12 oz., birthday cake with one candle 1.00 1.50

☐ **Happy New Year 1980,** Garden State, 12 oz., Father Time and infant, reads "Premium Beer" near bottom.. .90 1.20

☐ **Harlequin Dark Beer,** Walter Brewing, 12 oz., gold, cream, red and gold, brand name in red on cream background, "Dark" in black lettering underneath brand name......................... 4.50 5.50

☐ **Hauenstein New Ulm,** Grain Belt, 12 oz., red and white .... .65 .85

☐ **Hauenstein New Ulm,** Hauenstein, 12 oz., silver, red and white, silver at top and bottom, brand name in red lettering outlined in silver 3.00 4.00

☐ **Hauenstein New Ulm,** Hauenstein, 12 oz., red and white .... .90 1.35

☐ **Hauenstein New Ulm,** Heileman, 12 oz., red and white .... .40 .65

☐ **Hausbrau Lager,** Maier, 12 oz., red, white and blue, snow-capped mountain peak 35.00 45.00

Price Range

☐ **Hedrick Lager,** Hedrick, 12 oz., gold, red and white, canned at Williamsett, Massachusetts, top of can not pinched in at rim 8.00   12.00

☐ **Hedrick Lager,** Hedrick, 12 oz., gold, red and white, canned at Albany, New York 12.00   16.00

☐ **Hedrick Lager,** Hedrick, 12 oz., gold, burgundy and white, canned at Hammonton, New Jersey .85   1.35

☐ **Heibrau,** Heibrau, 12 oz., black, gold and blue .. 23.00   30.00

☐ **Hedrick Lager,** Hedrick, 12 oz., gold, red and white, canned at Williamsett, Massachusetts, top of can pinched in at rim .... .85   1.35

☐ **Heidelberg,** Carling, 12 oz., gold and red, brand name in small lettering, lower two-thirds of can solid gold 5.00   6.00

☐ **Heidelberg,** Carling, 12 oz., dark gold and red, brand name in medallion at center, does not read "Aluminum Recyclable Can" 6.50   8.50

☐ **Heidelberg,** Carling, 12 oz., dark gold and red, brand name in medallion at center, reads "Aluminum Recyclable Can" at bottom 4.00   5.00

☐ **Heidelberg,** Carling, 12 oz., dark blue, white, gold bands at top and bottom..................... 4.50   5.75

☐ **Heidelberg,** Carling, 16 oz., gold and white, large brand name in red, "Carling" in black 20.00   25.00

☐ **Heidelberg Light Pilsener,** Carling Brewing, 12 oz., gold, white and brown, brand name in brown on white background, small illustration above brand name of German-style home 6.00   7.00

☐ **Heidelberg Light Pilsener,** Carling Brewing, 16 oz., gold, white and brown, same design as the 12 oz. 15.00   20.00

☐ **Heidelberg Light Pilsener,** Carling, 12 oz., grey and gold 7.50   10.50

☐ **Heileman's Old Style,** Heileman, 12 oz., red, white and blue, red ribbon behind brand name .40   .65

☐ **Heileman's Old Style,** Heileman, 12 oz., red, white and blue, no red ribbon behind brand name .85   1.35

☐ **Heileman's Sparkling Stite,** Heileman, 12 oz., white 1.85   2.30

☐ **Heileman's Special Export,** Heileman, 12 oz., green and white .... .90   1.35

☐ **Heritage House Fine Light,** Falstaff, 12 oz., yellow and red 1.75   2.25

☐ **Heritage House Premium,** Pittsburgh Brewing, 12 oz., yellow and red .... .40   .65

Price Range

☐ **Heritage House Premium,** Pittsburgh Brewing, 12 oz., yellow and red .... .60 .90

☐ **Heritage House Premium,** Queen City, 12 oz., yellow and red 1.75 2.25

☐ **Heritage House Premium Fine Light,** General, 12 oz., yellow and red .... .90 1.35

☐ **Heublein Velvet Glove Malt Liquor,** Hamm Brewing, 12 oz., white, black and yellow, "Heublein" in white on black background, "Velvet Glove" in black on yellow background, illustration of red glove in bottom center of label 40.00 50.00

☐ **Hi Brau,** Huber, 12 oz., gold, red and black, brand name in white 1.00 1.75

☐ **Hien Brau,** Tivoli, 12 oz., brown and white 20.00 25.00

☐ **Highlander,** Highlander, 12 oz., white and blue, foaming glass at center, no wide silver stripe at bottom 4.00 5.00

☐ **Highlander,** Rheinlander, 12 oz., white and blue, foaming glass at center, wide silver stripe at bottom .... .85 1.15

☐ **High Life,** Miller, 12 oz., gold, white and red ... .40 .65

☐ **Hof-Brau,** General, 12 oz., red and white, brand name in grey-blue lettering 2.50 3.50

☐ **Hof-Brau,** General, 12 oz., red and white, brand name in bright blue lettering, bright blue frame around medallion .... .85 1.30

☐ **Hof-Brau,** Maier, 12 oz., red and white, brand name in grey-blue lettering 5.00 6.25

☐ **Hofbrau,** Hofbrau, 12 oz., cream white and red, illustration of German village inn 12.00 16.00

☐ **Hoffman House,** Walter, 12 oz., white, brown and red 2.25 3.25

☐ **Holiday,** Holiday, 12 oz., white and red 1.80 2.25

☐ **Holiday,** Huber, 12 oz., white and red 1.00 1.30

☐ **Holiday Bock,** Holiday, 12 oz., bright tomato red with illustration of ram 6.00 9.00

☐ **Holihan's Pilsener,** Diamond Spring, 12 oz., white, dark brown and gold, brand name at center surrounded by brown and gold circles 12.00 16.00

☐ **Holihan's Pilsener,** Diamond Spring, 12 oz., white, brand name repeated several times within circles 1.85 2.25

☐ **Home Dry Lager,** Heileman, 12 oz., white, red and gold 8.00 12.00

☐ **Home Pilsner,** Pocono, 12 oz., yellow and dark brown .... .90 1.35

Price Range

☐ **Hop'n Gator,** Pittsburgh, 12 oz., white and brown, illustration of glass of beer, "Flavored Beer" at bottom 90   1.35

☐ **Hop'n Gator Malt Liquor,** Pittsburgh, 12 oz., white, shot glass and palm tree 4.50   6.00

☐ **Horlacher Premium,** Horlacher, 12 oz., gold and black 1.00   1.75

☐ **Horseshoe Curve,** Pittsburgh, 12 oz., illustration of railroad tracks with "horseshoe curve" 75   1.25

☐ **Huber,** Huber, 12 oz., white and red, gold band at top and bottom 1.75   2.50

☐ **Huber Bock,** Huber, 12 oz., white and burgundy red, medallion at upper left with illustration of ram's head 2.00   3.00

☐ **Hudepohl,** Hudepohl, 12 oz., white, red and gold, predominant color is white 6.00   7.25

☐ **Hudepohl,** Hudepohl, 12 oz., gold and white, green badge reading "14K" above brand name   6.00   8.00

☐ **Hudepohl,** Hudepohl, 12 oz., yellow and brown, pictorial baseball scene 1.50   2.25

☐ **Hudepohl,** Hudepohl, 12 oz., white and light brown 85   1.35

☐ **Hudepohl,** Hudepohl, 12 oz., red, white and gold, designed to resemble beer barrel 5.25   6.50

☐ **Hull's Export,** Hull, 12 oz., white with brand name in black, "Export" in red 2.75   3.50

☐ **Hynne Premium Quality,** Walter, 12 oz., cream white and red with mountain scene 6.00   7.25

☐ **Imperial Pilsener,** Hofbrau, 12 oz., white, brown and red 90   1.20

☐ **India,** Cervecia San Juan, 12 oz., white, blue and red, brand name appears repetitively around can   2.00   3.00

☐ **Innsbrau Lager,** Innsbrau, 12 oz., gold and blue   6.00   8.00

☐ **Iron City,** Pittsburgh, 12 oz., white and red, "No.1" at top, "With the Snap Top" at bottom 12.00   16.00

☐ **Iron City,** Pittsburgh, 16 oz., "The Big Iron" 1.25   2.00

☐ **Iron City,** Pittsburgh, 12 oz., Iron City Salutes the 1979 World Champion Pirates 1.25   2.00

☐ **Iron City,** Pittsburgh, 12 oz., Paul Revere's Ride (from American Bicentennial series) 1.00   1.75

☐ **Iron City,** Pittsburgh, 12 oz., Signing of the Declaration of Independence (from American Bicentennial series) 1.00   1.75

☐ **Iron City,** Pittsburgh, 12 oz., Spirit of '76 (from American Bicentennial series) 1.00   1.75

Price Range

☐ **Iron City Draft,** Pittsburgh, 12 oz., white and red, "Draft Beer" in black lettering 2.50 3.25

☐ **Iron City Draft,** Pittsburgh, 12 oz., white and red, "Draft Beer" in red lettering .... .90 1.35

☐ **Iroquois,** Iroquois, 12 oz., red and white, portrait of Indian, brand name in red 5.00 6.25

☐ **Iroquois,** Iroquois, 12 oz., red and white, portrait of Indian, brand name in red, canned at Columbus, Ohio 2.75 3.50

☐ **Iroquois,** Iroquois, 12 oz., red and white, portrait of Indian, brand name in red, canned at Toledo, Ohio 1.50 2.25

☐ **Iroquois,** Iroquois, 12 oz., red and white, portrait of Indian, brand name in red, canned at Erie, Pennsylvania .... .65 .90

☐ **Iroquois,** International, 12 oz., red and white, portrait of Indian, brand name in red 4.00 6.00

☐ **Iroquois Draft,** Iroquois, 12 oz., red, white and blue 1.85 2.30

☐ **Iroquois Draft Brewed,** Iroquois, 12 oz., red, white and blue 1.75 2.25

☐ **Iroquois Draft Ale,** Iroquois, 12 oz., green and white, profile portrait of Indian 17.50 25.00

☐ **Ivy League,** Ivy League, 12 oz., white, gold and yellow 1.00 1.50

☐ **Jacob Ruppert,** Ruppert, 12 oz., light blue and dark blue .... .85 1.30

☐ **Jaguar Malt Liquor,** Jaguar, 12 oz., black and gold, leopard-skin pattern 65.00 80.00

☐ **Jaguar,** Jaguar, 12 oz., red, black and gold, leopard-skin pattern 75.00 90.00

☐ **Jaguar Malt Liquor,** Standard Rochester, 12 oz., black and gold, leopard-skin pattern 65.00 80.00

☐ **Jamaica Sun Premium,** Jamaica, 12 oz., white and gold 22.50 30.00

☐ **Jax,** Jackson, 10 oz., top half white, bottom half gold, brand name in red 10.00 14.00

☐ **Jax,** Jackson, 12 oz., white, blue and red, brand name in red, wide blue ribbon placed vertically behind brand name 7.50 10.00

☐ **Jax,** Jackson, 12 oz., white, red and gold 7.00 9.00

☐ **Jax,** Jackson, 12 oz., gold, white and red, white scrolling at either side of pictorial medallion, "The Fabacher Family Brew" in large white lettering 2.50 3.25

☐ **Jax,** Pearl, 12 oz., gold, red and white .... .90 1.35

☐ **Jax Draft,** Jax, 12 oz., gold and brown 50.00 60.00

Price Range

☐ **Jet Malt Liquor,** Westminster Brewing, 12 oz., white, silver and red, brand name in red on white background, logo of a plane across center of can, | 15.00 | 20.00

☐ **Jet Malt Liquor,** Westminster Brewing, 16 oz., white, silver and red, same design as 12 oz. with "King Size" in red across upper center of can .. | 8.00 | 12.00

☐ **Jet Malt Liquor,** Tivoli Brewing, 12 oz., white silver and red, same design as Westminster Brewing can .... | 15.00 | 20.00

☐ **Johnny Dollar's Saloon and Dance Hall,** Pittsburgh, 12 oz., steer horns near top .... | .75 | 1.25

☐ **Jr, J.R. Erwing's Private Stock,** Pearl, 12 oz., belt buckle and stars, signed message from J.R. Ewing, statement "Imported from Texas" ...... | .90 | 1.35

☐ **K and B,** Premium, 12 oz., silver and violet ...... | .85 | 1.15

☐ **Kappy's Premium,** Eastern, 12 oz., dark brown and white .... | 1.00 | 1.75

☐ **Karlsbrau,** Gold Spring, 12 oz., red, white and brown .... | .65 | .90

☐ **Karlsbrau,** Heileman, 12 oz., red, white and brown | 1.85 | 2.50

☐ **Kassel,** Jackson Brewing, 12 oz., gold, red and black, brand name in black on red banner diagonally across center of can, large illustration of lion | 1.00 | 2.00

☐ **Kassel,** Pearl Brewing, 12 oz., gold, red and black, same design as Jackson Brewing can .... | .75 | 1.50

☐ **Katz,** Associated, 12 oz., red and white, small brand name, no caricature of cat .... | 4.25 | 5.25

☐ **Katz,** Associated, 12 oz., red and white, very large red medallon with brand name, surmounted by caricature of cat .... | 7.00 | 9.00

☐ **Katz,** Pearl, 12 oz., red and white, small brand name, no caricature of cat .... | .90 | 1.25

☐ **Keg,** American, 16 oz. .... | 7.00 | 10.00

☐ **Keg Natural Flavor,** American, 12 oz., white, red and yellow .... | 10.00 | 14.00

☐ **Keg Natural Flavor,** General, 12 oz., white, red and violet .... | .40 | .60

☐ **Keg Natural Flavor,** General, 12 oz., pink, red and white .... | .85 | 1.10

☐ **Keg Natural Flavor,** General, 16 oz., red and white .... | 10.00 | 14.00

☐ **Keg Natural Flavor,** Maier, 12 oz., pink, red and white .... | 5.50 | 7.50

☐ **Kegle Brau,** Cold Spring, 12 oz., gold near bottom | 1.50 | 2.00

☐ **King Snedley's,** General, 12 oz., silver and black | 1.25 | 2.00

☐ **King Snedley's,** Lucky, 12 oz., silver and black | 12.00 | 16.00

Top, Left to Right: **Iron City Steelers** *(1975 Super Bowl), 12 oz.,* **$1–$2;** **Koehler,** *12 oz.,* **$1–$2.** *Bottom, Left to Right:* **Leinenkugels,** *12 oz.,* **$2.50–$3.50;** **Miller Lite** *(early design), 12 oz.,* **$2.50–$3.50.**

Price Range

☐ **King's Premium,** King's, 12 oz., white and blue   15.00   20.00
☐ **Kingsbury,** Heileman, 12 oz., white and red, does not state "Recyclable Aluminum" 1.00   1.75
☐ **Kingsbury,** Kingsbury, 12 oz., red and white, brand name in red against white shield 2.75   3.75
☐ **Kingsbury,** Kingsbury, 12 oz., red and white, brand name in white against red shield 8.00   12.00
☐ **Kingsbury Brew Near Beer,** Heileman, 12 oz., pale buff, red and gold 75   1.25
☐ **Kingsbury Brew Near Beer,** Kingsbury, 12 oz., pale buff, red and gold 1.50   2.25
☐ **Kingsbury Pale,** Kingsbury, 12 oz., red, white and gold, brand name in red, "Pale Beer" in blue ...   5.75   7.75
☐ **Kingsbury Real Draft,** Kingsbury, 12 oz., white, brown and red, lower portion of can has woodgrain finish 5.50   7.50
☐ **Kingsbury Wisconsin Pale,** Kingsbury, 12 oz., red, white and blue 5.00   6.25
☐ **Knickerbocker Natural,** Jacob Ruppert, 7 oz., white with red and blue ribbons, blue lettering ..   5.00   6.25
☐ **Knickerbocker Natural,** Jacob Ruppert, 16 oz.   2.25   3.25
☐ **Knickerbocker Natural,** Jacob Ruppert, 12 oz., white, blue and brown, ribbons at center are dark blue and brown 90   1.35
☐ **Knickerbocker,** Jacob Ruppert, 12 oz., gold, red, white and blue, without "Beer" beneath blue ribbon 5.00   6.50
☐ **Knickerbocker,** Jacob Ruppert, 12 oz., gold, red, white and blue, without "Beer" beneath blue ribbon 2.75   3.50
☐ **Knickerbocker Natural,** Jacob Ruppert, 12 oz., red, white and blue, ribbons at center are red and blue 40   .65
☐ **Knickerbocker Natural,** Jacob Ruppert, 12 oz., red, white and blue, ribbons at center are blue, yellow and red 65   .90
☐ **Koch's Golden Anniversary,** Koch, 12 oz., white, red and gold 5.75   7.75
☐ **Koch's Golden Anniversary,** Koch, 12 oz., red, white and gold, "The Best in Flavor" at top of can   .40   .65
☐ **Kodiak Ale,** Schmidt, 12 oz., blue and gold, illustration of mountain peaks 90   1.35
☐ **Koehler,** Erie, 12 oz., dark blue and white, no bright orange trim around brand name 12.50   17.50
☐ **Koehler,** Erie, 12 oz., dark blue and white, bright orange trim around brand name 2.75   3.50

Price Range

☐ **Koehler,** Erie, 12 oz., blue and white, Bicentennial	.90	1.35
☐ **Koehler,** Erie, 12 oz., red and white, Bicentennial	.90	1.35
☐ **Koenig Brau,** Koenig Brau, 12 oz., gold and white	6.00	8.00
☐ **Kol,** Cumberland, 12 oz., gold and blue	25.00	32.50
☐ **Kol,** Warsaw, 12 oz., gold and blue	30.00	40.00
☐ **Krewes,** Premium, 12 oz., light blue, dark blue and red, figure of lion, heraldry emblem	.85	1.30
☐ **Krewes,** Royal, 12 oz., illustration of heraldic lion	.75	1.25
☐ **Krewes,** Royal, 12 oz., light blue, dark blue and red, figure of lion, heraldry emblem	.50	.70
☐ **Krueger,** Krueger, 12 oz., red, white and pale violet	12.00	16.00
☐ **Krueger,** Krueger, 12 oz., red and white, flat bottom	10.00	14.00
☐ **Krueger,** Krueger, 12 oz., red and white, rounded bottom	1.00	1.75
☐ **Krueger Ale,** Krueger, 12 oz., black and white with gold bands at top and bottom, "Ale" in white . .	11.00	15.00
☐ **Krueger Ale,** Krueger, 16 oz.	9.00	13.00
☐ **Krueger Draft,** Krueger, 12 oz., brown, white and gray, "Draft" in red at upper left	10.00	14.00
☐ **Krueger Pilsner,** Falstaff, 12 oz., brown, white and gray	4.00	6.00
☐ **Krueger Pilsner,** Krueger Pilsner, 12 oz., brown, white and gray	7.00	9.00
☐ **Krueger Pilsner,** Krueger, 12 oz., white, gray and red	5.00	7.00
☐ **Labatt's,** General, 12 oz., red, white and blue . .	30.00	40.00
☐ **Lanser's,** Arizona Brewing, 12 oz., red, white, blue and green, brand name in black on white background, "A-1 Beer" directly underneath, blue band around top	35.00	45.00
☐ **Lanser's,** Arizona Brewing, 16 oz., red, white, blue and green, same design as 12 oz.	60.00	75.00
☐ **Leinenkugel's,** Leinenkugel, 12 oz., white, burgundy and gold	2.75	3.50
☐ **Leinenkugel's,** Leinenkugel, 12 oz., white, burgundy and silver	.40	.65
☐ **Liebotschaner Cream Ale,** Lion, 12 oz., green, white and black	.90	1.35
☐ **Light,** Peter Hand, 12 oz., white and blue	.40	.65
☐ **Lime Lager,** Lone Star, 12 oz., green and silver	8.00	12.00
☐ **Lite,** C. Feigenspan, 12 oz., white and blue	6.00	8.00
☐ **Lite,** Meister Brau, 12 oz., blue and white, "Meister Brau" on same line	9.50	13.50

Price Range

☐ **Lite,** Meister Brau, 12 oz., white, gold and blue, "Lite" in blue script lettering, small emblem at top   1.50   2.25

☐ **Lite,** Meister Brau, 12 oz., blue and white, "Meister" in arched lettering atop "Brau" 6.50   8.75

☐ **Lite,** Miller, 12 oz., white, gold and blue, "Lite" in blue script lettering, small emblem at top 65   .90

☐ **Lite,** Miller, 12 oz., white, red and black, "A Fine Pilsner" in white lettering 40   .60

☐ **Lite,** Meister Brau, 16 oz., brand name in blue . .   11.00   15.00

☐ **Little King,** Horlacher Brewing, 12 oz., white and red, fanciful illustration of a little king in upper center of can 35.00   45.00

☐ **Lone Star,** Lone Star, 12 oz., red, white and gold, large red badge-type medallion with brand name in white, small lettering at bottom in red 8.00   12.00

☐ **Lone Star,** Lone Star, 12 oz., red, white and gold, large red badge-type medallion with brand name in white, small lettering at bottom in blue 6.50   8.00

☐ **Lone Star,** Lone Star, 12 oz., cream white with brand name in small badge medallions repeated across can 5.50   6.00

☐ **Lone Star,** Lone Star, 12 oz., white, red, brown and gold, brand name in red badge-type medallion   1.00   1.50

☐ **Lone Star Draft,** Lone Star, 12 oz., silver, "Charcoal Filtered" directly above "Draft" 40   .60

☐ **Lone Star Draft,** Lone Star, 12 oz., silver, with green star over emblem, reads "Pasteurized" at bottom 4.25   5.50

☐ **Lone Star Draft,** Lone Star, 12 oz., silver, "Honest to Goodness" directly above "Draft" 2.50   3.25

☐ **Lone Star Draft,** Lone Star, 12 oz., gold, red and black 200.00   265.00

☐ **Lucky Draft,** General, 12 oz., white and tan, pictorial illustration and lengthy text 1.25   1.75

☐ **Lucky Draft,** Lucky, 12 oz., white and gold, pictorial illustration and lengthy text 3.25   4.50

☐ **Lucky Draft,** Lucky, 16 oz., wide gold band at bottom 15.00   20.00

☐ **Lucky Draft,** Lucky, 16 oz., brand name in glossy gold 5.00   7.00

☐ **Lucky Lager,** General, 12 oz., pale blue and gold, brand name slightly curved 3.50   4.75

☐ **Lucky Lager,** General, 16 oz., "Lager Beer" in red   1.35   1.80

☐ **Lucky Lager,** General, 16 oz., "Lager Beer" in black 70   1.00

Price Range

☐ **Lucky Lager,** Lucky Lager, 7 oz., pale beige with red cross at center 12.00 16.00

☐ **Lucky Dark Continental Beer,** General Brewing, 12 oz., brown and beige, brand name in beige on brown banner diagonally across upper center, illustration of brewery in the mountains in center .75 1.25

☐ **Lucky Bock,** General Brewing, 12 oz., white, green and red, brand name in green script on white background in upper center, "Bock Beer" in red lettering in center 1.00 1.75

☐ **Lucky Bock,** General Brewing, 12 oz., green, gold and white, upper half of can is white, lower half in green, brand name in gold on white background in upper center, illustration of a ram's head in lower center 8.00 12.00

☐ **Lucky Light Draft,** General, 12 oz., white and tan, pictorial illustration and lengthy text .... .90 1.20

☐ **Lucky Malt Liquor,** Lucky, 16 oz. 15.00 20.00

☐ **Lucky Red Carpet,** General, 12 oz., red and white .90 1.20

☐ **Maier Select,** Maier, 12 oz., red, white and blue, blue leaf near top 4.00 6.00

☐ **Malt Duck Grape,** National, 12 oz., purple and white 21.00 25.00

☐ **Manheim,** Reading, 12 oz., red and white 8.00 12.00

☐ **Mannchester,** Maier, 16 oz. 80.00 105.00

☐ **Mark Meister Premium Lager,** Eastern, 12 oz., blue and white 5.00 7.00

☐ **Mark V,** Pittsburgh, 12 oz., red, white and blue, brand name in black 1.75 2.35

☐ **Mark V,** Pittsburgh, 12 oz., red, white and blue, brand name in blue .... .65 .85

☐ **Mark V,** Wagner, 12 oz., white, blue, red and silver, scrollwork beside emblem atop brand name, silver band at bottom 12.00 16.00

☐ **Master Brew,** Walter, 12 oz., red and white, large emblem with lion .... .55 .70

☐ **Master Brew,** Walter, 12 oz., white and gold, gold bands at top and bottom .... .90 1.20

☐ **Matterhorn,** Burgermeister, 12 oz., blue and white, illustration of mountain peak 17.00 22.00

☐ **Matterhorn,** Hamm, 12 oz., blue and white, illustration of mountain peak 9.50 13.50

☐ **Matts Premium Lager,** West End, 12 oz., white, green and gold 9.50 13.50

☐ **Matts Premium Lager,** West End, 12 oz., gold, red and white................................ 2.00 2.50

Price Range

☐ **McSorley's Non-Alcoholic Brew (Near Bear),** Forrest, 12 oz., white, yellow and gold, illustration of foaming glass of beer 1.40   1.85

☐ **Mein,** Mein, 12 oz., multi-colored with waterfall scene 4.25   6.25

☐ **Meister Brau Bock,** Meister Brau, 12 oz., white, black and gold 7.00   9.00

☐ **Meister Brau Bock,** Miller, 12 oz., white, red and gray, brand name in gray 1.75   2.25

☐ **Meister Brau Draft,** Meister Brau, 12 oz., brown and pale blue, word "Draft" appears above brand name 2.50   3.25

☐ **Meister Brau Draft,** Miller, 12 oz., brown, white and yellow, illustration of pitcher 1.00   1.35

☐ **Meister Brau Draft,** Peter Hand, 12 oz., light brown, dark brown and black, textured to resemble beer keg, white bands at top and bottom . . . 4.00   6.00

☐ **Meister Brau Lite,** Meister Brau, 12 oz., blue and white, "Meister Brau" on same line 9.50   13.50

☐ **Meister Brau Lite,** Meister Brau, 12 oz., blue and white, "Meister" in arched lettering atop "Brau" 6.25   8.50

☐ **Meister Brau Premium,** Miller, 16 oz. 1.60   2.00

☐ **Meister Brau Premium Lager,** Miller, 16 oz. 90   1.20

☐ **Metbrew Near Beer,** Metropolis, 12 oz., brown, gold and pastel blue, illustration of stein 60   .80

☐ **Metz,** Walter, 12 oz., white, blue, red and gold . . 3.50   5.00

☐ **Metz,** Walter, 16 oz. 9.00   10.00

☐ **Michelob,** Anheuser Busch, 12 oz., red and gold, brand name in raised lettering 4.25   5.50

☐ **Michelob,** Anheuser Busch, 12 oz., red and gold, brand name not in raised lettering 40   .60

☐ **Mickey's Malt Liquor,** Associated, 12 oz., green and white 7.50   10.75

☐ **Mickey's Malt Liquor,** Heileman, 12 oz., white, red and blue 85   1.15

☐ **Mickey's Malt Liquor,** Sterling, 12 oz., green and white 20.00   30.00

☐ **Mickey's Malt Liquor,** Sterling, 16 oz. 9.00   12.00

☐ **Mile Hi,** Tivoli, 12 oz., red, white and blue, illustration of Colorado mountain, reads "Light Premium Quality" in bands at bottom, mountain illustration has dark blue background 35.00   45.00

☐ **Miller,** Miller, 8 oz., cream white and brown 3.00   5.00

☐ **Miller,** Miller, 10 oz., gold .85   1.15

☐ **Miller High Life,** Miller, 12 oz., gold, white and red .40   .60

☐ **Miller High Life,** Miller, 16 oz. brand name in cross 13.50   17.50

Top, Left to Right: **Meister Brau Bock,** *12 oz.,* **$2.25–$3.25;** *Mizzou Brew (one of a three-can set commemorating University of Missouri's football program), 12 oz.,* **$1–$2.** *Bottom, Left to Right:* **Mizzou Brew,** *12 oz.,* **$1–$2;** *Mizzou Brew,* *12 oz.,* **$1–$2.**

	Price Range	
☐ **Miller Malt Liquor,** Miller, 16 oz.	4.50	6.00
☐ **Milwaukee's Best,** Miller, 12 oz., red and white, illustration of stein against burnt orange background	4.00	5.25
☐ **Milwaukee's Best,** Miller, 12 oz., pale blue, black and red, pair of steins	.70	1.00
☐ **Milwaukee Extra,** Miller, 12 oz., red, white and blue	9.50	13.50
☐ **Milwaukee Premium,** Waukee, 12 oz., pale blue, red and gold	.90	1.25
☐ **Molson Golden,** Molson, 12 oz., gold and white, heraldic figure of lion	.90	1.25
☐ **Monticello Ale,** Monticello, 12 oz., red and white, illustration of Thomas Jefferson home	20.00	30.00
☐ **Mountain Brew,** Queen City, 12 oz., red and white	12.00	16.00
☐ **Muhlheim Draft,** Muhlheim, 12 oz., red, white and brown, illustration of keg in upper center	12.00	16.00
☐ **Mule Malt Liquor,** General, 16 oz.	8.00	12.00
☐ **Munich Light Lager,** Feigenspan, 12 oz., white, blue and gold, canned at Cranston, Rhode Island	.40	.65
☐ **Mustang Malt Lager,** Pittsburgh Brewing, 12 oz., red and gold, brand name in thin block letters, "Malt Lager" in red	12.00	16.00
☐ **Mustang Malt Lager,** Pittsburgh Brewing, 12 oz., red, white and black, illustration of rearing horse, "Malt Lager" in black lettering	4.50	6.00
☐ **Mustang Malt Lager,** Pittsburgh, 16 oz.	12.00	16.00
☐ **Mustang Malt Liquor,** Pittsburgh Brewing, 12 oz., red, white and black, illustration of rearing horse	.90	1.35
☐ **Mustang Malt Liquor,** Pittsburgh, 16 oz.	12.00	16.00
☐ **My Beer,** My Brewing, 12 oz., red, white and blue, "My" in red lettering on white banner around center of can	45.00	55.00
☐ **Narragansett,** Falstaff, 12 oz., white, yellow and red	.40	.60
☐ **Narragansett,** Falstaff, 12 oz., red, white and blue, American flag and Liberty Bell	.90	1.45
☐ **Narragansett,** Narragansett, 12 oz., white, yellow and red	.95	1.45
☐ **Narragansett,** Narragansett, 12 oz., gray and white, no red band at bottom	8.00	12.00
☐ **Narragansett,** Narragansett, 12 oz., yellow, white and red, red band at bottom	7.50	10.00
☐ **Narragansett 96 Extra Light,** Narragansett, 12 oz., lengthy printed message at lower half	.50	.90

Price Range

☐ **Narragansett Ale,** Narragansett, 12 oz., white, green and orange	5.00	7.00
☐ **Narragansett Draft,** Narragansett, 12 oz., yellow, white and red	100.00	135.00
☐ **Narragansett Lager,** Narragansett, 16 oz., brand name centerized on can	20.00	30.00
☐ **Narragansett Lager,** Narragansett, 16 oz., ship emblem has blue background	2.00	3.00
☐ **National Bohemian,** National, 8 oz., squat, cream white with white lettering on brown medallion, orange trim at top and bottom	.85	1.35
☐ **National Bohemian,** National, 8 oz., squat, white with horizontal banding, white lettering on red . .	6.75	9.50
☐ **National Bohemian,** National, 8 oz., white with horizontal banding, white lettering on red	6.75	9.50
☐ **National Bohemian,** National, 8 oz., cream white with white lettering on brown medallion, orange trim at top and bottom	2.50	3.50
☐ **National Bohemian,** National, 12 oz., cream white and red, thin gold bands at top and bottom	1.25	2.00
☐ **National Bohemian,** National, 12 oz., cream white, black and red, red bands at top and bottom	.40	.65
☐ **National Bohemian Bock,** National, 12 oz., black, white and red, illustration of ram's head	12.00	16.00
☐ **National Bohemian Light,** National, 12 oz., red, white and black, without caricature of one-eyed man	16.00	21.00
☐ **National Draft,** National, 12 oz., white, red and gold, large illustration of foaming glass	2.75	3.50
☐ **National Premium,** National, 12 oz., white, black and gold, heraldic shield supported by lions, embossed steel	3.50	4.75
☐ **Near Beer,** Pearl Brewing, 12 oz., white, gold, yellow and red, "Near" in white on red background, "Beer" in white on yellow background, "pale" appears in gold above brand name	6.00	9.00
☐ **Neuweiler Light Lager,** Neuweiler, 12 oz., blue and gold	10.50	14.50
☐ **Nine-O-Five (905),** Associated, 12 oz., red, white and blue, illustration of horse and rider	2.50	3.50
☐ **Nine-O-Five (905),** Heileman, 12 oz., red, white and blue, illustration of horse and rider	.85	1.15
☐ **Northern,** Cold Spring, 12 oz., white, red and gold	.90	1.20
☐ **North Star,** Associated, 12 oz., red, white and blue	2.50	3.25

Price Range

☐ **North Star,** Associated, 12 oz., dark blue, white and red, three small white crosses over "Beer" at bottom	1.75	2.50
☐ **North Star,** Cold Spring, 12 oz., dark blue, white and red, three small white crosses over "Beer" at bottom	.50	.85
☐ **North Star,** Heileman, 12 oz., dark blue, white and red	.70	1.00
☐ **North Star,** Associated, 16 oz.	11.50	15.50
☐ **Norvic,** DuBois Brewing, 12 oz., white and red	17.50	22.50
☐ **Norvic,** Regional, 12 oz., white and gold, brand name in red	20.00	25.00
☐ **Oconto,** Oconto, 12 oz., blue, white and gold . .	16.00	21.00
☐ **Oertel's '92,** Heileman, 12 oz., white and red . . .	.80	1.10
☐ **Oertel's '92,** Heileman, 16 oz.	8.00	12.00
☐ **Oertel's '92,** Oertel, 16 oz.	22.50	27.50
☐ **Oertel's Real Draft,** Oertel, 12 oz., red, black and gold, illustration of beer in glass, foam not spilling from top of glass	15.00	20.00
☐ **Oertel's Real Draft,** Oertel, 12 oz., red, black and gold, illustration of beer in glass, foam spilling from top of glass	17.50	22.50
☐ **Old Bohemian Bock,** Eastern, 12 oz., white and blue	1.00	1.50
☐ **Old Bohemian Light,** Eastern, 12 oz., white, red and silver	.90	1.20
☐ **Old Bohemian Light,** Eastern, 16 oz.	1.80	2.25
☐ **Oldbru,** Hamm, 16 oz.	15.00	20.00
☐ **Old Chicago,** Peter Hand Brewing, 16 oz., dark gold, white and red, brand name in white on red label, thin gold band around bottom, thicker gold band around top, illustration of Chicago near turn of the century	2.00	3.00
☐ **Old Chicago Lager,** Peter Hand, 12 oz., cream white, brown and red, statement of contents in white lettering against brown band at bottom . . .	.50	.75
☐ **Old Chicago Lager,** Peter Hand, 12 oz., cream white, brown and red, statement of contents in small red type at bottom	.90	1.15
☐ **Old Crown,** Old Crown, 12 oz., white and red, without symbol (figure of man)	.90	1.20
☐ **Old Crown,** Old Crown, 12 oz., white and red, with symbol (figure of man)	2.00	2.50
☐ **Old Crown Bock,** Old Crown, 12 oz., brown and white, illustration of ram's head	1.75	2.50

Price Range

☐ **Old Crown Premium Quality Ale,** Old Crown, 12 oz., gold, black and white .... .80 1.10

☐ **Old Crown,** Peter Hand, 12 oz., white and red, with symbol (figure of man) .... .40 .65

☐ **Old Dutch,** Associated, 12 oz., multi-colored pictorial, scene of people dining at table, yellow background, slogan "The Good Beer" 2.75 3.50

☐ **Old Dutch,** Pittsburgh Brewing, 12 oz., multi-colored pictorial, scene of people dining at table, yellow background, slogan "The Good Beer" ... .65 .85

☐ **Old Dutch,** Queen City, 12 oz., multi-colored pictorial, scene of people dining at table, yellow background, slogan "The Good Beer" 1.00 1.50

☐ **Old Export,** Cumberland Brewing, 12 oz., white, red and black, brand name in black on white shield-shaped label, brewer's logo in upper center 2.00 3.00

☐ **Old Export,** Cumberland Brewing, 16 oz., same design except with black bands at top and bottom 10.00 14.00

☐ **Old German,** Eastern, 16 oz. 1.50 2.25

☐ **Old German,** Eastern, 12 oz., red, white and black .45 .65

☐ **Old German,** Peter Hand, 12 oz., red and gold .85 1.10

☐ **Old German,** Queen City, 16 oz. 5.25 6.75

☐ **Old German,** Renner, 12 oz., white and red, brand name on red ribbon 3.25 4.25

☐ **Old German Premium Lager,** Queen City, 12 oz., red and white, symbol of Alpine Boy at upper left, no blue bands at top and bottom .... .75 1.25

☐ **Old German Premium Lager,** Queen City, 12 oz., red and white, symbol of Alpine Boy at upper left 1.50 2.25

☐ **Old German Premium Lager,** Queen City, 12 oz., red and white, symbol of world globe at upper left 4.50 6.00

☐ **Old Heidelbrau,** General, 12 oz., red, white and blue, illustration of stein 8.00 12.00

☐ **Old Milwaukee,** Schlitz, 12 oz., red and white, "Tap Top" in circle to left of, and below, brand name 4.00 5.00

☐ **Old Milwaukee,** Schlitz, 12 oz., red and white, "Pop Top" in circle to left of, and below, brand name 3.50 4.50

☐ **Old Milwaukee Draft,** Schlitz, 12 oz., white and red, silver bands at top and bottom 2.50 3.50

☐ **Old Milwaukee Draft,** Schlitz, 12 oz., white and red, pale grey band at top 1.00 1.75

☐ **Old Milwaukee Genuine Draft,** Schlitz, 16 oz., large "16" above brand name 2.50 3.25

Top, Left to Right: **Olde Frothingslosh,** *12 oz.,* **$1–$2;** *Olde Frothingslosh,* *12 oz.,* **$.80–$1.30.** *Bottom, Left to Right:* **Old Style,** *12 oz.,* **$1–$2;** *Our,* *12 oz.,* **$.80–$1.30.**

Price Range

☐ **Old Style,** Heileman, 12 oz., red, white and blue, no red ribbon behind brand name .... .85 1.10

☐ **Old Style,** Heileman, 12 oz., red, white and blue, red ribbon behind brand name .... .40 .65

☐ **Old Style,** Heileman, 16 oz., no ribbon behind brand name 3.00 4.00

☐ **Old Tankard Ale,** Pabst, 12 oz., gold, white and red, illustration of man with shield and stein 3.50 3.50

☐ **Old Tap,** Pabst, 12 oz., brown and gold, red lettering, illustration of end of wooden keg, wood graining not detailed on keg 1.75 2.50

☐ **Old Tap,** Pabst, 12 oz., brown and gold, red lettering, illustration of end of wooden keg, sharply detailed wood graining on keg 1.25 2.00

☐ **Old Timer's Lager,** Walter, 12 oz., red and white, shield motif with "Superior Quality" in white script .60 .90

☐ **Old Timer's Lager,** Walter, 12 oz., white with multicolored pictorial scene of men in olden costume around table .... .75 1.25

☐ **Old Timer's Lager,** West Bend, 12 oz., white with multi-colored pictorial scene of men in olden costume around table .... .75 1.25

☐ **Old Vienna,** Maier, 12 oz., white and yellow, reads "6 for 87¢" in red across top of can 20.00 30.00

☐ **Oldbru,** Burgermeister, 12 oz., white and red ... 65.00 75.00

☐ **Olde English 600 Malt Liquor,** Blitz Weinhard, 12 oz., burgundy gold and white 25.00 35.00

☐ **Olde English 600 Malt Liquor,** Blitz Weinhard, 16 oz. 45.00 55.00

☐ **Olde English 800 Malt Liquor,** Blitz Weinhard, 12 oz., burgundy and gold, canned at Newark, New Jersey 3.00 4.00

☐ **Olde English 800 Malt Liquor,** Blitz Weinhard, 12 oz., burgundy and gold, canned at Portland, Oregon .... .40 .60

☐ **Olde Frothingslosh,** Pittsburgh, 12 oz., silver with black-and-white photographic illustration of very plump woman in swimsuit (satirical) 1.00 1.75

☐ **Olde Frothingslosh,** Pittsburgh, 12 oz., white with blue photographic illustration of very plump woman in swimsuit (satirical) 1.00 1.75

☐ **Olde Frontingslosh,** Pittsburgh, 12 oz., red with black-and-white photographic illustration of very plump woman in swimsuit (satirical) 3.25 4.00

Price Range

☐ **Olde Frothingslosh,** Pittsburgh, 12 oz., orange with black-and-white photographic illustration of very plump woman in swimsuit (satirical) 10.00   15.00

☐ **Olde Frothingslosh,** Pittsburgh, 12 oz., blue with black-and-white photographic illustration of very plump woman in swimsuit (satirical) 10.00   15.00

☐ **Olde Frothingslosh,** Pittsburgh, 12 oz., dark brown with black-and-white photographic illustration of very plump woman in swimsuit (satirical)   3.75   4.75

☐ **Olympia,** Olympia, 7 oz., white and salmon with silver bands at top and bottom 2.00   3.00

☐ **Olympia,** Olympia, 7 oz., white and salmon (no silver bands) 1.00   1.50

☐ **Olympia,** Olympia, 12 oz., white, brown and gold, gold band at top and bottom 1.85   2.25

☐ **Olympia Light,** Olympia, 7 oz., white with greenish black at bottom 20.00   27.50

☐ **Olympia Light,** Olympia, 12 oz., white, brown and gold 75   1.25

☐ **Olympia Light,** Olympia, 16 oz. 2.00   3.00

☐ **One-O-Two (102),** General, 12 oz., black, white and gold, illustration of foaming glass against black background 75   1.25

☐ **One-O-Two (102),** Maier, black, white and gold, illustration of foaming glass against black background, "6 for 99¢" 4.75   6.00

☐ **One-O-Two (102),** Maier, black, white and gold, illustration of foaming glass against black background "6 for $1.09" 5.50   7.50

☐ **One-O-Two (102) Dark,** Maier, 12 oz., white and red with basketweave background, reads "Continental" (alluding to the fact that dark beer is more popular in Europe than in America) 75.00   100.00

☐ **One-O-Two (102) Draft,** Maier, 12 oz., blue and white, "Draft" in red 10.00   14.00

☐ **One-O-Two (102) Genuine Draft,** Maier, 16 oz.   11.00   15.00

☐ **One-O-Two (102) Pale Dry Brew,** Maier, 16 oz., "6 for $1.25" 5.00   6.50

☐ **One-O-Two (102) Pale Dry Brew,** Maier, 16 oz., "6 for $1.35" 2.50   3.25

☐ **One-O-Two (102) Pale Dry Brew,** General, 16 oz., "6 for $1.54" 1.00   1.75

☐ **One-O-Two (102) Pale Dry Brew,** General, 16 oz., "6 for $1.79" 75   1.25

☐ **One-O-Two (102) Stout Malt Liquor,** General, 16 oz. 11.50   14.75

Price Range

☐ **007 Special Blend Malt Liquor,** National Brewing, 12 oz., set of seven different cans, illustrations of starlets from James Bond films, brand name in white 225.00   275.00

☐ **Original $1000 Natural Process,** Miller, 12 oz., yellow, black and white 7.00   10.00

☐ **Ortlieb's,** Ortlieb Brewing, 12 oz., brand name in white on oval red label, brewer's logo in upper left 2.00   3.00

☐ **Ortlieb's,** Ortlieb, 12 oz., red and white, small brand name, with lengthy message from company president 2.00   2.50

☐ **Ortlieb's,** Ortlieb, 12 oz., white and burgundy . . . 14.00   19.00

☐ **Ortlieb's,** Ortlieb Brewing, 12 oz., Collector's Series, a set of 12 cans showing scenes from the revolutionary war and colonial America, brand name in white on red oval label, illustration of Liberty Bell (This series was released at the Bicentennial.) . . 1.00   1.50

☐ **Ortlieb's Genuine Draft,** Ortlieb Brewing, 12 oz., red, white and blue, brand name in white on red oval label, "Genuine Draft Beer" in blue, "ice-capped" lettering in center of can 2.00   3.00

☐ **Our,** Huber, 12 oz., maroon, gold and red 85   1.10

☐ **Ox Bow,** Walter, 12 oz., blue and gold, symbol of ox head in red 40.00   55.00

☐ **Oyster House,** Pittsburgh, 12 oz., dark brown, gold and silver 40   .65

☐ **Pabst,** Pabst, 7 oz., "Pabst Blue Ribbon" in white lettering, silver at top and bottom 40   .65

☐ **Pabst Blue Ribbon,** Pabst, 12 oz., red, white and blue 2.00   3.00

☐ **Pabst Blue Ribbon,** Pabst, 12 oz., brand name slightly below center of can, white circle inside ribbon 40   .65

☐ **Pabst Blue Ribbon Bock,** Pabst, 12 oz., white, red and blue, ram's head in white, large slogan at bottom 40   .65

☐ **Pabst Blue Ribbon Bock,** Pabst, 12 oz., white, red and blue, ram's head in white, small slogan at bottom 2.85   3.50

☐ **Pabst Blue Ribbon Bock,** Pabst, 12 oz., white, red and blue, two ram heads in red at top 4.00   5.00

☐ **Pabst's Eastside,** Pabst, 16 oz., large "16" near top, does not state "Half Quart" 2.00   2.75

☐ **Pabst Old Tankard Ale,** Pabst, 12 oz., gold, white and red, illustration of man with shield and stein 3.50   4.25

Price Range

☐ **Padre Pale Lager,** Maier, 12 oz., various shades
of brown, illustration of padre mission, canned at
Los Angeles, California 3.50   4.50

☐ **Pathmark Premium Lager,** Forrest Brewing, 12
oz., white and blue 1.00   1.50

☐ **Pathmark Premium Lager,** Hofbrau, 12 oz., white
and blue .... .85   1.15

☐ **Pearl,** Pearl, 12 oz., gold, red and white 11.00   14.75

☐ **Pearl,** Pearl, 12 oz., salmon and red with pictorial
illustration of stream and mountains 1.85   2.25

☐ **Pearl,** Pearl, 12 oz., cream and red with pictorial
illustration of stream and mountains .... .40   .60

☐ **Pearl Draft,** Pearl, 12 oz., gold and red 12.00   16.00

☐ **Pearl Draft,** Pearl, 12 oz., blue and red 22.50   27.50

☐ **Pearl Fine Light,** Pearl, 12 oz., red and white with
illustration of stream and mountains, small brand
name, gray mountains in background .... .90   1.20

☐ **Pearl Lager,** Pearl, 16 oz., upper two thirds of can
has white background 17.50   22.50

☐ **Pearl Lager,** Pearl, 12 oz., white and red with pictorial illustration of stream and mountains 5.00   7.00

☐ **Pearl Lager,** Pearl, 12 oz., white and red with pictorial illustration of stream and mountains 5.50   7.25

☐ **Pearl Light,** Pearl, 8 oz., white and red .... .75   1.00

☐ **Pearl Near Beer,** Pearl, 12 oz., white, dark orange
and yellow, brand name against solid-color (dark
orange) background .... .40   .60

☐ **Pearl Premium Light,** Pearl, 8 oz., white and red 1.75   2.50

☐ **Pearl Premium Light,** Pearl, 12 oz., red and white
with illustration of stream and mountains, large
brand name, pale blue mountain in background of
illustration 3.00   4.00

☐ **Pearl Premium Light,** Pearl, 12 oz., red and white
with illustration of stream and mountains, large
brand name, gray mountains in background of illustration .... .80   1.10

☐ **Peoples,** Peoples Brewing, 12 oz., blue, white and
silver, brand name in blue on white banner on
label, "Hits the Spot" in blue in upper center ... 2.00   3.00

☐ **Pfeiffer,** Associated, 12 oz., gold and white, illustration of buildings 8.00   12.00

☐ **Pfeiffer,** Heileman Brewing, 12 oz., white, gold
and red, brand name in red on white label, illustration in brown of brewery, "Quik-Chill" in top center, can made to look like keg .... .75   1.25

Price Range

☐ **Pfeiffer,** Heileman, 12 oz., brown, blue and gold, illustration of building .... .75   1.25

☐ **Pfeiffer,** Pfeiffer, 12 oz., red, white and blue, smiling glass 6.50   8.50

☐ **Phoenix Ariz. 100th Birthday,** National, 12 oz., white, gold and blue 20.00   25.00

☐ **Pickett's Premium,** Pickett, 12 oz., red, white and blue 1.00   1.50

☐ **Piel's Draft,** Piel, 12 oz., white, red and silver, silver trim at top and bottom 2.75   3.50

☐ **Piel's Draft,** Piel, 12 oz., white with brand name in red, reads "Keg Can" near top .... .65   .85

☐ **Piel's Draft Ale,** Piel, 12 oz., brown, white and black 40.00   50.00

☐ **Piel's Light Lager,** Piel, 12 oz. 4.50   6.00

☐ **Piels Real Draft,** Piel, 16 oz. .... .90   1.35

☐ **Pike's Peak Ale,** Walter, 12 oz., white and gold, illustration of Pike's Peak 30.00   40.00

☐ **Pike's Peak Malt Liquor,** Walter, 12 oz., white and gold 12.00   16.00

☐ **Pike's Peak Malt Liquor,** Walter, 16 oz. 12.00   16.00

☐ **Pilsener Club Premium,** Pearl, 12 oz., blue, white and gold 1.85   2.25

☐ **Pilsener Club Premium,** Storz, 12 oz., blue, white and gold 2.75   3.50

☐ **Pilsener Club Select,** Storz, 12 oz., red, white and blue, small emblem, brand name in red 4.00   6.00

☐ **P.O.C.,** Pilsener, 12 oz., white, gold and red, no gold bands at top and bottom .... .40   .60

☐ **P.O.C.,** Pilsener, 12 oz., white, gold and red, statement of contents on front above gold band at bottom 1.85   2.35

☐ **Point,** Stevens Point, 12 oz., blue, red and white, "Beer" printed horizontally 1.65   2.00

☐ **Point,** Stevens Point, 12 oz., red, white and blue, eagle in red 1.75   2.10

☐ **Polar,** Polar, 12 oz., red, white and blue .... .90   1.20

☐ **Potosi,** Potosi, 12 oz., red, white and gold 1.85   2.25

☐ **Prager Bohemian,** Associated Breweries, 12 oz., white and red, illustration of musicians and man dancing 1.00   1.50

☐ **Preferred Stock,** Hamm, 12 oz., white and black, illustration of city scene 1.75   2.35

Top, Left to Right: **Olde Pub Tavern Brew**, *12 oz.,* **$1.85–$2.30;** *Padre Pale Lager, 12 oz.,* **$2–$2.75.** *Bottom, Left to Right:* **Penn State Iron City,** *12 oz.,* **$2.50–$3.50;** *Point Beer, 12 oz.,* **$1–$2.**

Price Range

☐ **Price Chopper,** Forrest, 12 oz., red and white ..	1.65	2.00
☐ **Primo,** Schlitz, 12 oz., blue and white, brand name in white on blue background, "Hawaiian Beer" in black lettering directly under brand name, small illustration of man in traditional Hawaiian headdress	.75	1.25
☐ **Primo,** Schlitz, 12 oz., gold and white, similar design to above can	2.00	3.00
☐ **Prinz Brau,** Prinz Brau, 12 oz., figures of polar bears on opposite sides of shield with letter P, slogan "The only one brewed with pure Alaska waters"	2.00	3.00
☐ **Prior,** Prior Brewing, 12 oz., white, red and gold, brand name in red on white background, gold heraldic lions above brand name	.75	1.25
☐ **Prior Lager,** Valley Forge, 12 oz., white and black, "Liquid Luxury"	10.00	13.00
☐ **Prizer Extra Dry,** Reading, 12 oz., white, red and gold illustration of stein	.90	1.20
☐ **Pub Malt Liquor,** Home Brewing, 12 oz., brown and beige, brand name in white, illustration of pub takes up entire face of can	2.00	3.50
☐ **Queen's Brau,** Queen City, 12 oz., black, white and gold	3.00	5.00
☐ **Rahr's,** Rahr, 12 oz., dark reddish gold and white	11.00	14.00
☐ **Rainier,** Rainier, 16 oz., bottom one-third of can gold	.90	1.20
☐ **Rainier Ale,** Rainier, 12 oz., green and silver "Ale" in large white lettering	1.40	1.75
☐ **Rainier Ale,** Rainier, 12 oz., green and blue, lengthy message	6.00	8.00
☐ **Rainier Ale,** Rainier, 12 oz., gold and blue double-sided can with same design on both sides	.60	.90
☐ **Rainier Ale,** Sicks, 12 oz., yellow and black	7.50	10.00
☐ **Rainier Bold Malt Liquor,** Rainier, 12 oz., black, white, red and gold, brand name in white on black background, gold unicorn above brand name	9.75	13.75
☐ **Rainier Not So Light,** Sicks, 12 oz., blue and white, gold bands at top and bottom	50.00	65.00
☐ **Rainier Old Stock Ale,** Sicks, 16 oz., brand name in yellow oval	8.00	12.00
☐ **Ram's Head Ale,** Schmidt, 12 oz., gold and black	.40	.60
☐ **Ram's Head Ale,** Schmidt, 12 oz., gold and green	7.00	10.00
☐ **Reading Light,** Reading, 12 oz., red, white and blue	.90	1.20
☐ **Reading Premium,** Reading, 12 oz., black, white and gold	1.40	1.75

Price Range

☐ **Reading Premium,** Reading, 16 oz., blue center, gold rings 1.85   2.25

☐ **Reading Premium,** Reading, 16 oz., blue center, gold rings 90   1.20

☐ **Reading Premium,** Reading, 16 oz., red center, blue rings 3.75   4.75

☐ **Red Cap Ale,** Carling, 12 oz., black, light beige and white, "Red Cap" in large black letters topped by illustration of a red cap, no portrait of man, "Ale" in very thin red script lettering 6.50   8.50

☐ **Red Cap Ale,** Carling, 12 oz., green, very light brown (yellowish brown), and red. "Red Cap" in red letters, portrait of man wearing red cap at lower center, canned at Natick, Massachusetts   1.35   1.80

☐ **Red Cap Ale,** Carling, 12 oz., green, very light brown (yellowish brown) and red, "Red Cap" in red letters, portrait of man wearing red cap at lower center, canned at Baltimore, Maryland . . .   1.85   2.35

☐ **Red Lion Malt Liquor,** Red Lion, 12 oz., dark reddish gold and white 9.75   13.75

☐ **Red Top,** Associated, 12 oz., black and red 5.00   6.50

☐ **Red Top,** Drewry, 12 oz., black and red 5.25   6.75

☐ **Red, White and Blue,** Pabst, 12 oz., red, white and blue, narrow medallion with brand name . . .   1.00   1.50

☐ **Red, White and Blue,** Pabst, 12 oz., red, white and blue, medallion with brand name 40   .60

☐ **Regal,** Pickett, 12 oz., red and white 1.50   2.00

☐ **Regal,** Regal, 12 oz., blue and white 90   1.20

☐ **Regal Brau,** Huber, 12 oz., white, black and gold   .40   .60

☐ **Regal Premium,** Regal, 16 oz. 3.25   4.25

☐ **Regal Select,** General, 12 oz., red, white and blue, "6 for 99¢" 4.00   5.00

☐ **Regal Select,** General, 12 oz., red, white and blue, "6 for $1.09" 3.50   4.50

☐ **Regal Select,** General, 12 oz., red, white and blue, "6 for $1.29" 1.75   2.10

☐ **Regal Select,** General, 12 oz., red, white and blue, no indication of price 75   1.25

☐ **Regal Select,** Maier, 16 oz., "6 for $1.29" 3.00   5.00

☐ **Regal Select,** Maier, 16 oz., "6 for $1.54" 1.75   2.25

☐ **Regal Select,** General, 16 oz., slogan "Recognized as One of America's Two Great Beers" (which was the other one?) 75   1.25

☐ **Regal Select Draft,** Maier, 12 oz., black, white and gold 12.00   16.00

Price Range

☐ **Regency,** Maier, 12 oz., white and red 25.00   35.00
☐ **Regency,** Maier, 12 oz., yellow and white, brand
name in white on red ribbon 20.00   25.00
☐ **Regent Premium,** Champale, 12 oz., red and
white, "Brewery Fresh" 4.50   6.00
☐ **Renner Golden Amber,** Renner, 12 oz., red, gold
and white 4.75   6.50
☐ **Rex,** Fitger, 12 oz., yellow and red 2.50   3.25
☐ **Rex,** Schell, 12 oz., yellow and red 2.50   3.25
☐ **Rheingold Extra Dry,** Rheingold, 7 oz., white and
red 1.00   1.50
☐ **Rheingold Extra Dry Lager,** Rheingold, 12 oz.,
red and white 40   .65
☐ **Rheinlander,** Huber, 12 oz., silver, white and or-
ange, illustration of snow-laden field with trees,
brand name in small letters 6.00   8.00
☐ **Rheinlander,** Rheinlander, 12 oz., white, yellow
and orange, brand name centerized, no silver
bands at top or bottom 2.00   2.75
☐ **Rheinlander,** Rheinlander, 12 oz., white, yellow
and orange, brand name centerized, silver bands
at top and bottom 75   1.25
☐ **Richbrau Premium,** Home, 12 oz., white, black
and red, canned at Richmond, Va. 4.75   6.00
☐ **Richbrau Premium,** Home, 16 oz. 7.50   10.50
☐ **Rock And Roll,** Royal, 12 oz., reverse pictures
leatherjacketed youth of 1950's era, with caption
"I sold my soul for rock and roll" 90   1.20
☐ **Rolling Meadows Anniversary Beer,** Leinenku-
gel, 12 oz., reads "25 Years, 1955–1980" 2.50   3.50
☐ **Rolling Rock,** Latrobe, 12 oz., dark green and
white, brand name centerized in large letters,
reads "Extra Pale" 2.50   3.50
☐ **Rolling Rock Premium Beer,** Latrobe, 7 oz.,
squat, dark green, script lettering 1.00   1.75
☐ **Rolling Rock Premium,** Latrobe, 12 oz., dark
green and white, illustration of waterfall centerized
beneath brand name 40   .65
☐ **Rolling Rock Premium,** Latrobe, 12 oz., dark
green and white, illustration of waterfall to left of
brand name 2.00   2.75
☐ **Royal Amber,** Heileman, 12 oz., gold and white   .75   1.25
☐ **Royal 58,** Heileman Brewing, 12 oz., white, blue
and gold, brand name in blue lettering across top
center, "58" shown in label above a glass of beer   90.00   130.00

Price Range

☐ **Royal Hibernia,** Yuengling, 12 oz., illustration of man with lute serenading woman at window .... .90 1.35

☐ **Schaefer,** Schaefer, 10 oz., white with rows of circular medallions in black, gold and white 1.75 2.75

☐ **Schaefer,** Schaefer, 12 oz., white, red and gold, brand name repeated in balloons around can .. 4.00 5.00

☐ **Schaefer,** Schaefer, 12 oz., white, red and gold, brand name repeated in balloons around can, carries plug for Schaefer Center at New York's World's Fair (1964)........................... 22.50 27.50

☐ **Schaefer,** Schaefer, 12 oz., white, red and gold, revised version of the original "multi balloon" design, now with fewer but larger balloons .... .40 .65

☐ **Schaefer,** Schaefer, 16 oz., reads "One Pint" in white lettering on gold background at top ...... .75 1.25

☐ **Schell,** Schell, 12 oz., black, illustration of moose head against silver background .... .40 .65

☐ **Schell,** Schell, 12 oz., white, light brown and dark brown 20.00 27.50

☐ **Schell,** Schell, 12 oz., black and multicolors, illustration of moose head, reads "It's a Good Old Beer" in pink lettering 1.85 2.20

☐ **Schell,** Schell, 12 oz., black and multicolors, illustration of moose head, reads "It's a Good Ole Beer" in white lettering 1.75 2.50

☐ **Schlitz,** Schlitz, 10 oz., white and maroon ...... .60 .85

☐ **Schlitz,** Schlitz, 12 oz., white and brown, slogan "The Beer That Made Milwaukee Famous" is printed in dark brown script letters .... .90 1.35

☐ **Schlitz,** Schlitz, 12 oz., white and brown, slogan "The Beer That Made Milwaukee Famous" is printed in dark brown script letters, dated 1971 .80 1.05

☐ **Schlitz,** Schlitz, 12 oz., white and brown, slogan "The Beer That Made Milwaukee Famous" is printed in dark brown script letters, dated 1973 .60 .90

☐ **Schlitz,** Schlitz, 12 oz., white and brown, slogan "The Beer That Made Milwaukee Famous" is printed in dark brown script letters, dated 1975 .40 .70

☐ **Schlitz,** Schlitz, 12 oz., white and brown, reads "Pop Top" in brown 2.25 3.00

☐ **Schlitz Light,** Schlitz, 10 oz., cream white, blue artwork and lettering .... .90 1.35

☐ **Schlitz Light,** Schlitz, 12 oz., cream white and blue .... .75 1.25

☐ **Schlitz Malt Liquor,** Schlitz, 8 oz., squat, white, silver and blue, dated 1968 .... 3.00 4.00

Price Range

☐ **Schlitz Malt Liquor,** Schlitz, 8 oz., squat, white, silver and blue, dated 1969 .... 2.50   3.25

☐ **Schlitz Malt Liquor,** Schlitz, 8 oz., white, silver and blue, dated 1970 .... 3.00   4.00

☐ **Schlitz Malt Liquor,** Schlitz, 8 oz., white and silver with blue bull .... .90   1.15

☐ **Schlitz Malt Liquor,** Schlitz, 12 oz., blue, black and white, illustration .... .75   1.25

☐ **Schlitz Malt Liquor,** Schlitz, 16 oz., dark blue bull   .75   1.25

☐ **Schlitz Stout Malt Liquor,** Schlitz, 12 oz., white and gold, blue lettering, "Stout" positioned above "Malt Liquor" instead of all on one line 3.00   4.00

☐ **Schlitz Stout Malt Liquor,** Schlitz, 12 oz., white and gold, blue lettering 4.00   5.50

☐ **Schlitz Stout Malt Liquor,** Schlitz, 16 oz. ...... .90   1.20

☐ **Schmidt's,** Schmidt, 12 oz., antelope (from a later edition of Schmidt's Wildlife Series, originally issued by Associated) 1.00   1.65

☐ **Schmidt's,** Schmidt, 12 oz., auto racing (from a later edition of Schmidt's Wildlife Series, originally issued by Associated) 1.00   1.65

☐ **Schmidt,** Schmidt, 12 oz., ice fishing (from a later edition of Schmidt's Wildlife Series, originally issued by Associated) 1.00   1.65

☐ **Schmidt,** Schmidt, 12 oz., pheasants (from a later edition of Schmidt's Wildlife Series, originally issued by Associated) 1.00   1.65

☐ **Schmidt,** Schmidt, 12 oz., water skiing (from a later edition of Schmidt's Wildlife Series, originally issued by Associated) 1.00   1.65

☐ **Schmidt,** Schmidt, 12 oz., Battle of Germantown at Chew Mansion, Germantown, Pa., October 4, 1777 (from Bicentennial Series, reads "The Beer for the Bicentennial" on front) 1.00   1.65

☐ **Schmidt,** Schmidt, 12 oz., Betsy Ross House, Philadelphia, Pa., Where the First U.S. Flag was made (from Bicentennial Series, reads "The Beer for the Bicentennial" on front) 1.00   1.65

☐ **Schmidt,** Schmidt, 12 oz., Cornwallis Surrenders (from Bicentennial Series, reads "The Beer for the Bicentennial" on front) 1.00   1.65

☐ **Schmidt,** Schmidt, 12 oz., Drafting the Declaration of Independence (from Bicentennial Series, reads "The Beer for the Bicentennial" on front) 1.00   1.65

Top, Left to Right: **Schmidt** *(one of a set of 21 cans depicting outdoor sporting and wildlife scenes), 12 oz.,* **$1–$2;** **Schmidt** *(one of a set of 21 cans depicting outdoor sporting and wildlife scenes), 12 oz.,* **$1–$2.** *Bottom, Left to Right:* **Schmidt** *(one of a set of 21 cans depicting outdoor sporting and wildlife scenes), 12 oz.,* **$1–$2;** **Star,** *12 oz.,* **$.75–$1.25.**

Price Range

☐ **Schmidt,** Schmidt, 12 oz., Elfreth's Alley, Philadelphia, Pa., the Nation's Oldest Colonial Street (from Bicentennial Series, reads "The Beer for the Bicentennial" on front) 1.00   1.65

☐ **Schmidt,** Schmidt, 12 oz., Head House, Philadelphia, Pa., Early Colonial Marketplace (from Bicentennial Series, reads "The Beer for the Bicentennial" on front) 1.00   1.65

☐ **Schmidt,** Schmidt, 12 oz., The Spirit of '76 (from Bicentennial Series, reads "The Beer for the Bicentennial" on front) 1.00   1.65

☐ **Schmidt,** Schmidt, 12 oz., Winter at Valley Forge (from Bicentennial Series, reads "The Beer for the Bicentennial" on front) 1.00   1.65

☐ **Schmidt,** Schmidt, 16 oz., Cornwallis Surrenders (from Bicentennial Series, reads "The Beer for the Bicentennial" on front) 2.00   3.00

☐ **Schmidt,** Schmidt, 16 oz., Drafting Declaration of Independence (from Bicentennial Series, reads "The Beer for the Bicentennial" on front) 2.00   3.00

☐ **Schmidt,** Schmidt, 16 oz., Winter at Valley Forge (from Bicentennial Series, reads "The Beer for the Bicentennial" on front) 2.00   3.00

☐ **Schmidt's Bock,** Schmidt, 12 oz., red, white and gold, illustration of ram's head 37.50   47.50

☐ **Schmidt Draft,** Associated, 12 oz., red and white, "Draft" in large yellow letters near top 3.50   4.50

☐ **Schmidt Draft,** Associated, 16 oz., "16" under brand name 8.00   12.00

☐ **Schmidt Draft,** Heileman, 12 oz., red and white, "Draft Brewed" in yellow letters near top ...... .40   .65

☐ **Schmidt Draft,** Associated, 16 oz., moose (from pictorial series) 12.00   16.00

☐ **Schmidt Draft,** Associated, 16 oz., wild horses (from pictorial series) 12.00   16.00

☐ **Schmidt Draft,** Associated, 16 oz., covered wagon (from pictorial series) 12.00   16.00

☐ **Schmidt Draft,** Heileman, 12 oz., red and white, "Draft" in large yellow letters near top .... .85   1.15

☐ **Schmidt Draft,** Heileman, 16 oz., "Half Quart" under brand name .... .90   1.35

☐ **Schmidt Draft,** Heileman, 16 oz., "16" under brand name 1.35   1.85

☐ **Schmidt's Extra Special,** Associated, 12 oz., blue and white 2.75   3.50

Price Range

☐ **Schmidt's Light,** Schmidt, 12 oz., gold, red and white	4.75	6.50
☐ **Schmidt's Light,** Schmidt, 12 oz., pale gold, red and white, coat-of-arms not in colors, words "Light Beer" both appear on same line	.75	1.25
☐ **Schmidt's Light,** Schmidt, 16 oz., words "Light" and "Beer" appear on separate lines	1.00	3.00
☐ **Schmidt's Select Near Beer,** Associated, 12 oz., blue, white and gold	2.75	3.75
☐ **Schmidt's Select Near Beer,** Heileman, 12 oz., blue, white and gold	.40	.65
☐ **Schoenling Lager,** Schoenling, 12 oz., red and white, statement of contents near top	.90	1.20
☐ **Schoenling Lager,** Schoenling, 12 oz., red and white, statement of contents near bottom	4.50	6.00
☐ **Schoenling Lager,** Schoenling, 12 oz., red, white and gold	9.50	12.50
☐ **Schwegmann Premium Light,** Buckeye, 12 oz., purple and white	17.50	22.50
☐ **Schwegmann Premium Light,** Cumberland, 12 oz., purple and white	15.00	20.00
☐ **Schwegmann Premium Light,** Cumberland, 12 oz., purple and white	15.00	20.00
☐ **Scotch Buy Light,** Falstaff, 12 oz., Scotch plaid and smiling face near top	.75	1.25
☐ **Select 20 Grand Cream Ale,** Associated, 12 oz., green and yellow	8.00	10.00
☐ **Seven Eleven (7-11),** Garden State, 12 oz., gold and red, canned for sale at 7-11 Convenience stores	20.00	25.00
☐ **Seven Springs Mountain,** Pittsburgh Brewing, 12 oz., blue and white	1.00	1.35
☐ **SGA,** Associated, 12 oz., gold and white	2.75	3.50
☐ **SGA,** Heileman, 12 oz., gold and white	2.00	2.50
☐ **SGA,** Heileman, 12 oz., red, white and blue	.40	.60
☐ **Shell's City Pilsener Premium,** S.C., 12 oz., white and red, globe of world	26.00	32.00
☐ **Shenanigan's Premium,** Yuengling, 12 oz., multi-colored pictorial	.90	1.20
☐ **Sheridan,** Walter, 12 oz., gold, white and red, illustration of bucking bronco	10.00	14.00
☐ **Shiner,** Spoetzl, 12 oz., gold, white and red, small brand name	1.85	2.30
☐ **Shiner,** Spoetzl, 12 oz., gold, white and red, large brand name	3.00	4.00

Price Range

☐ **Shiner,** Spoetzl, 12 oz., gold and red	.75	1.25
☐ **Shop Rite,** Eastern, 12 oz., gold, red and white, brand name in circle near top, made for sale in Shop Rite supermarket chain	.75	1.25
☐ **Shopwell Premium,** Colonial, 12 oz., red and gold, brand name in diamond	1.00	1.40
☐ **Silver Peak,** Falstaff, 12 oz., blue and white, no blue band at bottom	2.45	3.00
☐ **Silver Peak,** Tivoli, 12 oz., blue and white	10.00	13.25
☐ **Silver Top Old Time Lager,** Duquesne, 12 oz., red and silver, brand name in thick lettering	3.00	5.00
☐ **Silver Top Old Time Lager,** Duquesne, 12 oz., red and silver, brand name in thin lettering	3.00	5.00
☐ **Ski Country Premium,** Walter, 12 oz., white, green, red and blue, illustration of snow-covered mountains	22.50	27.50
☐ **Slim Price,** Pearl, 12 oz.	.80	1.10
☐ **Slim Price Light,** Pearl, 12 oz.	.80	1.10
☐ **Soul "Mellow Yellow",** Maier, 12 oz.	275.00	325.00
☐ **Soul Stout,** Maier, 12 oz.	230.00	270.00
☐ **Sparkling Stite,** Heileman, 8 oz., squat, with red band near top	1.75	2.50
☐ **Sparkling Stite,** Heileman, 12 oz., white	1.85	2.30
☐ **Spearman Ale,** Century Brewing, 12 oz., white, green and red, brand name in white on red banner in center, illustration of man in upper center holding a glass	20.00	27.50
☐ **Special Export,** Heileman, 12 oz., green and white	.75	1.25
☐ **Spike Driver,** Walter, 12 oz.	.75	1.25
☐ **Sportsman,** Maier, 12 oz., gold, white and red . .	23.00	30.00
☐ **Spring,** General, 12 oz., light blue and dark blue, does not state price	1.40	1.90
☐ **Spring,** General, 12 oz., light blue and dark blue, "6 for 89¢", c. 1962	10.00	14.00
☐ **Springfield,** General, 12 oz., white and gold	.40	.65
☐ **Springfield Fine Light,** Falstaff, 12 oz., white and gold	1.00	1.65
☐ **Spur Stout Malt Liquor,** Sicks, 12 oz., white, brown and red	35.00	45.00
☐ **Spur Stout Malt Liquor,** Sicks, 16 oz.	30.00	40.00
☐ **Stag,** Carling, 12 oz., gold, white and red, brand name in large lettering, directly at center of can	1.75	2.25
☐ **Stag,** Carling, 12 oz., gold, white and red, brand name in large lettering, slightly below center of can	2.75	3.75

Price Range

☐ **Stag,** Stag, 12 oz., gold, white and red, small brand name .... .40 .65

☐ **Stag,** Carling, 16 oz., "Half Quart" in large white letters near top 4.50 6.00

☐ **Stag,** Carling, 16 oz., does not state "Half Quart" 1.75 2.50

☐ **Stag Light,** Carling, 12 oz., deer head symbol, slogan "A Brewing Heritage Since 1851" 1.00 1.65

☐ **Stallion XII,** Gold Medal, 12 oz., gold, white and red, illustration of horse 50.00 60.00

☐ **Standard Cream Ale,** Standard Rochester, 12 oz., green, white and gold 14.00 19.00

☐ **Standard Dry Ale,** Eastern, 12 oz., blue, white and gold .... .85 1.25

☐ **Standard Dry Ale,** Standard Rochester, 12 oz., blue, white and gold 3.75 4.75

☐ **State Fair Premium,** Fuhrmann and Schmidt, 12 oz., silver and blue 40.00 50.00

☐ **Stegmaier Gold Medal,** Stegmaier, 12 oz., gold and white .... .75 1.25

☐ **Steinbrau Genuine Draft,** Maier, 12 oz., black, red and gold 20.00 27.50

☐ **Steinbrau Pale Dry Lager,** General, 12 oz., white and red, illustration of stein, canned at Los Angeles, California 1.85 2.30

☐ **Steinbrau Pale Dry Lager,** General, 16 oz. 15.00 20.00

☐ **Steinbrau Malt Beverage, Near Beer,** Eastern, 12 oz., white and red .... .40 .65

☐ **Steinhaus,** Schell Brewing, 12 oz., white, blue and gold, brand name in red on gold background, illustration of two men sitting at a table holding beer steins 20.00 25.00

☐ **Steinhaus,** Schell, 12 oz., white and yellow 2.85 3.35

☐ **Steinhaus,** Steinhaus, 12 oz., white and yellow 20.00 30.00

☐ **Sterling,** Associated, 16 oz., red "16" near top 3.50 4.50

☐ **Sterling,** Heileman, 16 oz., red "16" near top .. 2.50 3.50

☐ **Sterling,** Sterling, 12 oz., light silver, maroon and black, statement of contents appears to right of vertical ribbon 2.50 3.50

☐ **Sterling,** Sterling, 16 oz., speckled 8.00 11.00

☐ **Sterling,** Sterling, 16 oz., red "16" near top 5.50 7.00

☐ **Sterling Premium Draft,** Sterling, 12 oz., brown, blue and red, grained to resemble keg 9.75 12.50

☐ **Sterling Premium Pilsener,** Sterling, 12 oz., silver, blue and red, reads "Premium" above brand name, red oval behind brand name is narrow ... 4.00 5.25

Price Range

☐ **Sterling Premium Pilsener,** Sterling, 12 oz., silver, maroon and white, speckled can 3.25 5.00

☐ **Stoney's Pilsener,** Jones, 12 oz., gold, white and red, brand name in red 1.00 1.65

☐ **Storz,** Storz Brewing, 12 oz., white, blue, red and gold, brand name in white on red banner in center of can, gold bands at bottom and top 5.00 7.00

☐ **Storz Draft,** Storz Brewing, 12 oz., white, red and blue, brand name in white on red banner in upper center, "draft" in large block lettering in center of can 10.00 14.00

☐ **Stroh's Bohemian Style,** Stroh, 16 oz., does not state "Half Quart" 1.35 2.00

☐ **Stroh's Bohemian Style,** Stroh, 12 oz., white and gold, states "12 Fl. Oz." in dark letters near bottom of can .... .40 .65

☐ **Stroh's Bohemian Style,** Stroh, 12 oz., white and gold, brand name in script lettering .... .70 1.00

☐ **Sunshine Premium,** Sunshine, 12 oz., white and red with thin gold band at top and bottom, does not read "Extra Dry" above brand name 25.00 35.00

☐ **Sunshine Premium,** Sunshine, 12 oz., white and red with thin gold band at top and bottom, reads "Extra Dry" above brand name 20.00 25.00

☐ **Sunshine Premium,** Sunshine, 12 oz., white with yellow and orange sun symbol 20.00 27.50

☐ **Supreme Pilsner,** Maier, 16 oz. 11.50 15.50

☐ **Swinger Malt Liquor,** Maier, 12 oz., blue and white, "6 for $1.29" 35.00 45.00

☐ **Tap, Bohemian,** Burger, 12 oz., dark brown with brand name in white pyramid 5.00 7.00

☐ **Tap Genuine Draft,** Storz, 12 oz., brown and white, made to resemble keg 9.75 13.75

☐ **Tech Premium,** Pittsburgh, 12 oz., white, red and Scotch plaid 1.85 2.50

☐ **Tech Premium,** Pittsburgh, 12 oz., white and red, brand name in small letters .... .75 1.25

☐ **Tennent's,** Tennent, 12 oz., Penny in the Morning, foreign can .... .75 1.25

☐ **Tennent's,** Tennent, 12 oz., Penny at Noon, foreign can .... .75 1.25

☐ **Tennent's,** Tennent, 12 oz., Penny in the Evening, foreign can .... .75 1.25

☐ **Tex Super Light Lager,** Jackson, 12 oz., silver and blue 14.00 18.50

Price Range

☐ **Texas Pride Extra Light,** Pearl, 12 oz., blue, white
and silver, map of Texas in white 1.35   1.85
☐ **Texas Pride Extra Light,** Pearl, 12 oz., blue, white
and silver, map of Texas in silver 90   1.35
☐ **Time Saver,** Royal, 12 oz., salmon, gold and red   .90   1.35
☐ **Tivoli,** Falstaff, 12 oz., white and blue 1.50   2.30
☐ **Tivoli,** General, 12 oz., white and blue 2.00   2.65
☐ **Tivoli Gardens Light Colorado,** Tivoli, 12 oz.,
white and blue 90.00   115.00
*Note: Tivoli Gardens is an amusement resort in
Copenhagen, Denmark.*
☐ **Tomahawk Ale,** International Brewing, 12 oz.,
white and green 100.00   125.00
☐ **Topper Light Dry Pilsener,** Eastern, 12 oz., white
and red 75   1.25
☐ **Topper Real Draft,** Standard Rochester, 12 oz.,
white, red and black 11.00   15.00
☐ **Triumph,** Storz, 12 oz., white, red, blue and gold   .90   1.20
☐ **Tropical Ale,** Associated, 12 oz., green, white and
gold 9.50   13.50
☐ **Tubor,** Carling, 12 oz., dark gold and dark red . .   .40   .65
☐ **Tubor,** Carling, 12 oz., gold and red, lettering near
bottom in dark type 2.00   3.00
☐ **Tubor,** Carling, 16 oz. 90   1.20
☐ **Tuborg,** Carling, 10 oz., gold with red medallion
topped by crown 8.00   12.00
☐ **Tuborg Gold,** Carling, 16 oz., gold 90   1.35
☐ **Tudor Ale,** Cumberland, 12 oz., green and white,
small red "A & P" logo above brand name 1.85   2.65
☐ **Tudor Ale,** Valley Forge, 12 oz., green and white,
small red "A & P" logo above brand name 75   1.25
☐ **Tudor Pilsner,** Cumberland, 12 oz., white and red,
"A & P" logo above brand name 4.00   5.00
☐ **Tudor Premium,** Cumberland, 12 oz., gold and
black, red "A & P" logo above brand name 90   1.35
☐ **Twenty Grand Cream Ale,** Associated, 12 oz.,
green and yellow 15.00   20.00
☐ **Utica Club Cream Ale,** West End, 12 oz., cream
and dark brown, does not state "Extra Dry" 75   1.25
☐ **Utica Club Extra Dry Cream Ale,** West End, 12
oz., gold, white and green, brand name in green   5.00   6.25
☐ **Utica Club Extra Dry Cream Ale,** West End, 12
oz., gold and black 20.00   25.00
☐ **Utica Club Pilsener Lager,** West End, 12 oz., gold
and pale blue 8.00   12.00

Price Range

☐ **Utica Club Pilsener Lager,** West End, 16 oz., red
at top with "16 ozs." in white, repetively printed   1.00   1.65
☐ **Utica Club Pilsener Lager,** West End, 16 oz., gold
at top 1.80   2.30
☐ **Valley Forge Old Tavern,** Schmidt, 12 oz., gold,
white and red 1.75   2.25
☐ **Value Line Premium Lager,** General, 12 oz., red,
yellow and white 5.75   7.25
☐ **Value Line Premium Lager,** Hamm, 12 oz., silver,
blue and white 16.00   20.00
☐ **Van Dyke Export,** Van Dyke, 12 oz., blue, white
and silver 22.00   28.00
☐ **Van Dyke Lager,** Van Dyke, 12 oz., red and white,
portrait of Van Dyke (Dutch artist of 17th century)   20.00   25.00
☐ **Van Merritt,** Peter Hand, 12 oz., green and white,
multicolor illustration of windmill 90   1.20
☐ **Velvet Glove Malt Liquor,** Hamm, 12 oz., white,
dark brown and yellow 15.00   20.00
☐ **Velvet Glove Malt Liquor,** Heublein, 16 oz. 24.00   31.00
☐ **Velvet Glow,** General, 12 oz., white, yellow and
red 2.75   3.50
☐ **Velvet Glow,** Maier, 12 oz., white, gold and red,
brand name in white lettering 5.50   7.25
☐ **Velvet Glow,** Maier, 16 oz. 40.00   50.00
☐ **Waldbaum's Premium Lager,** Eastern, 12 oz.,
red, white and gold 25.00   32.00
☐ **Walter's,** Walter, 12 oz., red, white and black . .   5.00   7.00
☐ **Walter's,** Walter, 12 oz., gold, white and red,
brand name in white on red background 2.00   2.50
☐ **Walter's Bock,** Walter, 12 oz., white, green and
red, pictorial scene, red medallion with ram's head   16.00   20.00
☐ **Walter's Colorado,** Walter, 12 oz., white and red,
illustration of rocky mountains, slogan "Pure
Rocky Mountain Water" 2.00   2.50
☐ **Walter's Light Ale,** Walter, 12 oz., red, white and
blue, Bicentennial issue 1.00   1.35
☐ **Walter's Premium,** Walter, 16 oz. 2.75   3.50
☐ **Weisbrod The Pearless Pilsener,** Old Dutch, 12
oz., salmon and white, trademark of German eagle   12.00   15.00
☐ **Weiss Bavarian Pilsener,** General, 12 oz., red,
white and blue, illustration of mountain peak . . .   3.50   4.25
☐ **Weiss Bavarian Pilsner,** Maier, 12 oz., red, white
and blue, illustration of mountain peak 7.00   10.00
☐ **Wellington Malt Liquor,** Walter, 12 oz., pale blue
and black 4.75   6.00

Price Range

☐ **Wellington Malt Liquor,** Walter, 16 oz.	3.00	5.00
☐ **Western,** Cold Spring, 12 oz., red, white and black	.90	1.25
☐ **Westover Premium Light,** Eastern, 12 oz., white and red	110.00	145.00
☐ **Westover Premium Light,** Old Dutch, 12 oz., white and red	130.00	160.00
☐ **West Virginia Pilsner,** Little Switzerland, 12 oz., white, red and gold	3.00	4.00
☐ **Wiedeman,** Heileman, 12 oz., red, white and blue, thick red frame around brand name	1.50	2.30
☐ **Wiedemann Genuine Draft,** Weidemann, 12 oz., red and white	2.15	2.65
☐ **Whale's White Ale,** National, 12 oz., black and white	15.00	20.00
☐ **Whale's White Ale,** National, 16 oz.	12.00	16.00
☐ **Wilco,** Colonial, 12 oz., blue and green	14.00	19.00
☐ **Winchester Malt Liquor,** Walter, 12 oz., pale blue	4.50	5.75
☐ **Winchester Malt Liquor,** Walter, 16 oz.	3.00	4.50
☐ **Winchester Stout,** Walter, 12 oz., cream white and gold	45.00	60.00
☐ **Wisconsin Club Premium Pilsner,** Huber, 12 oz., white and gold, brand name in white	1.00	1.65
☐ **Wisconsin Gold Label,** Huber, 12 oz., white and gold, brand name in gold, very ornate gold designing	.75	1.25
☐ **Wisconsin Gold Label Premium,** Huber, 12 oz., gold and white	5.75	7.25
☐ **Wisconsin Holiday,** Huber, 12 oz., white and red	1.00	1.30
☐ **Wisconsin Premium,** Heileman, 12 oz., white, red and blue, small map of Wisconsin	1.00	1.30
☐ **Wunderbar,** Minneapolis Brewing, 12 oz., light gold and dark gold with blue and white	9.50	13.50
☐ **Wunderbrau Malt Beverage, Near Beer,** Erie, 12 oz., blue and white, coat of arms	11.00	15.00
☐ **Yuengling Premium,** Yuengling, 12 oz., silver and red, eagle symbol near top, in red	.90	1.35

BREWERIANA MARKET REVIEW

The first thing that anyone unfamiliar with the breweriana market should know is that it is a completely separate hobby from beer cans. The two fields occasionally overlap in collections or on dealer lists but this is usually kept at a minimum. It is enough of a challenge to collect one or the other, much less both.

Top, Left to Right: **Schlitz**, *12 oz.,* **$2.25–$3;** **Schmidt's Extra Special**, *12 oz.,* **$2.75–$3.50.** *Bottom, Left to Right:* **Topper Light Dry Pilsener**, *12 oz.,* **$ .85–$1.10;** **Triumph**, *12 oz.,* **$ .90–$1.20.**

Top, Left to Right: **Walters Colorado**, *12 oz.,* **$1.50–$2.50;** **WEIR Radio** *(a Pittsburgh radio station), 12 oz.,* **$.75–$1.25.** *Bottom, Left to Right:* **World-Wide Charter Membership Can** *(produced in limited quantities for now defunct club), 12 oz.,* **$12.50–$17.50;** **World-Wide 1975 Membership Can,** *12 oz.,* **$8–$12.**

Breweriana is doing well according to most dealers in the field. Prices are increasing slowly but steadily, and supply is staying fairly constant. Dealers are also reporting a healthy growth in the number of new collectors.

Breweriana from the pre-World War II era is doing very well, especially those items that picture a specific brewery. This includes trays, paper or tin signs and beer glasses. Coasters from that period are also very strong, although coasters tend to be a real specialty field. Coaster collectors generally tend to collect nothing else. There's such a variety of them that you can spend a lot of time just in that area. Prices on coasters have been steadily increasing. There have been several $200 coasters recently; a trend that should continue. Pieces from before 1920 are especially in demand. These items often have illustrations of children or pretty girls. These are very popular. Look for continued growth in the entire pre-World War II field.

Items from 1940 up until the present have not enjoyed the same growth as the earlier items. However, the market on these items has stayed stable and a smart purchase will usually turn out to be a sound investment. The post-1940 items are more often bought simply for use or enjoyment than the pre-1940 breweriana. Having a bar in the basement is becoming increasingly popular, so demand from that quarter is on the rise. Regional collecting is also very common in the more recent items. For instance, a resident of New York City might specialize in breweriana from the Jacob Ruppert Brewery.

The smaller fields, such as tap knobs, openers or calendars, continue to have their separate followings, but they are limited. In many of these areas, the supply of collectible items is very limited, which will certainly inhibit the number of new collectors. In other small fields (e.g. payroll checks from breweries) collector interest is just not very strong. These fields will always have their collectors but will probably not grow very much.

What should you collect from today's breweriana? A good rule of thumb is that the cheaper items will generally not become valuable. It's usually a better investment to buy one $100 item than four at $25 a piece. A $100 item will usually appreciate in value more than one for $25. The collector's enjoyment of the piece should always be the deciding factor, however. Beer bottle caps are really starting to increase in value. These are low-priced items and will probably never exceed more than a few dollars for one, but they are numerous and fun to collect.

Look for continued growth in the breweriana market overall. If you haven't already, join one of the two breweriana associations listed in the "Organizations" section in this book. They will assist you in your hobby. Most of all, have fun.

ABOUT THE BREWERIANA PRICES

Prices for the breweriana collectibles in this section are for specimens showing signs of use and age, but *without* serious defects of any kind. Actual mint specimens, which are hardly ever found among the older items, sell for higher prices than those listed. Damaged or restored specimens bring lower prices.

ASHTRAYS

Ashtrays represent one more article from the vast array of those made for breweries to be used in taverns and restaurants. In a sense this was a tray of another kind—like the serving tray and tip tray—and could be designed along precisely the same lines. All it required was a lip on the rim and a few grooves for resting cigarettes or cigars. Beer-related ashtrays are found in various metals as well as ceramic and glass, and also the hard non-scorchable plastic from which many ordinary commercial ashtrays are made. They are *not* found in celluloid, a highly flammable substance.

Not every tavern or restaurant patron was a smoker, but an ashtray was sure to be on the table anyway. So it was another ideal advertising vehicle. Obviously it would not attract as much notice as a 14" serving tray. But there is the matter of competition to be considered. The serving tray that arrived at your table might advertise X's beer, while the ashtray advertised Y's. If Y's ashtray was not on your table you would only get X's advertising message. It was considered appropriate to attack from all sides.

Since ashtrays were scrubbed hard in cleaning, some specimens have their designs partly or very badly worn off. This is particularly true of glass, where a good scrubbing with a wire brush would remove the whole design in a few seconds. The mint specimen is the exception, but is seldom available if the ashtray is old. In that case, most hobbyists will settle for one showing nothing more alarming than a few scratches.

	Price Range	
☐ **Arrow,** arrow shaped, silver finish with brand name in red	20.00	30.00
☐ **Bass,** brass, square, with brand logo at one corner, wording "Bass in Bottles," made in England, 5½"	30.00	40.00
☐ **Bavarian,** clear glass, red lettering, "Bavarian Premium Beer, Mount Carbon Brewery, Pottsville, Pa."	3.50	5.00
☐ **Carlsberg,** ceramic, illustration of Copenhagen skyline, wording, "Carlsberg, Brewed in Copenhagen, City of Beautiful Towers," made in Britain	2.00	3.00
☐ **Columbia,** clear glass, wording "Columbia Premium Beer, Columbia Brewing Co., Shenandoah, Pa.," late 1960's	7.00	10.00
☐ **Coors,** ceramic, white, circular, with wording "Coor's, America's Fine Light Beer, Brewed with Pure Rocky Mountain Spring Water," 6"	4.00	5.00
☐ **Dinkel Acker,** plastic, white, yellow and black border, with logo	1.00	1.50
☐ **Holsten,** ceramic, white, circular, wording "Holsten Beer" in black, 4", made in Germany	20.00	25.00

	Price Range	
☐ **Mackeson,** ceramic, square, black with red lettering, wording "At a Time Like This . . . Mackeson," 5″, made in Britain	5.00	7.00
☐ **Old Shay Ale,** tin, silver colored, black lettering, wording "Old Shay Ale, Product of the Fort Pitt Brewing Co., Jeanette, Pa. Plant," believed to date from the mid 1950's	15.00	20.00
☐ **Stegmaier's,** tin, lettering is stamped, reads "Stegmaier's Gold Medal Beer, Since 1857. Stegmaier Brewing Co., Wilkes-Barre, Pa."	5.00	7.00
☐ **Tuborg,** ceramic, circular, red, lettering in white, 6″, made in Denmark	10.00	15.00
☐ **Weinhard's,** imitation pewter, circular, wording "Drink Weinhard's Beer, Portland, Ore.," also "Purity is Health"	20.00	25.00
☐ **Whitebread,** plastic, circular, blue, lettering in multicolors, reads, "Whitebread Tankard Helps Me Excel," large 9″ tray, made in Britain	5.00	7.00

BEER STEINS

The earliest decorated drinking ware that has come to light in our time was made in Europe during the Bronze age. The ornamentation was crude by later standards, but they are the first attempts at combining art and utility in a drinking vessel. The Northern people of Europe were especially adept at producing beautiful drinking wares. They used gold as well as bronze and other materials. Many fine specimens have been found in ancient Norse graves.

The next flowering of this art was during the Renaissance. Every European nation developed its own style of drinking stein. The Swiss and Germans were especially fond of figural steins made of silver and wood.

The craft has survived to the present day, especially in Germany, Switzerland and Austria.

A stein is defined as a drinking vessel with a lid and a handle, but collectors will usually accept an attractive piece that doesn't necessarily fit the requirements.

Note: All prices are for items in very good condition. In the older steins, some small imperfections are tolerated.

	Price Range	
☐ **Blown Glass Stein,** German, etched decoration, knobbed finial, pewter lid, height 9½″	100.00	150.00
☐ **Blown Glass Stein,** English, green glass, enamel decor of King Arthur, winged helmet lid, height 14½″	350.00	450.00

Price Range

☐ **Capo-Di-Monte Style Stein,** relief decoration of a lion hunt, lion finial, capacity 1 liter, height 8½" *(Capo-Di-Monte was a porcelain factory in Naples, Italy that produced pieces of great complexity and detail usually in high relief.)* 500.00 700.00

☐ **Cut Glass Stein,** German, shows a silhouette of Frankfurt, Germany, capacity ½ liter, height 5½" 225.00 275.00

☐ **Cut Glass Stein,** English, etched design of a ship "HMS Pelikan 1895/98," gilded lip, pewter lid, height 16½" 250.00 300.00

☐ **Cut Glass Stein,** Swiss, etched decoration of pastoral scene, pewter lid, capacity ½ liter, height 12" 175.00 225.00

☐ **Cut Glass Stein,** German, ribbed body, pewter lid with brass "4-F" design, thumblift, capacity ½ liter, height 6" 75.00 100.00

☐ **Faience Stein,** Dutch (Goudy), landscape illustration, capacity ½ liter, height 6" 150.00 200.00

☐ **Faience Stein,** German, modern reproduction, glazed flower design, ball finial, capacity 1 liter, height 7½" 150.00 200.00

Character Stein, German, *post World War II, porcelain, potrays Bismarck, capacity ½ liter, height 7¼",* **$75–$100.**

Price Range

☐ **Faience Stein,** Austrian, pear-shaped, inscription in German, illustrations of flowers around inscription, small knobbed finial, capacity 1½″ liter, height 5½″ 175.00   225.00

☐ **Faience Stein,** German, dated 1804, knobbed finial, capacity 1 liter, height 7″ 75.00   125.00

Rare Ivory Stein, dates from 1700's, very high relief on design, stein rests on mask feet, finial portrays abduction of Sabine woman, height 22″, *$5000–$8000.*

Price Range

☐ **Meissen Stein,** German, dates from the 18th century, floral decoration, domed lid, knobbed finial, no handle, capacity ½ liter, height 6″ *(Meissen was a firm that specialized in making very delicate and fine porcelain pieces. The firm was especially successful in the 18th and 19th centuries.)* 2250.00   2750.00

☐ **Meissen Stein,** German, dates from the 19th century, white body with crossed swords and crowned shield, blue glaze, pewter lid, capacity ½ liter, height 6″ 325.00   425.00

☐ **Meissen Stein,** German, dates from 18th century, crossed swords, marked "MP" beneath swords in blue glaze, capacity 1 liter, height 7½″ 300.00   500.00

☐ **Mettlach Stein,** German, Villeroy & Boch # 675, barrel design, inlaid lid, ball finial, horizontal ribbing, capacity ½ liter, height 5¼″ *(Mettlach was the town in Germany where the firm of Villeroy & Boch made their steins.)* 75.00   100.00

☐ **Mettlach Stein,** German, Villeroy & Boch # 2632, etched design, inlaid lid, illustration of men in a tavern, capacity ½ liter, height 8″ 100.00   150.00

☐ **Occupational Stein,** German, porcelain, lithophane of a butcher, capacity ½ liter, height 10″ *(Occupational steins were items made to be given as awards to employees for long years of service. There are steins illustrating nearly every occupation.)* 100.00   175.00

☐ **Porcelain Tankard,** German, handpainted illustrations of lovers, brass fittings, figural handle, lid painted inside and out, warriors depicted on the interior, capacity ½ liter, height 8″ 1400.00   1900.00

☐ **Porcelain Stein,** Swiss, handpainted scene of woman bowing to warrior, lid painted inside and out, capacity ½ liter, height 6″ 1000.00   1400.00

☐ **Westerwald Stoneware Stein,** German, saltglazed, dates from the 18th century, capacity ½ liter, height 6″ *(The Westerwald is a region in Germany that was very important in early stoneware production. These items can date back to the early 16th century. Salt glazing is a technique where salt is thrown into the kiln during firing. The pieces are covered with a finely mottled glaze.)* 100.00   150.00

☐ **Westerwald Stoneware Stein,** German, marked "Hanke" relief decoration, capacity 1 liter, height 10″ 75.00   100.00

Mettlach Stein, German, Villeroy & Boch, # 1498, etched decoration of man in traditional garb, pewter lid, capacity 5½ liter, height 21", **$800–$1100.**

	Price Range	
☐ **Westerwald Stoneware Stein,** German, dates from about 1900, relief decoration of musicians, capacity ½ liter, height 8½"	75.00	100.00
☐ **Westerwald Stoneware Stein,** German, dates from about 1900, relief decoration of two women and a man talking, also a music box, capacity ½ liter, height 11"	125.00	175.00

Porcelain Pouring Jug, *possibly Scandinavian, face illustrated on neck, ball finial, height 12¼", $100–$165.*

CALENDARS

Both wall and desk calendars were issued by breweries, in a variety of sizes. They were considered a marvelous advertising tool, as they were inexpensive to produce and would remain on view for one full year. Collectors should realize that despite the large quantities that were printed of most brewery calendars (and advertising calendars in general), the survival rate was quite low. This was the type of item that got discarded when it had served its purpose. Hardly anybody would bother to put away, for posterity, an outdated calendar. And certainly nobody in the earlier decades of this century could have imagined that such things would become desirable items for collectors.

Westerwald Stoneware Stein, *German, marked "Reinhold Merkelbach," capacity 1 liter, height 11", **$100–$165.***

Whether a calendar is a wall or desk model, it will be one of two basic types. It will either be the "fold over" variety, in which a page is turned each month to reveal a new picture and new month; or the so-called stationary type which has just one picture to serve for the whole year. Most brewery calendars were of the latter kind. The months and days were printed on a light grade of white paper and arranged like a writing tablet, one on top of the other, and stapled or otherwise attached at the lower portion of the calendar. At the end of the month, the sheet representing the expired month was merely torn off. It should be needless to point out that such calendars are very difficult to get in good condition.

Though any kind of good artwork is desirable on a brewery calendar, collectors are particularly interested in those picturing the brewery's factory. Also desirable are those showing early beer cans. But many brewers made a special effort to avoid giving their calendars the appearance of an advertisement.

Price Range

☐ **Flanagan Nay Brewing Co.,** 1935, non-pictorial, has name in diamond frame at top with tear-off pages, 8" x 11" 20.00   30.00

☐ **Ruppert,** 1950, picture of the Statue of Liberty with New York City skyline at evening 20.00   30.00

☐ **Schmidt's of Philadelphia,** 1978, plastic on cardboard, 15" x 10" 2.00   3.00

☐ **Shiner Beer,** 1977, satirical drawing of dogs playing cards and drinking beer, 18" x 28" 10.00   15.00

CHECKS

Checks issued by brewing companies are highly collectible. They are often very decorative, with the company logo and sometimes an engraving of the headquarters or other pictorial work. The general rule with checks is, "the older the better," but this applies mainly to checks issued by the same brewery. If the issuing brewery was minor and short-lived, the check could be quite valuable even if not particularly early. Collectors are more interested in checks from the small breweries than those of the giants as these tend to be the rare ones. By the same token a plain check (no pictorial decoration) can outsell a fancy one, depending on the issuing brewery. Whenever you see a check dating before 1900 from a brewery whose name you do not recognize, it is very likely to have at least a moderate value.

Brewery checks can be bought from the breweriana dealers and via breweriana auction sales. These are not your only potential sources of supply, however. While such items as beer cans and tap knobs are "pure breweriana," checks overlap into another popular hobby: "financial Americana." This hobby centers on checks, stock certificates, and anything pertaining to financial investment. There are many dealers in this field, who, like the breweriana dealers, also issue price lists and run auction sales. You will discover some brewery-related items among their offerings and on occasion the prices will be low, as these sellers are not catering to a breweriana-oriented clientele. It is also worth checking the lists issued by autograph dealers, and even those put out by dealers in paper money.

Price Range

☐ **Becker Brewing and Malting Co.,** name printed in large gothic lettering, 1901 .... 8.00   12.00

☐ **Becker Brewing and Malting Co.,** engraving of company headquarters, 1911 .... 8.00   12.00

Price Range

☐ **Blatz Brewing Co.,** Philadelphia, ornamental
blank check (unused) from the 1870's 15.00   20.00

CLOCKS

☐ **Carling,** electric, 14″ x 18″ 22.00   29.00
☐ **Falls City,** dated 1956 ....   30.00   40.00
☐ **Pabst Blue Ribbon,** wood, pictorial glass, over-
hanging lamp at top, 11″ x 23″ 40.00   55.00

COASTERS

Coaster collecting has witnessed a sharp rise in interest and prices recently. In breweriana auctions, rare coasters are now drawing just about as much attention as rare early serving trays, and the prices are not too much lower. In the Brau Haus auction #6, a gala sale of breweriana accompanied by a lavish catalogue, no less than five coasters brought prices in excess of $200. This was all the more noteworthy, in light of the fact that the Brau Haus auctions are strictly postal-bid and "phone in" sales, with no floor competition. As recently as five years ago, the sale of a single coaster for $200 would have been headline news in the hobby.

Coasters are small trays, usually made of enameled tin. Though still manufactured (often of plastic, these days), the purpose they serve today is no longer as significant as in the past. When coasters first came into use, most taverns had polished wood bar-tops and tables with wood tops and no table cloths. The moisture from a beer bottle or drinking glass could easily mar such a surface. Even if it did no actual damage, it necessitated frequent polishing and repolishing to remove the stain marks. So the coasters came in handy. Today, with formica and other substitutes for wood, moisture staining is no real problem; but the use of coasters is deeply ingrained into tavern life and will probably continue.

Most coasters, old and new, are circular. Rectangular or square ones seem peculiar, since there were never any rectangular or square beer bottles. Yet, some coasters of these shapes were made. Pfeiffer's had a square coaster which has become a prime collector favorite—it shows three men seated around a pitcher of beer, and the drawing is so quaint that it could pass for folk art. Goebel also had a square coaster which is now popular and expensive, and there have been others. The fact that a coaster is an odd shape does not add to its value, it just so happens that some of the "non-circulars" are scarce and therefore desirable.

To a beginner, coasters might seem like just a bit of memorabilia in the hobby. In fact this is a highly specialized pursuit, enjoyed by many advanced collectors.

Price Range

☐ **Bozeman Beer,** a plain simple design with the brand name and word BEER in thick block capitals, separated from each other by a pair of dots at the left and right; at the center is an illustration of an open field with rows of pine trees; the illustration gives the impression of having been adapted from a linoleum cut. There is no other lettering: no slogan, no company address 225.00   275.00
Note: Be careful on this one. It looks too recent to be valuable, but is actually one of the highest priced of all coasters.

☐ **Drink Schwartz Beer,** brand name in modern gothic lettering, a non-pictorial coaster which consists of wording exclusively; beneath the brand name in small letters is "Brewed at Hartford, Wis.," and then in larger letters, enclosed within brackets, "Finest of Aged Beers." Beneath this is the company name and address, along with the phone number 85.00   115.00

☐ **Glacier Special Beer,** brand name in block lettering on banner crossing the center of the coaster horizontally, the letters are designed to appear "icy" with icicles forming beneath them; the word BEER appears in larger lettering than the brand name and directly below it in the background is a small illustration of snow-capped mountains, surmounted by a heraldic-like shield bearing the initials K.M.B. Co. At the lower portion of the design is the slogan, "The finest beer in town" 225.00   275.00

☐ **Goebel Beer, square coaster,** the brand name in decorative script lettering set against a shield, above the brand name appears the wording PURE FOOD; the shield is located at the upper right corner of the coaster, which consists chiefly of an illustration of a man seated at a dining table, smiling broadly as he hoists a glass; the table is arrayed with foods of various sorts, plus a tall beer bottle 30.00   45.00

☐ **Golden Age Beer,** the brand name appears twice in this design (very unusual for a coaster), both times in period gothic style; it is set in large letters in a semi-circle around the upper portion of the design, and then in tiny letters upon a banner at the center, superimposed on a gothic-style shield of arms. At the lower portion are the slogans, "Fully Aged" and "No Headaches" 28.00   34.00

Coaster, Budweiser, green and red, 4½", **$12–$20.**

Coaster, Budweiser, green and red with scalloped edge, 4", **$14–$16.**

Price Range

Note: The slogan "no headaches" was not meant in the sense of "no problems," but literally, no headaches. Temperance groups often charged that beer, among its other supposed evils, constricted the blood vessels and caused headaches.

☐ **Goldenrod Beer/Ale,** Comicaps coaster (special design with promotional tie-in), brand name at top, words BEER and ALE at either side of the design, at the center the wording "A New Game—Ask Your Dealer." Arranged in a circle are small portraits of comic characters 100.00   150.00

Note: At the time this tray was current, probably the 1940's, Goldenrod was placing "Comicaps" on its beer bottles. Each cap carried a picture of a newspaper comic strip character. Details on the nature of the promotion are lacking, but since this was advertised as "A New Game" we can probably presume that the public received some sort of prize for collecting all the different specimens.

☐ **Greenway's Mild Mellow Ale-Lager,** the brand name in large block capitals, the words MILD and MELLOW in block capitals of about half the size, arranged in a circular pattern which frames a small central illustration of a horse and rider, enclosed within a circle. There is no additional wording .. 225.00   275.00

☐ **Haberle's Black Bass Ale,** the brand name in wide block capitals, at the top appears the wording EXTRA PALE, at the bottom DRY HOP, both in small lettering, at the upper center is an illustration of a bass (fish) struggling to free itself of a fisherman's line. The design is enclosed in a slightly oval frame, wider than tall (but a quick glance will give the impression that the frame is circular) 225.00   275.00

☐ **Hop Gold Beer,** the words HOP GOLD in squat modernistic capitals (a style of lettering used frequently in advertising in the Art Deco era), the word BEER in script with an exaggerated ascender on the letter B, all enclosed within a five-pointed star and set against a circular frame background. No other wording appears on the design, nor any illustration 18.00   23.00

☐ **Independent Brewing Co.,** Pittsburgh, Pale Export Beer, company name on banner, slogan "Not a Headache in a Barrel," 4½", c. 1915 .... 75.00   90.00

Coaster, *Independent Brewing Co., 4½" diameter, c. 1915,* **$75–$90.**

Coaster, *Michel Beer, Ebling Brewing Co., blue and white on orange, 4½", c. 1930,* **$20–$24.**

Price Range

(About twenty years later, Lucky Strike Cigarettes used a twist on this slogan, "Not a Cough in a Carload.")

☐ **Kips-Bay Ale/Porter, Extra Beer,** brand name in script lettering at top, EXTRA BEER in block lettering at bottom; ALE at left, PORTER at right, in the center a circular frame with illustration of sailboat and company address: 1st Ave. between 37th and 38th Streets, N.Y. 275.00   350.00
Note: This is the most valuable of all beer coasters, of those which have established price records based on actual sales. Although Kips Bay is a neighborhood in Brooklyn, N.Y., the brewery was located across the river in Manhattan. The initials K.B.B.Co. appear on one of the sails of the sailboat.

☐ **Moose Beer & Ale,** the brand name in decorative script lettering toward the upper portion of the design, which is superimposed over an illustration of a moose standing on a riverbank. Directly beneath the illustration appears the slogan "Pride of the Monongahela Valley," then, at the very bottom of the design, "Moose Brewing Co., Roscoe, Pa."   75.00   100.00

☐ **Pacific Beer,** the brand name in thin old-style capitals arranged in semi-circular form in the upper portion of the design, in the lower portion appears the word TACOMA (headquarters of the brewery), in the central portion is the wording, "Those who reprove us are more valuable friends than those who flatter us." At either side are small vine-like motifs 35.00   50.00

☐ **Par-Ex Lager,** brand name in thin, slanting script lettering of decorative calligraphic style, the brand name is set horizontally at the center; above it appears the wording "Syracuse Brewery, Inc.," and beneath it, "Syracuse, N.Y." At the very top is a decorative script-style letter S between a pair of heraldic lions 70.00   90.00

☐ **Pfeiffer's Bottled Beer, square coaster,** the brand name in modern gothic lettering on one line, beneath this in standard lettering appears the company location—Detroit, Mich.; the upper portion of the design is comprised of an illustration of three men at a table, all wearing large hats, with a pitcher of beer prominently displayed on the table 35.00   45.00

Coaster, Michelob, brown, gold and red, 4¼", **$12–$20.**

Coaster, Michelob, green and red, 4", **$4–$8.**

Price Range

☐ **Pointer Beer,** the brand name in decorative script with a large flourish beneath POINTER, set at the upper portion of the design; in the central portion appears an illustration of a pointer (hunting dog) facing right with its right foreleg raised in a striding motion; beneath the illustration is the wording "Pointer Brewing Company, Clinton, Iowa" 20.00   25.00

☐ **Royal Pilsen Old Glory,** brand name in wide block capitals arranged in a circle to frame a central motif of heraldic type; at the top of the design appears the wording "One of America's Finest Beers," and this is repeated again at the bottom, both in semicircles. Small dots are set at either side of the design 105.00   130.00

☐ **Schmidt's Famous Beer,** brand name in thin script lettering, the words FAMOUS BEER in block capitals, at top of design the wording "America's Finest Beer," at the bottom, "Made in Detroit." The brand name is enclosed within a circle which also carries the phone number TEmple 2-7200 and "Est. 1873." To the right is a small emblem 26.00   33.00

FIGURES

☐ **Elfenbrau,** C. and J. Michel Brewing Co., statuette of elf holding bottle of the company's product, chalkware, fully modeled, on tall cylindrical base, 20″ 500.00   550.00

☐ **Non-Advertising,** figure of man standing at bar, holding mug, reads, "Beer Drinkers Make Better Lovers," 5″ 4.50   6.00
This was part of a series, all with "Make Better Lovers" captions, showing golfers, tennis players, etc.

☐ **Schmidt's,** waiter, metallic with bronze wash, he holds a tray, behind the figure is a bottle holder, 10″ 22.00   30.00

FOAM SCRAPERS

These are not nearly as abundant as many of the other breweriana items, but they do exist in greater numbers than a beginner or non-collector is apt to suspect. As the name implies, this is an implement used to remove the froth or foam which rises above the top of a beer mug. The shape is something like

Figures, Rolling Rock Premium Beer, chalk bar piece, Latrobe Brewing Co., **$30–$90.**

Foam Scraper, Jetter Brew'g Co., closed in 1911, black on off white, 8", **$10–$20.**
Courtesy of Paul Michel, Buffalo, NY.

Beer Scraper, Budweiser, celluloid, gold letters and logo outlined in black, **$12–$20.**

a wide letter-opener, with a rounded or blunt end. You will not find foam scrapers in too many taverns any longer. Today they are mainly restricted to taverns with a "gay nineties" decor, which attempt to recreate the mood of that era. And that was, unquestionably, the glory age of the foam scraper.

Foam scrapers have a colorful history. In the late 1800's, huge bushy mustaches were the fashion for American males. Men were proud of their mustaches and took pains to keep them immaculate, with mustache wax and special mustache brushes and combs. As a result drinking posed problems. The makers of drinking mugs and cups responded with the "mustache cup," now a familiar item in the antiques shops but otherwise gone from the American scene. These were specially designed cups with an extra piece added along the top, to prevent mustache and liquid from coming into contact. Mustache cups were far more than just a novelty item. They had huge sales and remained on the market for years. They were not effective with beer as the foam would simply rise up over the special protective piece.

The solution to the dilemma of how to drink beer and keep your mustache reasonably dry was the foam scraper. Of course, one must understand that the approach to beer drinking has changed a bit since then. Today, quite a few people like the foam, but in the 1890's, foam was considered nothing more than an indication that the beer was fresh and properly brewed. It was relished by few beer drinkers.

There was an art to foam scraping, and a deft scraper prided himself on his abilities as much as a karate expert breaking bricks with his hands. You had to be quick, and you had to hold the scraper at the precisely right angle. A slight miscalculation of the wrist, and the foam cascaded down the sides of the mug. In successful foam scraping, the scraper must come into contact with the rim of the mug or glass, and remain there until the scraper has passed completely over the mug. If done right—and if the beer has just been poured from a fresh bottle—the foam comes off in one clump like cotton candy.

Customers who did not trust bartenders to have scrapers on hand—or to do the job correctly—carried their own and did it themselves. It was largely because of the "do-it-yourselfers" that breweries considered the foam scraper to be a good advertising vehicle.

	Price Range	
☐ **Ballantine,** white with red lettering, smiling mug with company logo and wording, "Ballantine Draught Beer," dated 1964	9.00	12.00
☐ **Haberle,** red with gold lettering, 1960's	9.00	12.00
☐ **Knickerbocker,** white with blue and red lettering, reads "Ruppert Knickerbocker Beer," believed to date from the 1960's	9.00	12.00
☐ **Ram's Head Ale,** double-sided scraper, red with gold lettering, one side reads "Scheidt's Ram's Head Ale," the other "Scheidt's Valley Forge Beer, Adam Scheidt's Brewing Co., Norristown, Pa."	9.00	12.00

Price Range

☐ **Rheingold,** white with red and black lettering, reads "Rheingold Extra Dry, Liebmann Breweries Inc., New York, N.Y." 9.00   12.00

☐ **Ruppert Old Knickerbocker Beer,** maroon with gold lettering 9.00   12.00

☐ **Schaefer,** orange with white lettering 9.00   12.00

MINIATURE BEER BOTTLES

☐ **Blatz,** 4″ 14.00   19.00

☐ **Fehr's Darby Ale** 70.00   90.00

MUGS

☐ **Germania Brewing Co.,** made by Villory and Bach, ceramic, cylindrical with slight inward sloping at mouth, hand painted, brand name in large script lettering, c.1900 . . . .   135.00   165.00
(The latest possible date for this item is 1912 as the brewery closed in that year.)

☐ **Iroquois Brewery,** ceramic, salt glazed, Indian head facing left with brand name in script lettering, pedestal style base, c.1900 . . . .   150.00   165.00

OPENERS

This is one of the older divisions of the breweriana hobby. Openers were actively collected before most of today's breweriana favorites came into prominence. It's believed that openers were first collected as an offshoot hobby by collectors of corkscrews—which are, after all, another type of "opener." Originally, no distinction was drawn between those advertising beer and those advertising soft drinks. In fact there was probably little distinction drawn between advertising and nonadvertising openers. The pioneer collectors just wanted to get ones they didn't already have, and if they were attractive and a bit unusual, so much the better. Some impetus was also given to this hobby by the collectors of bottle caps—which, in the 1920's and 1930's, included about half the juvenile population of this country.

Openers became a necessity as soon as beverages began to be bottled with the modern type of scalloped-edged cap. This dates all the way back to the late 1800's, for both the soft drink and beer industries. Other types of bottle closures were tried, some of them quite elaborate and complicated, but nothing served the purpose nearly as well. Every home had one or more bottle openers, from as early as 1890.

Mug, *Germania Brewing Co.,*
hand painted, by Villory & Bach,
c. 1900, ***$150–$170.***

Mug, *Iroquois Brewery, salt*
glazes, c. 1900, ***$140–$165.***

Most of the pioneer openers were plain steel and sold for less than 5¢. You
can find them listed in old Sears Roebuck catalogues. They did not advertise
anything, and they did nothing but open bottles. It was not long, however, before
the wide-reaching potential of bottle openers began to be recognized. Soon
the market was flooded with novelty openers of all kinds, on which the opposite
end was a wrench or a hole-puncher or some other kind of tool. Openers were
also set into pocket knives, along with corkscrews. Well and good—but what
about the shank? Why let the shank go to waste? With a little more thought,

manufacturers came up with ideas for utilizing the shank. Some turned it into a nail file. Others sold advertising space for it. When that got started, it was a whole new ballgame.

Advertising messages of all the major breweries of the 20th century, and many lesser ones, can be found on openers. These include relatively plain ones as well as novelty types and others that are truly works of art. Some were so unusual and decorative that you have to look twice to realize that the item is really a bottle opener. Pacific Brewing Co. placed its name on models in which the opener was the eraser-holder on a pencil. These had long steel shanks, so you could grasp the shank while opening the bottle and not break the pencil. International Breweries had one in the likeness of an Indian, which must be turned over to discover that it's an opener. There were quite a few retractable openers, too, in which the opening tool slid out from a holder and could be retracted when finished. The idea for these was derived from the retractable-lead pencil, which was being manufactured at the same time. And of course there were many openers in the shape and color of beer bottles.

	Price Range	
☐ **Ballantine,** front reads "Drink Ballantine Ale, Beer," back blank	7.00	10.00
☐ **Ballantine,** copper plated, front reads "Ballantine Ale, Beer" with logo, reverse repeats wording on front but adds "Vaughn USA 1,996,550"	5.00	7.00
☐ **Ballantine Ale and Beer,** combination bottle and can opener, small	1.00	1.75
☐ **Budweiser,** wooden bottle with Bud label	10.00	15.00
☐ **Budweiser, King of Beers,** combination bottle and can opener, small	1.00	1.25
☐ **Carling,** combination bottle and can opener, small	1.00	1.25
☐ **Columbia,** both sides read "Columbia Preferred Beer"	3.50	5.00
☐ **Dubois,** reads "Original Dubois, Dubois Beers, Let's Meet and Be Friends"	7.00	10.00
☐ **Duquesne,** combination bottle and can opener, small	1.00	1.25
☐ **Duquesne Pilsener,** Silver Top Beer, wire	1.75	2.25
☐ **Esslinger's,** reads "Esslinger's Premium Beer, Over the Top"	9.00	12.00
☐ **Gunther,** front side reads "Gunther's Premium Dry Beer," back reads "Gunther Brewing Co., Inc., Balto., Md."	3.00	4.00
☐ **Hamm's,** front side reads "Hamm's Beer, Refreshing as the Land of Sky Blue Waters," back reads "Theo. Hamm Brg. Co., Baltimore, Md., Vaughn USA 60"	4.00	6.00
☐ **Harvard,** handle reads "Harvard," around opener end is wording "Beer, Ale, Porter," c. 1960	7.00	10.00

Corkscrew Opener, *Anheuser Busch, metal and wood with varnished handle, **$60–$75.***

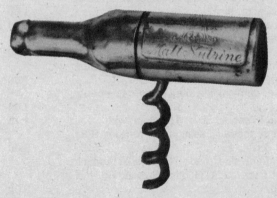

Corkscrew Opener, *nickel plated, in shape of beer bottle, **$40–$55.***

Price Range

☐ **Horlacher,** double sided opener with same wording on both sides, "Horlacher Pilsner Beer," picture of penguin 2.00   2.50

☐ **Hudepohl,** reads "Drink Hudepohl Beer" 6.00   9.00

☐ **Kaier's,** reads "Kaier's Outstanding Beer" on both sides 4.50   6.00

☐ **Knickerbocker,** reads "Jacob Ruppert, Brewer—New York—The Brew That Satisfies—Save This Opener—Order by the Case" 20.00   25.00

☐ **Lucky Lager,** reads "Lucky Lager, Lucky Ale" .. 4.50   6.00

☐ **National,** reads "National Premium Beer, The National Brewing Co., Baltimore, Md." 3.50   5.00

☐ **Neuweiler's,** front reads "Louis F. Neuweiler's Sons, Allentown, Pa.," back reads "Neuweiler's Beer" 6.00   8.00

☐ **Oertel's 92,** reads "Cheer Up with Oertel's 92 Beer, Oertel Brewing Co., Louisville, Ky." 9.00   12.00

☐ **Ortlieb,** double sided opener with same wording on both sides, "Ortlieb's Premium Beer, Henry Ortlieb Brewing Co., Phila., Pa." 2.00   3.00

*Corkscrew, Buffalo Co-op Brewing Co., c. 1900, **$20–$25.***

Price Range

☐ **Pickwick,** reads "Pickwick Ale, America's Finest Ale, Haffenreffer & Co., Brewers Since 1870, Pickwick Stout, Brewers Since 1870, Boston" 30.00   40.00

☐ **Queen City Brewing Co.,** Old German Beer, wire   1.50   2.50

☐ **Rheingold,** double sided opener, both sides read, "Rheingold Extra Dry Lager Beer, Handy Wilen, Inc., NYC NY." 2.00   2.50

☐ **Schaefer,** double sided opener, both sides read "Schaefer, America's Oldest Lager Beer" 3.00   4.00

☐ **Scheidt,** reads "Adam Scheidt Brewing Co., Norristown, Pa." 5.00   7.00

☐ **Schlitz,** combination bottle and can opener, small   1.00   1.75

☐ **Schmidt,** reads "Schmidt's of Philadelphia, Brewers Since 1860" 5.00   7.00

☐ **Schmidt's of Philadelphia,** combination bottle and can opener, small 1.00   1.25

☐ **Schmidt's of Philadelphia,** wire 1.50   2.50

☐ **Senate Beer,** front reads "Chr. Heurich Brewing Co., Wash., D.C., Senate," back reads "Vaughn, Chicago, Pat. 143,327—1,996,550 Made in USA"   5.00   7.00

☐ **Smith's Ale,** reads "Say Smith's For An Honest Ale" 7.00   10.00

☐ **Stegmaier,** wooden handle, reads "Stegmaier Brewing Co., Wilkes-Barre, Pa., Stegmaier's Gold Medal Beer" 20.00   25.00

☐ **Sunshine,** reads "Sunshine Beer, Ales, Porter—Keep Sunshine in Your Home" 8.00   12.00

☐ **Valley Forge,** front reads "Valley Forge, A Beer Worthy of its Famous Name," back reads "Ram's Head, Aristocrat of Ales, Adam Scheidt Brewing Co., Norristown, Pa. CMI/APR, Vaughn, USA 58"   4.00   6.00

☐ **Yuengling,** reads "Drink Yuengling's Beer, Ale—D.G. Yuengling & Son, Inc., Pottsville, Pa."   8.00   11.00

POSTERS

☐ **American Beer,** "American Woman," 19″ x 26″   8.00   12.00
Note: This price is for a reprint of this poster, which was originally published in 1893 and is virtually impossible to get in the original edition.

☐ **Arrow Beer,** nude girl with blonde hair against black background, caption "Matchless Body," 16″ x 26″ 8.00   12.00
Note: This price is for a reprint of this famous and rare poster, which is very expensive in the original.

☐ **Brunswick Bock,** ram's head with wording "Brunswick Bock Beer," green background, 23″ x 34″ **65.00** **85.00**
Note: Probably dates from around 1940.
☐ **Busch,** snow-capped mountain with reflection of Busch can in lake, 23″ x 34″ **2.00** **4.00**
☐ **Coors,** Gibson girl, wording "Coors Golden Brewery, Golden, Colo.," 14″ x 19″ **8.00** **12.00**
Note: This is a reprint poster.
☐ **Falstaff,** serving maid pouring beer into stein, wording, "An Old Friend, Falstaff Beer, The Choicest Product of the Brewer's Art," 22″ x 11″ **70.00** **90.00**
☐ **Genesee Beer,** 26″ x 43″ **1.00** **1.75**
☐ **Genesee, Taste Invaders,** space ship with cans of Genesee beer, Genesee ale, and Genesee Light, 20½″ x 28″ **2.00** **3.00**
Note: Inspired by the game "Space Invaders."
☐ **Maximus Super,** girl on couch, wording, "Relax, Then Have a Max," 18″ x 23″ **1.00** **1.75**
☐ **Maximum Super,** girl with blonde hair holding Max can, wording, "Send your pix to Max, 1976 photo contest to become Ms. Max," 22″ x 17½″ **1.00** **1.75**
☐ **Munich Oktoberfest Bier,** picture of German waitress holding four beer mugs, wording "Munich Oktoberfest Bier," 18″ x 30″ **2.00** **3.00**
☐ **Old German Beer,** no-deposit glass bottle, 14″ x 21″ **1.00** **1.50**
☐ **Old German/Old Export,** banner style, 18″ x 44″ **1.00** **1.50**
☐ **Olympia Beer,** girl in Edwardian street costume, 18″ x 24″ **9.00** **12.00**
Note: This is a reprint.
☐ **Pabst,** woman in Edwardian outfit drinking glass of beer, wording, "Only When It's ... Pabst," 19″ x 23″ **9.00** **12.00**
Note: This is a reprint of a circa 1905 poster.
☐ **Schlitz,** wording "Best Little Can in Texas," dated 1980, 30″ x 20″ **2.00** **3.00**
☐ **Stroh,** picture of college students making pyramids with empty beer cans, one talks on phone and says, "Yeah, mom, I'm studying all about the pyramids," 14½″ x 21½″ **1.00** **1.50**
☐ **Stroh Light,** picture of sailboat, wording, "Looks like a Stroh Light night," 15½″ x 22″ **1.00** **1.50**

SERVING TRAYS

One of the fascinating aspects of the beer serving tray is that it has descended down through about 100 years without much change. Modern trays are not as artistic as those of granddad's time, but they are of approximately the same size, and made of the same material; and they still use lithographed illustrations. And they serve the same purpose as those of 1890—to place the product name before the public and hopefully influence future purchases.

The rapid growth of American breweries toward the close of the 19th century ushered in the advertising tray. With many breweries in competition against each other, any possible vehicle for advertising was not to be overlooked. Brewers advertised in magazines and newspapers, and via posters. But such advertising reached only a general audience, including many persons who were not potential users of the product. Any advertising that could be done in the taverns and restaurants themselves, where the beer drinkers were, stood to be much more rewarding.

Most of the early trays were produced under contract for specific breweries, which exercised full control over designs, messages, and styles of lettering. This was not the case with all trays, however. Some of them were "stock" designs prepared by the tray manufacturers. The manufacturers would select certain designs and prepare a quantity of trays depicting them. Then, the brand name and message—if any—were overprinted as instructed by the ordering brewery. Thus, stock designs show up with the names of various beer and breweries, and in general their collector interest is lower. However, there is an important factor at work here which serves to keep interest in stock-design trays from plummeting really low. Major breweries never used stock trays. They were used only by the smaller breweries, which did not want to incur the expense of making trays from scratch. Consequently, stock-design trays often carry the names of breweries from which hardly any other memorabilia is known. This in itself makes for collector appeal.

Dating a serving tray from its artwork is tricky business. On many trays, old and recent, the style of artwork is not typical of the era of manufacture. This is also true of the costuming, hairstyles, etc., of individuals that may be pictured in the design. After the initial popularity of serving trays (1895–1915), many brewers continued using their established designs, with minor changes or none at all. Quite a large percentage of 1920's trays were designed almost identically to those of 20 years earlier. Even into the thirties and forties, there were brewers who clung fast to their traditional designs, feeling that these designs had become trademarks of a sort.

	Price Range	
☐ **Ambassador,** G. Krueger, Newark, New Jersey, red and gold on blue background, 11¾"	16.00	20.00
☐ **Arrow,** multicolored, portrait of King Gambrinus in the midst of a bacchanalian feast, wording, "Arrow Beer, Mellowed by Nature, Strengthened by Repeal," 14"	55.00	70.00

Price Range

☐ **Arrow Gambrinus Rex,** by American Can Co., multicolor drinking scene, 13¼" 55.00 75.00

☐ **Ashland,** multicolored with black rim, large portrait of a young lady with smile, a three-quarter portrait facing to the left, picture is titled "The Invitation," tray also carries address of the brewery, "Ashland Brewing Co., Ashland, WI.," believed to date from about 1912 .... 260.00 320.00

☐ **Ballantine,** logo with rings and mug in red, blue and yellow on white background 7.00 10.00

☐ **Ballantine,** multicolored, harvest scene with glass of beer and Ballantine logo, wording "Golden mellow from the Golden Harvest," reads "Ballantine Beer" along inner and outer rims, 14" 11.00 15.00

☐ **Barbey's Sunshine,** blue with gold design, reads "Since 1861," rounded sides 31.00 39.00

☐ **Bavarian Premium Beer and Ale,** Mount Carbon Brewery 16.00 20.00

☐ **Beck's Brewing,** Buffalo, white and red, 13", believed to date from the 1950s 11.00 15.00

☐ **Beverwyck Beer and Ale,** Albany, New York, multicolor reading "Billy Beaver" 30.00 36.00

☐ **Bevo,** Busch Brewing Co., St. Louis, Missouri, pictures horse drawn wagon in full colors 75.00 100.00

☐ **Billy Baxter,** illustration of large red bird with wording, "The spoon is the enemy of the highball. Self starring Billy Baxter," 12" 28.00 35.00

☐ **Black Label,** red and white, Black Label label at center, circles with numbers one to eight surrounding logo, 14" 4.50 6.00

☐ **Breidt's Beer and Ale,** multicolor with slogans "It's Keg Mellowed" and "Quality Since 1867" 24.00 32.00

☐ **Broadway Brewing Co.,** red and black with gold gilt trimming, company name in bold letters encircling the upper portion of the design, "Buffalo, N.Y." at the lower, in the central portion a hand holding a metal ax of the type used in medieval warfare; at either side of the central illustration are the words "Pure" and "Beer" 275.00 350.00

☐ **Budweiser,** giant rectangular with curved sides, pictures horse drawn wagon with pictures of its breweries and founder, wording "100th Anniversary," 18¾" x 13½" 17.00 22.00

☐ **Budweiser,** reads "Where There's Life, There's Budweiser" 10.00 15.00

Price Range

☐ **Budweiser,** red and gold with wording "Duquoine State Fair, 50th Anniversary," 11¾" 13.00 17.00

☐ **Budweiser,** turquoise, wording "Where there's life . . . there's Bud," with logo and slogan, "King of Beers" on rim, 12" 4.00 6.00

☐ **Buffalo Brewing Co.,** stock tray picturing two St. Bernard dogs with playing cards and beer steins, c. 1910 . . . . 275.00 350.00

☐ **Buffalo Co-operative Brewing Co.,** Buffalo, N.Y., by Charles Shonk, pictures two beer bottles side by side with message at right, 12", c. 1915 150.00 200.00

☐ **Carlsberg,** multicolored, landscape scene with farmer in field, holding vegetables and tankard of beer, wording "Carlsberg, the Glorious Beer of Copenhagen," 11", made in Britain 8.00 12.00

☐ **Cerveza XX Dos Equis,** Mexican, pictures frothy stein and bottles 7.00 10.00

☐ **Columbia Five Star Beer,** red with white and gold, non-pictorial tray with brand name on banner across center in script lettering, "Beer" in block letters beneath, small shield emblem in the upper left 25.00 33.00

☐ **Columbia Five Star Brewery,** Shenandoah, Pennsylvania, shield with grain and hops, 13¼" 22.00 28.00

☐ **Conrad Siepp,** multicolored, portrait of smiling young girl with long hair, holding beer mug, posed against lush landscape background; the scene is set in late evening with moonlight reflecting off a lake, dated 1911 . . . . 350.00 450.00
Note: One of the most famous of all the pre-World War I beer serving trays. The Conrad Siepp Brewery was located in Chicago.

☐ **Coors,** plastic, waterfall in colors, 13¼" 5.00 7.00

☐ **Coors,** white lion on red striped background, slogan "America's Fine Light Beer" 7.00 10.00

☐ **Corona Cerveza Modelo,** Mexican, portrait of Mexican lady with pearls 7.00 10.00

☐ **Cremo Ale and Lager,** multicolored nonpictorial tray, brand name at upper center with long flourish on the initial letter, at the lower right is an illustration of a glass of beer, reads "Quality Ale and Lager," also "Cremo Brewing Co., Inc." 30.00 40.00

Tray, *Arrow Beer, features scene of "Gambrinus, King of Lager,"* **$125–$200.**

Serving Tray, *Buffalo Cooperative, by Charles Shonk, 12" diameter, c. 1915,* **$150–$175.**

Price Range

☐ **Daeufers Beer,** oval, red on yellow background, nonpictorial tray with brand name in broad script lettering, trademark symbol above it, wording "Brewed and bottled by Daeufer Lieberman Brewery, Allentown, Penna.," late 1930s 70.00 100.00

☐ **Daeufer's,** Allentown, Pennsylvania, pictures foaming glass with wording, "Since 1846" 22.50 27.50

☐ **Dotterweich Brewing Co.,** square, illustration of Indian on horseback pursuing buffalo, c. 1911 .. 425.00 500.00

☐ **Dotterweich Brewing Co.,** dark metallic colors with gold gilt edging, a view of Tokyo done in mock Japanese style, spelled "Tokio" 100.00 150.00
Note: The Dotterweich Brewing Co. of Dunkirk, New York, was in operation from 1900 to 1919. The spelling of Tokio for Tokyo was not unusual in the years before 1920.

☐ **DuBois Beer,** black background, brand name in block lettering, logo appears at the upper center, reads "Let's Meet and Be Friends" 35.00 45.00

☐ **DuBois Beer,** black background, nonpictorial tray with brand name in large gothic letters, at the center a small circle with "DuBois Brewing Co., DuBois, Pa." believed to date from 1935 .... 35.00 45.00

☐ **Duquesne Pilsener,** pictures prince hoisting glass in red/white/gold 17.50 22.50

☐ **Dutch Club,** Pittsburgh, pictures boy with steins on tray, logo and seal, 11¾" 55.00 75.00

☐ **Eagle Brewing Co.,** oval, multicolored, rim has fabric-work effect with red highlighting, profile portrait of woman with blonde hair, wearing flowers in her hair and a bluish green dress, undated ... 300.00 400.00
Note: The Eagle Brewing Co. was located in Waterbury, Connecticut.

☐ **East Buffalo Brewing Co.,** Buffalo, N.Y., by Baltimore Novelty Co., oval, porcelain on metal, company trademark of Buffalo in circle, wording "Lager Beer," 12", c.1890 .... 400.00 500.00

☐ **East Side Beer,** Los Angeles Brewery, picture of Yama Yama Boy 40.00 50.00

☐ **Edelweiss Beer,** multicolored with gold leafwork trim, portrait of a smiling young girl which covers nearly the entire tray, she has red hair and a blue dress, wording "Peter Schenhofen Brewing Co., Chicago," believed to date from about 1913 .... 325.00 425.00

☐ **Ehret's Hell Gate Brewery,** New York, oval with star, believed to date from the 1910–1920 era .. 175.00 225.00

Stock Tray, *Buffalo Brewing Co., c. 1910,* **$275–$350.**

Tray, *Canadian Ace, multicolored on woven background with gold trim,* **$40–$80.**

Price Range

☐ **Eichler's,** New York, N.Y., gold eagle with slogan, "Since 1862," 11¾" 35.00 45.00

☐ **El Dorado Brewing Co.,** rectangular, multicolored with glossy black rim and gold lettering, close-up portrait of sultry young girl holding beer glass, wording "Special Valley Brew" at top, at bottom, "Winner of Gold Medals" 300.00 400.00

☐ **Enterprise Brewing Co.,** San Francisco, California, pictures lady and horse, captioned "A Winner," c. 1915 .... 350.00 425.00

☐ **Enterprise Half Stock Ale,** rectangular, multicolored, brand name in script lettering at top with "Ale" in large capitals at right, the design consists of a portrait of an elderly man holding a glass of beer, his mouth is partially open as if exclaiming in delight, with the slogan, "It's Aged and Mellowed". 150.00 200.00

☐ **F & S Beer and Ale,** Shamokin, Pennsylvania, full color portrait of drum major 15.00 20.00

☐ **Falls City Brewing Co.,** pictures the brewery with wording "70th Anniversary," 11¾" 20.00 27.50

☐ **Falls City Lager,** oval with white and black on red 30.00 37.50

☐ **Fort Pitt,** blue and white with lettering in yellow, reads "Fort Pitt Special Beer," and on rim, "Fort Pitt Special," 14" 9.00 12.00

☐ **Fort Pitt Special,** blue with white and yellow wording 16.00 21.00

☐ **Fox Head Beer,** Waukesha Brewery, Waukesha, Wisconsin, fox's head against blue background, 13" 40.00 55.00

☐ **Frank Fehr Brewing Co.,** multicolored, picture of girl and boy, full-length in a landscape setting, locked in an embrace; the style of clothing suggests a period piece of a much earlier date than the manufacture of this tray, which was made in 1913. .... 375.00 450.00
Note: The Frank Fehr Brewing Co. was located in Louisville, Kentucky.

☐ **Genesee,** pheasant with glass and bottle on table in multi colors 16.00 20.00

☐ **Genesee,** portrait of female in black/yellow/white on red background, wording "Ask for Jenny" ... 14.00 18.00

Tray, *East Buffalo Brewing Co., by Baltimore Novelty Co., c. 1890,* **$400–$450.**

Tray, *German American Brewing Co., 13" square,* **$250–$300.**

Price Range

☐ **Genesee,** red and white with Genesee logo, numbers one through eight in circles surrounding logo, white rim with logo repeated, wording at bottom "The Genesee Brewing Co., Inc., Rochester, N.Y.," 12" 7.00 10.00

☐ **Gerhard Lang Brewery,** rectangular, cream lettering on woodgrain background, nonpictorial tray with a diamond at the center reading "Lang, Trade Mark," and, at the bottom "Buffalo" (the location of the brewery). There is a thin gold border along the inner rim and a broader one at the outer rim 200.00 250.00

☐ **German American Brewing Co.,** square, pictures two beer bottles standing side by side, reads "Imported" at left, 13" 250.00 300.00

☐ **Gibbons Mellow-Pure Beer and Ale,** Lion Brewing Co., Wilkes-Barre, Pennsylvania, red and white on black, 11¾" 12.50 17.50

☐ **Gibbons Premium,** white with red and black lettering, slogan "Gibbons is Good" 7.00 10.00

☐ **Goebel Beer,** multicolored, portrait of two Dutch girls in a field, one carries a basket of "Pure Food Goebel Beer," the inside rim is decorated with tiny renditions of Dutch scenes, believed to date from about 1913 .... 220.00 275.00

☐ **Goldenrod,** Brooklyn, N.Y., oval, view of the Hittelman Goldenrod Brewery 150.00 200.00

☐ **Grain Belt,** logo with mug, hops and grain, background pictures lake 12.00 16.00

☐ **Greater New York Brewery,** multicolored, reproduction of a painting by Herbert Bohnert showing a tavern interior with revelers of c. 1800, wording on rim "Fidelio Home Keg Service," 12" 85.00 115.00

☐ **Gretz Beer,** Philadelphia, picture of man riding Victorian-era high-wheel bicycle, 13" 42.00 53.00

☐ **Gunther's,** slogan "It's Dry and Beery" 25.00 32.00

☐ **Gustav C. Mammele,** stock tray with Dutch Girl with beer and food, titled "A Helping Hand," dated 1914 .... 40.00 55.00
(This stock tray was produced by American Artworks of Coshocton, Ohio.)

☐ **Hagerstown Brewing Co.,** rectangular, multicolored with gold lettering on a woodgrain finish rim, portrait entitled "Chrysanthemum Girl" 300.00 375.00

Serving Tray, Golden Age Beer, c. 1935, **$85–$110.**

Serving Tray, Hull's, blue background, 12", c. 1940, **$40–$65.**

Price Range

☐ **Hamm's,** crest with gold lion, white lettering 7.00   10.00

☐ **Hamm's Preferred Stock,** scenes of the brewery
in black and red on white background, two sided
tray 26.00   34.00

☐ **Heileman's Old Style,** pictures Alpine village with
revelers 7.00   10.00

☐ **Hinckel Brewing Co.,** multicolored with wine-red
rim and gold lettering, pictures an elaborate scene
of a shipwreck, the ship is called "Old Bourbon,"
also allegories of various elements from U.S. population (a negro, sailor, working man, etc.), very
detailed and suggestive of a Currier & Ives litho-
graph. At the bottom are the words, "Lager Beer,"
with the brand name in semi-circle at the top . . .   600.00   800.00

☐ **Hornung's,** red and yellow, wording "The beer
that Wins Awards . . . Hornung's Beer," also
"Jacob Hornung Brewing Co., Philadelphia, Pa.,"
14" 60.00   80.00

☐ **Hubner Toledo Beer,** small nonpictorial tray,
etched lettering on chrome with the brand name
in thick broad script, decorative rim has beadwork,
date uncertain 150.00   200.00

☐ **Hull's Export,** woodgrain background with stein
and logo 17.50   22.50

☐ **Iroquois,** cream and gold with gold edge, brand
name at top, "Buffalo" at bottom (location of the
brewery), at the center an illustration of three beer
bottles, each with different labels, reads "Iroquois
Fine Bottled Beers," pre-World War I 300.00   400.00

☐ **Iroquois Indian Head Beer,** Iroquois Brewery,
Buffalo, New York, head of Indian, 12" 85.00   115.00

☐ **Iroquois,** Iroquois Brewery, Buffalo, New York,
portrait of Indian facing left, 12", c.1905 . . . .   300.00   400.00

☐ **Jacob Leinenkugel,** pictures its breweries over
the years with portrait of founder and wording
"110th Anniversary" 15.00   20.00

☐ **Jacob Ruppert Beer and Ale,** Jacob Ruppert
Brewing Co., New York, N.Y., multicolored with
pair of hands holding steins, 11¾" 22.50   30.00

☐ **Jax,** plastic, slogan "Taste You Can Hold On To,"
13¼" 4.00   6.00

☐ **John Eichler Brewing Co.,** multicolored with
woodgrain rim, profile portrait of young lady with
her nose pressed against a bouquet of small flow-
ers, dated 1915 . . . .   350.00   450.00

Tray, *Iroquois, Niagara Litho. Co., Buffalo, NY, 15" diameter, c. 1915,* **$300–$325.**

Serving Tray, *Kings Beer by Electro-Chemical Engraving Co., Inc., blue background with gold trim, 11", c. 1935,* **$20–$30.**

Price Range

☐ **Kaier's,** red and black on white, wording "First Prize Seal," 11¾" 15.00   20.00

☐ **Knapstein Brewing Co. Red Band and Select Bottle Beer,** rectangular, gold on woodgrain background, full-length portrait of "little Dutch girl" in national costume holding serving tray with pitcher and glasses, she wears wooden shoes; the picture is entitled, "A Helping Hand," dated 1914   300.00   400.00

☐ **Krueger,** A Real Premium Beer, pictures Krueger man, 11¾" 10.00   15.00

☐ **Krueger Beer and Ale,** Newark, New Jersey, pictures Krueger Man with slogan "Since 1858," 11¾" 12.50   16.50

☐ **Krueger Pilsener,** lion crest in red/gold/black on white background, 11¾" 12.00   16.00

☐ **Laurentide,** blue and gold, Laurentide logo with wording, "Biere . . . Ale . . . Laurentide," 14" 4.50   6.00

☐ **Leinekugel,** multicolored, beer merchant gazing into stein, wording "J. Leinekugel Brewing Co., Chippewa Falls, Wis., Famous Since 1867," c. 1980 . . . .   9.00   12.00

☐ **Leinenkugel's,** logo with portrait of Indian maiden in red/black/gold on white background 9.00   12.00

☐ **Lone Star,** white with single-star logo in gold and red 10.00   15.00

☐ **Lowenbrau,** blue and gold with Lowenbrau logo and lion, wording "Special and Dark Special Beer," 14" 4.00   6.00

☐ **Maier Brewery,** Los Angeles, picture of lady in orange dress and ornamental hat, 12" 55.00   70.00
Note: Believed to date from the 1910–1920 era.

☐ **Mathie Brewing Co.,** multicolored, picture of South Seas native girl playing guitar, ocean and lush trees in background, wording "Red Ribbon Beer, Old Dutch Lager" 300.00   400.00

☐ **McSorley's Cream Stock Ale,** Greater New York Brewery, pictures four men at tavern table, dated 1936 . . . .   40.00   50.00

☐ **Miller,** gold and red with Miller logo in red, 12"   4.50   6.00

☐ **Miller High Life,** multicolored, brand name in thin slanted script lettering at top (slants toward right), picture of girl seated in quarter moon, in this version her face is in positive profile, her chin lifted, she holds glass of Miller at arm's length, there are abundant clouds in background; this version can

Serving Tray, Kips Bay by Electro-Chemical Engraving Co., Inc., NY, 12", c. 1930, $220–$250.

Tray, Knickerbocker, multicolored with cartoons, **$90–$150.**

Price Range

also be identified by the fact that the slogan, "The Champagne of Bottled Beer," is in large lettering 35.00 50.00
Note: Various versions of the "moon girl" design were used on Miller trays, for decades. This one dates from the 1930's.

☐ **Miller High Life,** multicolored, brand name in thin script lettering slanted toward right at top of design, picture of girl seated in quarter or eighth moon holding glass of Miller; this version can be distinguished by various features, such as the girl's face looking directly forward rather than in profile; her arm (holding glass) is bent rather than straight; there are few clouds in the background; the slogan, "The Champagne of Bottled Beer" appears in small lettering 20.00 30.00
Note: This is a late version of the "moon girl" motif, dating from 1945–1950.

☐ **Narragansett Ale,** red and gold with white, non-pictorial tray with brand name in decorative script lettering at the center (tilted semi-diagonally), reads "The Famous Old Narragansett," word "Ale" is in very large block letters, trademark symbol at top, vinework decoration encircling the rim 30.00 45.00

☐ **Neuweiler,** multicolored, picture of elderly brewmaster holding barley and tankard, wording "Louis F. Neuweiler's and Sons, Allentown, Pa.—Cream Ale, Pilsner, Porter," 14" 85.00 115.00

☐ **O'Keefe,** gold with red and cream white, O'Keefe and wording "Biere ... Ale," 14" 4.00 6.00

☐ **Old Catasauqua Dutch,** red with white and blue, brand name in block capitals running on semi-diagonal banner at center, at the upper center a small portrait of bald-headed man drinking from overflowing glass, reads "Eagle Brewing Co., Catasauqua, Pa." 130.00 170.00

☐ **Old Dutch Beer,** brown and black, brand name in gothic on curved banner at center, word "Beer" in block capitals at bottom, at the upper center is a drawing of a bald-headed man drinking from an overflowing glass. The background has a wood-grain finish 45.00 60.00

☐ **Old Milwaukee,** red mosaic with white lettering, dated 1968 .... 5.00 7.00

☐ **Old Reading Pennsylvania Dutch,** pictures heart with bird, 11¾" 20.00 26.00

Tray, Krueger, with K man, red background with white, red and black letters, **$120–$160.**

Tray, Neuweilers, features elderly German man, **$80–$120.**

Price Range

☐ **Olympia,** horseshoe with waterfall and hops in
gold on black background 17.00   22.00
☐ **Olympia,** portrait of Gibson Girl, cream colored
background 7.00   10.00
☐ **Olympia,** white with gold and black, Olympia logo
of forest scene with waterfall contained in lucky
horseshoe, wording "Olympia Beer . . . Pale Ex-
port Type . . . It's The Water," 14" 15.00   20.00
☐ **Olympia,** multicolored, an exclusively pictorial tray
which carries no wording whatsoever, however
the brand name is worked into the design as part
of the artwork: it shows a Dutch cavalier of the late
17th century, holding a bottle of Olympia Beer, the
coloring is florid 100.00   125.00
☐ **Ortlieb,** red with black and white, Ortlieb logo and
wording "Premium Lager Beer," also on rim "Or-
tlieb's . . . the WET Beer," 12" 8.00   12.00
☐ **Ortlieb,** red with yellow and white, lengthy mes-
sage reading "Ortlieb's Premium Lager Beer . . .
Ale Well Brewed and Aged . . . Phone Market 7-
4728 . . . Henry F. Ortlieb Brewing Company, Phila-
delphia," 12" 20.00   30.00
☐ **Pabst,** white with blue and gold, Pabst logo with
wording "Pabst Blue Ribbon . . . What'll You
Have?" framed by golden wheat stalks. On rim
wording "Finest Beer Served, Anywhere!!" 12"   10.00   15.00
☐ **Pabst Blue Ribbon,** portrait of 1920s flapper-style
girl 7.00   10.00
☐ **Pabst Blue Ribbon,** Limited Edition Bicentennial
tray with picture of the original Pabst brewery,
1976 . . . .   7.00   10.00
☐ **Phoenix Brewery by Charles Shonk,** large eagle
adapted from U.S. shield with wings spread, name
at top, 12" 300.00   350.00
☐ **Pickwick Ale,** picture of horse-drawn beer wagon
being led by man on foot, 12" 75.00   100.00
☐ **Piel's,** multicolored, Harry and Bert Piel (cartoon
characters) with wording "Enjoy Piel's Beer Now,
the Beer with a Barrel of Flavor Because it's Cool
Brewed," 14" 14.00   19.00
*Note: Radio comics Bob Elliot and Ray Goulding
did the voices of Bert and Harry Piel in commer-
cials.*
☐ **Piel's,** multicolored, elf carrying two glasses of
beer, wording "Piel's Light Beer . . . Tastes the
Best of All Because it's the Driest of All," 14" . .   18.00   23.00

Tray, *Ortlieb's, Henry F. Ortlieb, Philadelphia, PA, white, red and black,* **$20–$40.**

Serving Tray, *Ortlieb's, c. 1930,* **$70–$100.**

Price Range

☐ **Point Bicentennial,** logo with eagle in red/white/blue 15.00 20.00

☐ **Point Special,** pictures six of their old labels and gives dates, 13¼″ 12.00 16.00

☐ **Portsmouth Brewing and Ice Co.,** multicolored, gold leafwork rim, picture of woman with arm resting on tiger 175.00 225.00
Note: This design was used by other brewers for their trays, too, which detracts somewhat from the collector appeal and value. Nevertheless, hardly any memorabilia of the Portsmouth Brewing and Ice Co. exists, so it still ranks as a worthy item. This was an Ohio brewer.

☐ **Queen Quality,** a nonpictorial tray except for a small emblem of a moose head at the lower center, the brand name is in stylistic script lettering, wording "Deppen Brewing Company, Reading, Pa." 300.00 400.00

☐ **R&H Beer,** Rubsam & Horrmann Brewery, Staten Island, New York, gold lettering on brown background, 12″ 60.00 80.00

☐ **Rheingold Extra Dry Lager,** red and black logo on white background 7.00 10.00

☐ **Ruppert's Beer,** shows a pair of hands hoisting two mugs of beer, with eagle above, 13″ 60.00 80.00

☐ **Ruppert Knickerbocker,** full color portrait of Father Knickerbocker on white background 10.00 14.00
(Father Knickerbocker was a character in Washington Irving's "Knickerbocker's History of New York.")

☐ **Schaefer,** red and white, the red is an off-color which could be termed red/orange, reads "Schaefer Beer" at center, inner rim reads "Our hand has never lost its skill ... Established 1842 ... America's oldest lager beer," 12″ 15.00 20.00

☐ **Schaefer Brewery,** Brooklyn, N.Y., gold with white and red, 12″, believed to date from the 1950s 8.00 12.00

☐ **Scheidt's Ram's Head Ale,** pictures Valley Forge, winter headquarters of George Washington during American Revolution 20.00 30.00

☐ **Schlitz,** brown and cream, Schlitz logo in brown at center, 14″ 18.00 23.00

☐ **Schlitz Light,** sun-face and globe in black/silver/blue on beige background, 1976 ... 6.00 8.00

Tray, *Ortlieb's, white with red stripe, yellow background,* **$50–$80.**

Tray, *Pabst, Milwaukee, green, gold and red trademark with factory scene,* **$175–$220.**

Price Range

☐ **Schlitz Malt Liquor,** blue with bull and medals in white, 1971 .... 6.00   8.00

☐ **Schmidt's,** crest with tiger in multi colors on silver background, wording "Tiger Head Brand" 17.00   22.00

☐ **Schmidt's,** multicolored with silver and gold prominent, "Schmidt's Beer ... Ale" in blue lettering, picture of heraldic shield and tiger, 14" 28.00   37.00

☐ **Schwarzenbach Brewing Co.,** multicolored, picture of young girl at woodland fence alongside a horse; she reaches out to feed horse from her cupped hands. The view is titled "In Old Kentucky" by an uncredited artist and is dated 1912   175.00   225.00

☐ **Schwarzenbach Brewing Co.,** oval, multicolored, a large tray with an elaborate scene of a young girl and a horse and dog, the girl stands and reads a letter, all intricately and richly colored, titled "Loyal Friends." The picture is dated 1913 and copyrighted by American Art Works, 16" 350.00   450.00

☐ **Simon Pure,** logo with winged hops in red and black on white background 15.00   20.00

☐ **Simon Pure,** green with red and gold, picture of the firm's distinctive hops trademark, 13" 60.00   80.00

☐ **Stag,** oval, view of brewery with wording "125th Anniversary" 16.00   20.00

☐ **Star Union Brewing Co.,** multicolored with black lettering on gold rim, portrait of girl wearing a large elaborate fur hat and fur coat with prominent collar, she looks to the right, the picture is titled "Janice," accompanied by the slogan "The Beer that Pleases All," dated 1913 .... 400.00   525.00

☐ **Stegmaier,** multicolored, chipmunks at lake hold a bottle of Stegmaier beer, reads "Cold and Gold ... from the Poconos ... Brewed to the Taste of the Nations," 14" 15.00   20.00

☐ **Stegmaier,** multicolored, view of the brewery, 12"   40.00   55.00

☐ **Stegmaier's,** gold and black shield, slogans "Since 1857" and "Quality Beers" 20.00   30.00

☐ **Stoney's,** pictures man with 1890's style handlebar moustache in yellow/white/black on red background 15.00   20.00

☐ **Stroh's Bohemian,** pictures waiter with tray in multicolors, c. World War I era 140.00   165.00

☐ **Sunshine Beer,** wording "Wholesome as Sunshine," 13" 45.00   60.00

☐ **Superior,** Mexican, blonde girl holding glass and bottle 7.00   10.00

Serving Tray, Phoenix Brewery, by Charles Shonk, 12" diameter, **$300–$350.**

Serving Tray, Reading Beer, 11" and 13", c. 1930, **$70–$90.**

	Price Range	
☐ **Tam O'Shanter,** American Brewing Co., Rochester, New York, pictures Scotsman with tartan plaid (Tam O'Shanter was a poem by Robert Burns.)	30.00	45.00
☐ **Tru-Age,** Standard Brewing Co., Scranton, Pennsylvania, red/white/black portrait of king with foaming tankard, gold background	20.00	30.00
☐ **Utica Club,** pictures Schultz and Dooley (emblems of the brand), 11¾″	18.00	23.00
☐ **Utica Club Pale Lager,** full color portrait of "The Goddess of Grain," 10¾″	17.00	22.00
☐ **Valley Forge Beer,** illustration of Washington's winter headquarters, believed to date from the 1940s	40.00	55.00
☐ **Valley Forge Special,** picture of waitress, wording "As good as it looks." This is a rectangular tray	70.00	100.00
☐ **Wieland's Beer,** picture of young woman with roses, a rectangular tray	200.00	275.00
Note: Another version of this tray has a picture of a young woman reading a letter. The value is the same.		
☐ **Wooden Shoe Beer,** oval, multicolored, portrait of girl in Dutch costume wearing apron and carrying wickerwork basket, also wearing wooden shoes, reads "The Star Beverage Co., Minster, Ohio"	125.00	175.00
☐ **Yuengling Premium,** multicolored picture of glass and bottle	25.00	35.00

SIGNS, ILLUMINATED

Electrical signs are of two types, those employing ordinary bulbs and those utilizing neon for illumination. The neon ones require a transformer to be adaptable to most types of ordinary "house current," and can easily develop short circuits which lead to "blinking" or a portion of the sign going dark. For these reasons they are no longer in vogue, though their use has not been totally abandoned. As collector's items, it is quite another story. Hobbyists consider them desirable, as the hobbyist is not concerned about keeping them in continual operation—or operating them at all. Some of the older neon beer signs are very valuable, even when not in working order.

Illuminated beer signs developed roughly along the pattern set by serving trays. Here the concept of putting the brewery name and/or brand name before the public in a prominent manner was carried a step further. Advertising trays had already been in use for several decades before any of the breweries started making and distributing illuminated signs. There were no public opinion surveys in those days, but brewers were all in agreement that advertising trays had aided their business—so why not signs? The obstacle was the tavern keeper. He was glad to use advertising trays, since he had to use trays anyway. He did not have to use signs, other than those to advertise himself. At first this seemed like a major problem, but it was soon overcome. One solution, used by many of the breweries, was to prepare signs which did more than simply advertise their product. The product was, of course, advertised on the sign, but these signs carried additional wording which referred to the establishment: "ice-cold beer on tap," "draft beer sold here," and so on, which could apply to any tavern. Some even placed the phrase "and other popular brands" beneath the name of their brand—in much smaller letters. Another approach was to make the signs really decorative so that the tavern keepers would consider them irresistible for their windows: something sure to catch the eyes of passers-by and hopefully draw them in. As far as the brand name was concerned, most breweries used the same type of lettering that had become familiar on their bottle labels, trays and other advertising matters, or as closely as this distinctive lettering could be adapted to an illuminated sign. With neon signs this was often a problem, as the lettering had to be formed of continuous tubing and it was impossible to create overly decorative shapes and configurations. Signs lit by ordinary electric bulbs offered much greater latitude. Here it was simply a matter of creating a sign on glass or other substance that would allow light to shine through; the lettering could be painted or raised, and almost any kind of artwork could be used. Usually, "reverse painting" was used. In this technique the design and lettering are applied to the back, in mirror-image, rather than to the front. This serves two purposes. The coloring catches the light better this way and the enameling is protected from dust and scuff markings.

	Price Range	
☐ **Black Label,** porch light design with pair of lights, Black Label logo, 8", price for pair	23.00	30.00
☐ **Colt 45 Malt Liquor by National,** plastic, horseshoe with bucking Colt (horse) set against a blue velour backing, possibly a shelf sign as it stands unaided	8.00	11.00
☐ **Genesee,** neon, oval, white with red lettering, 12" high by 24" wide, comes with its own transformer	55.00	70.00
☐ **Miller,** plastic, gold colored, champagne holder with Miller logo at center, the logo lights up red, 8½"	9.00	12.00
☐ **National,** oval, plastic, in the style of stained glass, National label at center, multicolored, 15" high by 10" wide	11.00	15.00
☐ **Pabst,** plastic, blue with gold trim, in the style of a carriage light of the 19th century with the Pabst logo at the center	14.00	19.00
☐ **Ruppert,** glass with reverse painting, has collapsible wire frame stand, black with silver lettering, imitation wood frame, reads "Ruppert Beer, Ale—New York"	50.00	70.00

Price Range

☐ **Schaeffer,** neon, metallic frame and back, a circular design with the word Schaefer at the center,
entire sign illuminated by neon 35.00   45.00

☐ **Schlitz,** plastic, yellow and gold, in the form of half
a beer barrel, 8″ high, dated 1967 ....   9.00   12.00

SIGNS, NONILLUMINATED

This very extensive branch of the breweriana hobby includes signs of every type, except those that light up. The materials are cardboard, tin, wood, plastic, glass, celluloid, and others. Since they also range considerably in age—right up to the present time—the values start from very minimal figures (under $1 in some cases) but can go up into the hundreds.

From a pictorial standpoint, the simple poster-type sign offered the best possibilities for the least investment. Batches of large poster-type signs on cardboard could be printed up very inexpensively. Even today they represent the best advertising buy for the breweries. Other types have been made simply in the belief that variety is the spice of advertising. In the early days of non-illuminated signs, the late 1800's and early 1900's, the average poster-type sign was a real work of art, just like the serving trays of that era. They carried lithographic artwork in multicolors and were just as decorative as the framed prints of that time. Most of them were printed on very heavy stock, sometimes to a thickness of almost one-quarter of an inch. There was a purpose for the thickness. The tavern keeper was not expected to get a frame for them. If he was required to go to that much fuss, he would be apt to toss the sign into the trash. By printing them on extra thick stock, they could be tacked to a tavern wall without curling or buckling. Even if tacks were inserted only at the top, the sign would hang perfectly flat—for years and years. Do not expect to find vintage beer signs without tack-holes in them.

Instead of cardboard, some of the early signs were on wood—which in some cases was thinner than the cardboard! They were either flat slabs, or made with a raised rim around the edges to simulate a frame. It is important to keep in mind that the method of decoration on these wooden signs was precisely the same as that used for the cardboard ones. The sheet of printed paper was glued over the wood, instead of being glued over cardboard; you do not get a better grade of artwork with the wooden signs. Nevertheless, they are very attractive, especially those with the frame feature; and they tend to be scarcer than the cardboard ones, as apparently they were made in smaller quantities. Some of them are quite large, going up to two feet in height or even more. They were almost always rectangular, and in most cases vertical rather than horizontal.

Price Range

☐ **A-1 Beer,** cardboard in a wood frame, pictures cowboy asleep on a cloud with wording "Cowboy's Dream," 38″ x 25″ 110.00   140.00

☐ **American Brewery,** glass in wood frame, "Brewer's Best Premium," 13″ x 13″ 20.00   30.00

☐ **American Brewing Co.,** St. Louis, Missouri, lithographed paper, oval inset portrait of young girl in elaborate Edwardian dress holding glass of beer, 27″ x 19″ 450.00   550.00

☐ **Andeker,** square with picture of beer bottle and glass, name at bottom 8.00   12.00

☐ **Andeker,** vertical rectangular, brand name in large script lettering, pictures glass of beer, wording "Draught Supreme" at bottom 10.00   15.00

☐ **Andeker,** vertical rectangular picturing beer bottle   10.00   15.00

☐ **Arrow Premium,** Globe Brewery, Baltimore, Maryland, cardboard, 11″ x 14″ 1.00   1.75

☐ **M. Beck Brewing Co.,** lithographed paper on wooden board, varnished, pictures boy seated on beer barrel with girl standing alongside pouring a glass of beer, 16″ x 20″, c. 1899 . . . .   300.00   375.00
(It was not unusual at that time for alcoholic beverage signs, including those for liquor, to picture children.)

☐ **Black Horse Ale,** "Thoroughbred of Ales," 12″ x 14″ 4.00   6.00

☐ **Black Label,** horizontal rectangular with name at center surmounted by heraldic shield, the shield partially obscured 10.00   15.00

☐ **Blatz,** horizontal rectangular with pyramid rising from center, nonpictorial (name only) 20.00   30.00

☐ **Blatz Light,** triangular, reads, "Why Pay More For Less?" 4.00   6.00

☐ **Budweiser,** horizontal rectangular, name in block lettering 12.00   16.00

☐ **Budweiser,** in the shape of a tap knob, red, picturing horse drawn beer wagon 15.00   20.00

☐ **Consumers Park Brewing Co.,** Bock Beer, lithographed paper, pictures horse drawn wagon, c. 1890 . . . .   500.00   600.00

☐ **Copenhagen Castle Brand Beer,** Edelbrew Brewery, Brooklyn, N.Y., sheet tin, picture of bottle with king (of Denmark?) and Copenhagen landscape, 10″ x 12″ 25.00   35.00

☐ **Country Club,** in the shape of a very decorative tap knob 8.00   12.00

Price Range

☐ **Dewer's White Label,** double sided sign with picture of brewery on both sides, on one side the picture is in high relief, 13″ x 20″ 7.00   10.00

☐ **Dixie Light,** cardboard, 11½″ x 20½″ 1.25   1.75

☐ **Drewry's Sparkling Pure,** vertical rectangular with blunted corners, name in oval at center against ribbon background 10.00   15.00

☐ **East Buffalo Brewing Co.,** lithographed paper, tavern scene with group of customers, walls are hung with portraits and trophy heads, 22″ x 14″, c. 1900 . . . . 250.00   275.00

☐ **East Buffalo Brewing Co.,** lithographed paper, similar to above picturing the same tavern interior but with customers in different poses, mostly seated instead of standing, 22″ x 14″, c. 1900 250.00   275.00

☐ **Eastside Old Tap Lager,** celluloid, gold and black lettering on red background, 21″ x 9″ 35.00   45.00
Note: Believed to date from the 1930's.

☐ **Edelweiss,** heavy cardboard, multicolored with black circle in which price is intended to be handwritten, wording "Stop here for Edelweiss Light Beer, Schoenhofen Edelweiss Co., Chicago, Ill.," no information on size 25.00   35.00

☐ **Falstaff Beer,** cardboard, "The Big One, 32 Oz.," 13″ x 19″ 1.25   1.75

☐ **Genesee,** clear plastic, oval brand name, 14″ high 5.00   7.00

☐ **Genesee Beer on Tap,** red and black on gold plastic, 13″ x 21″ 5.00   7.00

☐ **Goetz,** cardboard, multicolored, picture of gentleman holding glass of beer, wording "Goodbye thirst . . . Goetz Country Club Beer . . . Famous for its Flavor," also "M. K. Goetz Co., St. Louis, Missouri," 18″ x 12″ with a thickness of nearly a quarter of an inch 20.00   25.00

☐ **Gold Label Beer,** cardboard with self-frame, picture of grizzled prospector and his mule, signed Peter Hurd, 20″ x 15″ 100.00   150.00

☐ **Hamm's,** vertical rectangular with scooped corners, pictures glass of beer 15.00   20.00

☐ **International Brewing Co.,** lithographed paper, globe of the world showing Western Hemisphere against background of clouds, moon and stars; globe reads "Pan-American" with slogan "Special Brew," 16″ x 20″, c. 1901 . . . . 300.00   350.00

Sign, American Brewing Co., St. Louis, MO, 27" x 19", **$450–$500.**

Sign, Chester Ale, tin, very scarce, 10", c. 1930, **$85–$105.**

Price Range

☐ **Iroquois Indian Head Beer and Ale,** lithographed sheet tin, vertical oval with Indian head facing left (updated version of the traditional portrait used by this firm for decades), c. 1930 .... 100.00 150.00

☐ **Kamm and Schellinger Brewing Co.,** Mishawaka, Indiana, lithographed paper, lion atop a globe of the world with wording "Challenge the World," 34″ x 26″ 240.00 270.00

☐ **Kato Beer,** convex glass, pictorial eagle motif, 15″ 110.00 140.00

☐ **Lake View Brewing Co.,** Buffalo, N.Y., reverse painting on glass, still-life with opened book, overturned mug and fruit on tabletop, title page of book gives brand name plus words "Ale and Porter," 16″ x 11″, c. 1905 .... 400.00 430.00
(Unsigned, but executed by someone with distinct artistic talents.)

☐ **Lowenbrau,** plastic, raised gold lion, 14″ x 16″ 15.00 20.00

☐ **Magnum Malt Liquor,** horizontal rectangular, name angled vertically with "Malt Liquor" in embossed lettering 20.00 30.00

☐ **Matt's Light Beer,** plastic, with plastic replica of Matt's Light bottle mounted on the sign 4.00 6.00

☐ **Miller Lite,** white plastic with blue lettering, 18″ x 14″ 4.00 5.00

☐ **Mt. Hood Brewery,** Oregon, brass, incised picture of landscape scene with mountain, 16″ x 26″ .. 300.00 400.00

☐ **Natural Light,** Anheuser Busch Brewing Co., elongated rectangle with badge at left 15.00 20.00

☐ **Natural Light,** in the form of a tap knob with name in script lettering 15.00 20.00

☐ **Old German Beer,** cardboard, "Welcome Sports Car Fans," 16″ x 20″ 1.00 1.75

☐ **Old German Beer,** cardboard, "What Is A Customer?," 20½″ x 14″ 2.00 3.00

☐ **Old German Presents State Lottery Winners,** cardboard, 11″ x 18″ 1.00 1.75

☐ **Old Milwaukee,** horizontal oval, nonpictorial (name only) 12.00 16.00

☐ **Old Style,** freeform in modified badge design, nonpictorial (name only), name in antique style script lettering 23.00 30.00

Sign, *Consumers Park Brewing Co., c. 1890,* **$500–$550.**

Sign, *East Buffalo Brewing Co., paper litho, 22" x 14", c. 1900,* **$250–$275.**

Price Range

☐ **Old Style Light,** badge shape with shield at center	12.00	16.00
☐ **Old Style Light,** in the shape of a tap knob, calls attention to caloric content	5.00	7.00
☐ **Old Style Welcome,** freeform with central design of a door knocker	14.00	18.00
☐ **Oly,** oval, banded rim, nonpictorial (name only)	22.00	29.00
☐ **Pabst Blue Ribbon,** square, name against ribbon background	23.00	30.00
☐ **Pabst Brewing Co.,** lithographed paper, panoramic view of its Milwaukee factory with wording "Capital Ten Million Dollars, Capacity Two Million Barrels Per Annum," 43" x 31", c. 1910	1100.00	1300.00
☐ **Pabst Extra Light,** square with view of keg end, word "Light" in script lettering	10.00	15.00
☐ **Pabst Blue Ribbon,** circular in the likeness of a serving tray, pictures black girl holding glass of beer, logo at bottom	10.00	15.00
☐ **Pabst Blue Ribbon,** elongated oval simulating the type of sign used in Victorian taverns, name set within embossed floral frame	10.00	15.00
☐ **Pabst Blue Ribbon,** in the form of an award mounted against a simulated woodgrain backing with projecting canopied top	14.00	18.00
☐ **Piel's,** oval, cardboard with cardboard stand and rope hanger, blue with gold lettering, wording "Piel's Fine Beer," 9" high by 11" wide	8.00	12.00
☐ **Rheingold Beer,** cardboard, picture of Miss Rheingold and fire engine, dates from the 1950's	14.00	19.00
☐ **Schaefer Cold Beer,** plastic (flexible), with gold metallic frame, wording, "F. M. Schaefer Brewing Co., New York, Albany, N.Y., and Baltimore, Md.," 24" x 8"	6.00	8.00
☐ **Schaefer,** "We Have Cold Beer to Take Home," 12" x 20"	6.00	8.00
☐ **Schlitz,** circular, cardboard, gold, in the likeness of a globe of the world with can of Schlitz at the center, 12" x 8"	8.00	12.00
☐ **Schlitz,** square, globe of the world encircled with a Schlitz ribbon, name in large block letters at bottom	17.00	23.00
☐ **Schlitz,** tin, picture of cone top can and beer glass with enameled decoration, slogan, "That famous flavor in the can that opens like a bottle," 11" x 15"	130.00	160.00
☐ **Schlitz Light,** rectangular, plastic, gold with blue and cream lettering, picture of Schlitz Light can	4.00	6.00

Sign, *Enterprise Brewing Co., c. 1915,* **$375–$400.**

Sign, *Hanley's Peerless Ale, reserve paint on glass, 20" x 16", c. 1930,* **$125–$140.**

Sign, International Brewing Co., paper litho, 16" x 20", c. 1901, **$320–$350.**

Sign, Iroquois Beer by American Art Works, c. 1908, **$40–$60.**

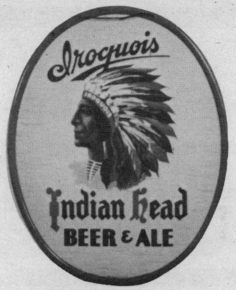

Sign, *Iroquois Beverage Corp., tin, c. 1930,* **$125–$150.**

Sign, *Kamm & Schellinger Brewing Co., paper litho, 34" x 26",* **$250–$260.**

Sign, Pabst Brewing Co., litho on paper, 43" x 31", c. 1910, **$1200–$1250.**

Sign, Silver Dime Beer, paper and wood, 13" across, c. 1930, **$40–$60.**

Sign, *Old Topper Ale,*
reverse paint on glass, 20"
x 16", c. 1930, **$125–$140.**

Sign, *Ox Head, Standard Brewing Co., Inc., reverse paint on glass*
except outlined letters where copper shows through, 20" x 16", c.
1930, **$125–$140.**

Sign, Yuengling's Cream Ale, tin over cardboard, 12″ x 6″, c. 1940, $35–$50.

	Price Range	
☐ **Schmidt's,** metallic, with wooden stand, reads "Schmidt's of Philadelphia, Beer/Ale," black background with silver lettering, 8″ wide by 6″ high	45.00	60.00
☐ **Special Export,** horizontal rectangular with projections at top and bottom, nonpictorial (name only)	23.00	30.00
☐ **Stegmaier Brewing Co.,** Wilkes-Barre, Pennsylvania, lithographed sheet tin, late Victorian parlor interior with husband, wife and child at table, being served by parlormaid, company logo appears on tablecloth, 30″ x 24″, c. 1900	1200.00	1275.00
☐ **Stroh's,** horizontal rectangular with projection at top, pictures sailboat, reads "Welcome Aboard," tip of sail extends beyond upper frame	13.00	17.00

Price Range

☐ **Stroh's For Beer Lovers,** freeform in the likeness of an ornately carved and gilded heraldic shield supported by lions at either side and surmounted by a crown 10.00   14.00

☐ **Sunshine Beer,** cardboard, lithographed, wood frame, pictures three winners of the horseracing "triple crown" (Kentucky Derby, Preakness, Belmont Stakes): Whirlaway, Sea Biscuit, Man O'War. Logo in red with wording "Sunshine Beer, it's Extra Light, it's Extra Good." Also "Barbey's Inc.," 18″ x 36″ 85.00   105.00
Note: The horses pictured would suggest a dating of about 1949.

☐ **Tuborg,** cardboard table sign reading "Tuborg Dark on Tap" 1.00   1.50

☐ **William Simon Brewery,** Buffalo, New York, reverse painting on glass, company logo of winged pineapple at center with wording "Simon Pure," gold and silver, 36″ x 26″, c. 1890 .... 900.00   975.00

☐ **Yuengling's Celebrated Pottsville Beer,** tin, picture of eagle, 13″ x 7″ 110.00   140.00
Note: This very early specimen is thought to date from around 1910.

STOCK CERTIFICATES

The value of a brewery stock certificate depends on (a) the brewery, (b) its age, (c) its ornamental qualities, if any, and (d) the physical condition of that particular specimen. While there is strong collector interest in certificates from the major breweries of the late 19th and early 20th centuries, the values of such specimens are generally lower than those of small breweries. It is easy to see why. The small breweries issued far fewer stock certificates. Some issued none at all, as they were sole proprietorships or private partnerships that never "went public" with their stock. All of the larger breweries were public corporations. So the first step in trying to obtain a stock certificate of an obscure brewery is to learn whether it ever issued any, and when it first issued its certificates. In some cases you will find that a brewery which opened its doors in 1870 did not have floating certificates until 1910 or 1920, so it is pointless to look for any earlier ones.

Price Range

☐ **ABC Brewing Corporation,** green with ornamental engraving, dated 1934 .... 9.00   12.00

☐ **Altes Brewing Co.,** brown, decorative sides, dated 1951 .... 9.00   12.00

Price Range

- ☐ **Mendota Brewing Co.,** black against white background with highlighting in gold, dated 1912 ....   25.00   35.00
- ☐ **Northampton Brewing Corporation,** orange engraving at sides, dated 1934 ....   18.00   23.00

TAP KNOBS

Tap knobs have been made of virtually every kind of known metal with the possible exception of silver and gold. Sometimes the metal is cast into a decorative design; sometimes it is set with another material, such as glass or celluloid (or plastic), with an enameled finish. Then there are specimens made of wood, and others made of (or containing) bone or marble. Even sizes and shapes are diverse. There are some traditional shapes such as oval and semi-rectangular, along with free-forms that are almost in the class of miniature sculptures. Most collectors like to mix the free-forms and standard shapes to show the contrast and evolution of tap knobs through the years.

Price Range

- ☐ **Bavarian's Old Style,** chrome ball with incised logo in blue, white enamel insert with blue lettering   40.00   50.00
- ☐ **Berlin Brewing Co.,** chrome ball, brand name in black lettering 40.00   55.00
- ☐ **Blatz Pilsener,** chrome ball, black on yellow enamel insert...........................   40.00   50.00
- ☐ **Enterprise Brewing Co.,** black ball with enamel insert, reads "Old Tap Select Stock Ale" in black lettering.....................................   22.00   28.00
- ☐ **Hamm's,** black ball with paper insert, light weight, brand name in white against blue background, transparent protective covering over insert 35.00   45.00
- ☐ **Narragansett,** chrome ball with enamel insert, brand name in light blue, reads "The Famous Narragansett," has patent number of design on face   45.00   60.00
- ☐ **Sicks Select,** copper on white enamel insert, chrome ball, incised logo with red "6" 30.00   38.00
- ☐ **Stevens Point Beverage Co.,** chrome ball, enamel insert with copper lettering, blue background.......................................   30.00   38.00

TIP TRAYS

Tip trays are small receptacles, used in restaurants and other establishments serving beer, on which the customer's check is placed and brought to his table. He deposits payment in the tray, and the tray is brought back to him with his change.

Beer Tap, Busch Bavarian Beer, wooden handle, A/Eagle logo in gold on white, bright blue, **$30–$50.**

Tap Knob, Horse Head by Gerhard Lang Brewery of Buffalo, NY, chrome ball with enamel on copper insert, c. 1940, **$20–$50.**

The majority of tip trays, like serving trays, are made of metal with an enamel finish. However, there are quite a few tip trays made of ceramic, and—more often these days—plastic or one of its by-products. The word "ceramic," when used in conjunction with tip trays, refers to all china/clay substances. There is no attempt, generally, to distinguish between the types (pottery, porcelain, etc.) such as is done by collectors of ceramics. Ceramic tip trays are very popular; they are not only good-looking but represent a dying species. All in all they tend to be scarcer individually, too, since there is the breakage factor with ceramic; the metallic and plastic specimens do not break. The plastic specimens are last on the list of collector popularity, and last in cash value; but this is not to say that they do not have their followers. Their low prices make them very appealing for beginners and others on a restricted budget.

	Price Range	
☐ **Budweiser,** red with white lettering, Budweiser logo and "King of Beers," 3″ x 7″	11.00	15.00
☐ **Cream Beer,** Oertel's Brewery, picture of lady and dove, 5″	70.00	90.00
☐ **Diehl Brewery,** picture of woman with arms raised, in the style of Maxfield Parrish (possibly by him but unsigned), wording "A New Diehl," 3″, 1930's	32.00	40.00
☐ **Hupful Brewery,** New York, with embossed trademark of H. D. Beach Co., 4″	50.00	65.00
Note: This tip tray is thought to date from the 1910–1920 era.		
☐ **Iroquois,** circular, red with the brand trademark (an Indian chief in elaborate headdress), wording "Iroquois Brewery, Buffalo," 4½″	110.00	140.00
Note: This is an old one, going back probably to about 1935.		
☐ **Krueger,** circular, red and gold, Krueger logo and wording "Beer . . . Ale . . . G. Krueger Brewing Co., Newark, N.J.," 4½″	32.00	41.00
☐ **Kuebler,** circular, orange and black, man in dress hat holding beer mug, wording "Kuebler Beer, Easton, Pa., 1852," 4½″	37.00	48.00
Note: The date 1852 refers to the founding of the brewery, not to the date of this tip tray.		
☐ **National Brewery Premium,** picture of crown and heraldic arms, a rectangular tip tray	10.00	14.00
☐ **Ruppert's Beer,** with Hans Flato cartoon, "people out on the town," 4″	40.00	52.00
☐ **Simon Pure,** picture of the famous company trademark of winged hops, a small 3″ tray	20.00	25.00

Tip Tray, *Buffalo Brewing Company by Kaufman-Strauss Co., NY, souvenir of San Francisco Exposition, 5", c. 1915,* ***$175–$220.***

Tip Tray, *Lager Beer, 5",* ***$125–$140.***

Tip Tray, *Magnus Beck Brewing Co., 5", c. 1915,* **$90–$110.**

Tip Tray, *Maltosia by Niagara Litho. Buffalo, NY, 5½", c. 1915,* **$45–$60.**

MISCELLANEOUS

Price Range

- [ ] **Car Plaque,** Old German Beer, 1911 Ford T Touring Car, 12″ x 14″ .... | 6.00 | 9.00
- [ ] **Cigarette Lighter,** Queen City Beer, 3″, c. 1941 | 13.00 | 17.00
- [ ] **Emery Board,** Old German Beer .... | .20 | .30
- [ ] **Eyeglass Cleaning Tissue,** Old German/Old Export, one pack .... | .40 | .60
- [ ] **Handkerchief,** Old German Beer .... | .25 | .35
- [ ] **Keg Pump,** non-advertising, 1920's .... | 26.00 | 34.00
- [ ] **License Holder (for tavern),** Old German Beer, wood frame with glass, 18″ x 28″ .... | 17.00 | 23.00
- [ ] **Lucky Penny,** Old German Beer .... | 1.00 | 1.50
- [ ] **Pen,** Old German Premium Lager, red .... | 4.00 | 6.00
- [ ] **Program,** Queen City Brewing Co. 70th Anniversary .... | .50 | .75
- [ ] **Tie Clip,** Old German Beer, picturing Herman .. | 13.00 | 18.00
- [ ] **Tie Clip,** Queen City Brewing Co., gold colored | 9.00 | 12.00

The HOUSE OF COLLECTIBLES Series

☐ Please send me the following price guides—
☐ I would like the most current edition of the books listed below.

THE OFFICIAL PRICE GUIDES TO:

☐ 753-3	American Folk Art (ID) 1st Ed.	$14.95
☐ 199-3	American Silver & Silver Plate 5th Ed.	11.95
☐ 513-1	Antique Clocks 3rd Ed.	10.95
☐ 283-3	Antique & Modern Dolls 3rd Ed.	10.95
☐ 287-6	Antique & Modern Firearms 6th Ed.	11.95
☐ 755-X	Antiques & Collectibles 9th Ed.	11.95
☐ 289-2	Antique Jewelry 5th Ed.	11.95
☐ 362-7	Art Deco (ID) 1st Ed.	14.95
☐ 447-X	Arts and Crafts: American Decorative Arts, 1894–1923 (ID) 1st Ed.	12.95
☐ 539-5	Beer Cans & Collectibles 4th Ed.	7.95
☐ 521-2	Bottles Old & New 10th Ed.	10.95
☐ 532-8	Carnival Glass 2nd Ed.	10.95
☐ 295-7	Collectible Cameras 2nd Ed.	10.95
☐ 548-4	Collectibles of the '50s & '60s 1st Ed.	9.95
☐ 740-1	Collectible Toys 4th Ed.	10.95
☐ 531-X	Collector Cars 7th Ed.	12.95
☐ 538-7	Collector Handguns 4th Ed.	14.95
☐ 748-7	Collector Knives 9th Ed.	12.95
☐ 361-9	Collector Plates 5th Ed.	11.95
☐ 296-5	Collector Prints 7th Ed.	12.95
☐ 001-6	Depression Glass 2nd Ed.	9.95
☐ 589-1	Fine Art 1st Ed.	19.95
☐ 311-2	Glassware 3rd Ed.	10.95
☐ 243-4	Hummel Figurines & Plates 6th Ed.	10.95
☐ 523-9	Kitchen Collectibles 2nd Ed.	10.95
☐ 080-6	Memorabilia of Elvis Presley and The Beatles 1st Ed.	10.95
☐ 291-4	Military Collectibles 5th Ed.	11.95
☐ 525-5	Music Collectibles 6th Ed.	11.95
☐ 313-9	Old Books & Autographs 7th Ed.	11.95
☐ 298-1	Oriental Collectibles 3rd Ed.	11.95
☐ 761-5	Overstreet Comic Book 18th Ed.	12.95
☐ 522-0	Paperbacks & Magazines 1st Ed.	10.95
☐ 297-3	Paper Collectibles 5th Ed.	10.95
☐ 744-4	Political Memorabilia 1st Ed.	10.95
☐ 529-8	Pottery & Porcelain 6th Ed.	11.95
☐ 524-7	Radio, TV & Movie Memorabilia 3rd Ed.	11.95
☐ 081-4	Records 8th Ed.	16.95
☐ 763-0	Royal Doulton 6th Ed.	12.95
☐ 280-9	Science Fiction & Fantasy Collectibles 2nd Ed.	10.95
☐ 747-9	Sewing Collectibles 1st Ed.	8.95
☐ 358-9	Star Trek/Star Wars Collectibles 2nd Ed.	8.95
☐ 086-5	Watches 8th Ed.	12.95
☐ 248-5	Wicker 3rd Ed.	10.95

THE OFFICIAL:

☐ 760-6	Directory to U.S. Flea Markets 2nd Ed.	5.95
☐ 365-1	Encyclopedia of Antiques 1st Ed.	9.95
☐ 369-4	Guide to Buying and Selling Antiques 1st Ed.	9.95
☐ 414-3	Identification Guide to Early American Furniture 1st Ed.	9.95
☐ 413-5	Identification Guide to Glassware 1st Ed.	9.95
☐ 412-7	Identification Guide to Pottery & Porcelain 1st Ed.	$9.95
☐ 415-1	Identification Guide to Victorian Furniture 1st Ed.	9.95

THE OFFICIAL (SMALL SIZE) PRICE GUIDES TO:

☐ 309-0	Antiques & Flea Markets 4th Ed.	4.95
☐ 269-8	Antique Jewelry 3rd Ed.	4.95
☐ 085-7	Baseball Cards 8th Ed.	4.95
☐ 647-2	Bottles 3rd Ed.	4.95
☐ 544-1	Cars & Trucks 3rd Ed.	5.95
☐ 519-0	Collectible Americana 2nd Ed.	4.95
☐ 294-9	Collectible Records 3rd Ed.	4.95
☐ 306-6	Dolls 4th Ed.	4.95
☐ 762-2	Football Cards 8th Ed.	4.95
☐ 540-9	Glassware 3rd Ed.	4.95
☐ 526-3	Hummels 4th Ed.	4.95
☐ 279-5	Military Collectibles 3rd Ed.	4.95
☐ 764-9	Overstreet Comic Book Companion 2nd Ed.	4.95
☐ 278-7	Pocket Knives 3rd Ed.	4.95
☐ 527-1	Scouting Collectibles 4th Ed.	4.95
☐ 494-1	Star Trek/Star Wars Collectibles 3rd Ed.	3.95
☐ 088-1	Toys 5th Ed.	4.95

THE OFFICIAL BLACKBOOK PRICE GUIDES OF:

☐ 092-X	U.S. Coins 27th Ed.	4.95
☐ 095-4	U.S. Paper Money 21st Ed.	4.95
☐ 098-9	U.S. Postage Stamps 11th Ed.	4.95

THE OFFICIAL INVESTORS GUIDE TO BUYING & SELLING:

☐ 534-4	Gold, Silver & Diamonds 2nd Ed.	12.95
☐ 535-2	Gold Coins 2nd Ed.	12.95
☐ 536-0	Silver Coins 2nd Ed.	12.95
☐ 537-9	Silver Dollars 2nd Ed.	12.95

THE OFFICIAL NUMISMATIC GUIDE SERIES:

☐ 254-X	The Official Guide to Detecting Counterfeit Money 2nd Ed.	7.95
☐ 257-4	The Official Guide to Mint Errors 4th Ed.	7.95

SPECIAL INTEREST SERIES:

☐ 506-9	From Hearth to Cookstove 3rd Ed.	17.95
☐ 504-2	On Method Acting 8th Printing	6.95

TOTAL		

SEE REVERSE SIDE FOR ORDERING INSTRUCTIONS

☐══════☐ FOR IMMEDIATE DELIVERY ☐══════☐

VISA & MASTER CARD CUSTOMERS
ORDER TOLL FREE!
1-800-733-3000

This number is for orders only; it is not tied into the customer service or business office. Customers not using charge cards must use mail for ordering since payment is required with the order—sorry, no C.O.D.'s.

OR SEND ORDERS TO

THE HOUSE OF COLLECTIBLES
201 East 50th Street
New York, New York 10022

──── POSTAGE & HANDLING RATES ────

First Book $1.00
Each Additional Copy or Title $0.50

Total from columns on order form. Quantity_____ $_____

☐ Check or money order enclosed $_____ (include postage and handling)

☐ Please charge $_____ to my: ☐ MASTERCARD ☐ VISA

Charge Card Customers Not Using Our Toll Free Number
Please Fill Out The Information Below

Account No. _____ Expiration Date_____
(All Digits)
Signature_____

NAME (please print)_____ PHONE_____

ADDRESS_____ APT. #_____

CITY_____ STATE_____ ZIP_____